WND Books

COLLECTOR'S EDITION

POLICE
STATE
USA

POLICE STATE

STATE

USA

HOW ORWELL'S NIGHTMARE IS BECOMING OUR REALITY

CHERYL K. CHUMLEY

 WND Books

POLICE STATE USA

Published by WND Books®, Washington, D.C. WND Books is a registered trademark of WorldNetDaily.com, Inc. ("WND")

Scripture quotations marked (NIV) are taken from the Holy Bible, New International Version®, NIV®. Copyright © 1973, 1978, 1984, 2011 by Biblica, Inc.™ Used by permission of Zondervan. All rights reserved worldwide. www.zondervan.com The "NIV" and "New International Version" are trademarks registered in the United States Patent and Trademark Office by Biblica, Inc.™

Scripture taken from the New King James Version®. Copyright © 1982 by Thomas Nelson, Inc. Used by permission. All rights reserved.

Jacket design by Mark Karis. Cover illustration by Michael Di Pietro.

WND Books are distributed to the trade by:
Midpoint Trade Books
27 West 20th Street, Suite 1102
New York, New York 10011
WND Books are available at special discounts for bulk purchases. WND Books, Inc., also publishes books in electronic formats. For more information call (541) 474-1776 or visit www.wndbooks.com.

First Edition
Hardcover ISBN: 978-1-936488-14-8
eBook ISBN: 978-1-936488-16-2

Library of Congress Cataloging-in-Publication Data
Chumley, Cheryl K., 1968-
Police state USA : how our out-of-control government is turning Orwell's nightmare into reality / Cheryl K. Chumley.
pages cm
ISBN 978-1-936488-14-8 (hardcover)
1. Civil rights--United States. 2. Liberty--United States. 3. Abuse of administrative power--United States. 4. United States--Politics and government--21st century. I. Title.
JC599.U5C5446 2014
323.4'90973--dc23
2013051145

Printed in the United States of America
14 15 16 17 18 19 MP 9 8 7 6 5 4 3 2 1

DEDICATION

For my Father, who art in heaven, in the name of Jesus Christ.
And for my husband, Doug, and our four children:
Savanna, Keith, Colvin, and Chloe.

CONTENTS

FOREWORD

"**W**hat has been will be again, what has been done will be done again; there is nothing new under the sun." This was Solomon's observation as the wisest of all kings. How does it apply here? Cheryl Chumley lays out clearly what is happening in this country now as has happened to countries in the past, and the consequences are clear.

People have liberty; people take their liberty for granted; people become apathetic; people lose their liberty. We are on that track, but detouring back to the freedom road is still possible.

Though there has never been a country in world history whose citizens have enjoyed the individual liberties found in the United States today, there have been countries whose citizens went from enjoying individual liberties to being oppressed by increasingly totalitarian rulers. Drawing from the available information around us, Cheryl points out the shocking usurpations of our freedoms.

Among the timely and tragic developments this book explores is the encroaching elimination of the expectation of privacy. If our Constitutional right to privacy is based upon what we can reasonably expect to remain private, then we may not have any privacy right at all. We know that there are all types of ways to peer through our windows—high magnification lenses, thermal imaging, magnetic resonance imaging, or sonar—or eavesdrop with listening devices that can listen through walls or our computers or our cell phones. You get the picture. So does the NSA.

Look at what we know the government already has accessed. Under Obamacare, the federal government now gets complete documentation of your deepest, darkest, most personal secrets in your medical records that only your doctor once knew until the government decided to help you. Your revelations to your doctor were completely secret, and our courts used to protect that precious doctor-patient relationship with full-blown privacy rights. Now, without a single Republican vote, the Democrats in the House and Senate decided that those full-blown rights should be fully blown up because the omniscient, ubiquitous, all-knowing, all-caring federal government needs to be in full control of our lives. Those Democrats are hoping that the governmental god in whom they trust will be more trustworthy in controlling our lives than it is in controlling and operating a website.

Thank goodness no one follows you around and watches every single thing you purchase. What you purchase, when you purchase it, and where you purchase it is your own business and no one else's—until now. As a result of a Democrat majority in the House and Senate and a Democrat in the White House, we have been forced to pay for a federal Consumer Finance Protection Bureau that will "protect" us from unscrupulous banks by that board's gathering all our debit and credit card information.

The IRS always had an awful lot of our financial information. But they certainly did not have it all. Now, the IRS wants to know even the content of our prayers, and what kind of books we read and movies we watch. Is it just me, or is this getting really creepy?

The NSA will "protect" us from evil people by getting information about every single call you make, how long you were on the call, and every bit of metadata about every single one of your calls.

While I was a freshman in Congress, we were assured during debate over renewal of the Patriot Act that it would never and could never be used that way. Oh no, we were assured that before the US government would gather information about a US citizen, that citizen would have to have had contact from a foreign member of a known terrorist organization. So Americans were safe from government monitoring, or so we were told.

The only good news is that though some people in the federal government have access to everything most personal and private about you, surely they would never use that information to manipulate, extort, or harass you. Or, perhaps, it has happened before and if it did, it is happening again.

The IRS actually prevented conservative organizations from pooling their members' money the way unions do for the purpose of getting like-minded people out to vote. They held up the tax status that would have allowed these groups to have as big an impact as Democrat organizations. The IRS did that under the gentle smile and nod of this administration. Who smiled and who nodded? Turns out that really is a secret. Absolutely everything you have or have done is not secret or private as far as the federal government is concerned, but when power-hungry federal officials move to take your freedoms and force you into submission to big brother, your secrets are theirs and their secrets are none of your business because they are "protecting" you. You may remember stories of how the mob used to "protect" people and businesses. All people had to do was pay a little protection money, and they did not get hurt by the collectors. Well, this is the same type of thing, except that the mob did not take nearly as high a percentage of taxes as the government takes today.

Remember, IRS official Lois Lerner was a leader of a group of government workers who intentionally targeted people opposed to the president. When she was caught in what certainly sounded like lies under penalty of perjury, others within the IRS who may have been tempted to use the IRS as their own political weapon waited to see what would happen to the irrepressible Lois Lerner. When there appeared to be no real consequences for her actions, the IRS seemed to pick right up where they left off and is now doubling down on their targeting of conservative groups.

If these actions weren't enough to make you fear your government, then along came Benghazi.

Examining what we know leaves the distinct impression that people were sent into a volatile, dangerous situation to do something secretly for this administration. And, while acting in that role, an attack, not a protest, began. Immediately, a call for help went out. Immediately, that information was relayed to the White House. But, there were campaign rallies, fund-raisers, and an image to keep up. After all, Al Qaeda was on the run. Al Qaeda and their related groups were on the run all right, running to kill our ambassador, an assistant, and two heroes who acted against orders and came to help them. Despite the immediate conveyance of the situation and urgent requests for help, they were abandoned until well after four deaths. Even after those deaths, it took many hours for their bosses in the US government to send help, because what happened in that attack did not fit the campaign rhetoric. After all, it was an election year and trying to save those lives might have lost the election. So they died without their bosses taking any official action to even try to save them.

The coming signs of tyranny are all around us. Fortunately they can be stopped before it is too late, but not without a courageous effort. This nation's founders risk absolutely everything to secure the blessings of freedom. We only risk some belittling by the mainstream and governmental harassment for preserving those freedoms. Bottom line, the data in this book concerns me and it should concern you. We can still save liberty for our children *if* and only *if*, America awakens.

—*Congressman Louie Gohmert*

ACKNOWLEDGMENTS

'd like to thank my agent, Craig Wiley, of the Craig Wiley Agency, for his enthusiastic embrace of my book proposal, and for his speedy and professional work in securing the contract. Here's to a long and successful partnership. And grateful nods to Joseph Farah and his excellent editing, publishing, designing, marketing, and promotional staff at WND Books for not only taking a chance on a first-time author, but for putting so much expertise and skill to work to bring this book across the finish line. Geoffrey Stone, you give editors a good name.

Special thanks to Kimberly Willingham, for such polite and speedy facilitation of my requests and messages. And to Rep. Louie Gohmert: It's truly an honor. Your principled service in the face of adversity is certainly an inspiration.

To John Taylor: your motivation served me well, and your friendship—along with that of your wife, Lynn—even better. Keep up the fight. Dennis and Ruth Zicko: your lifetime of guidance has certainly opened doors and paved paths, and for that, I'm grateful.

ACKNOWLEDGMENTS

Kudos to the staff and facilities at the John Musante Porter Branch library, the unwitting providers for much of my book's development.

And especial appreciation for my family's sacrifices and support: Colvin, for his unending faith in God and in me. Chloe, for her patient—sometimes—understanding when I couldn't play. Savanna and Keith, for holding down the fort and stepping up to more responsibility. And most of all, Doug, for guidance, honesty, and news sense, and without whom none of this would have been possible—or important.

AMERICA ISN'T IMMUNE TO TYRANNY

But what is government itself, but the greatest of all reflections on human nature?

—James Madison, Federalist No. 51

The last couple of years have certainly been interesting ones for freedom-loving Americans—especially for those who believe, as our country's founders did, that rights come from God, not government.

In June 2013, we learned through Edward Snowden that his former employer, the National Security Agency, had been collecting information on Americans—including tracking telephone communications and online activities via the servers of some of the nation's largest tech firms—through its PRISM program. PRISM is the code name for the government's top-secret data-collection program, SIGAD US-984XN, begun by President George W. Bush in 2007. Snowden's leak of its existence sparked an outrage that reverberated not just in the United States—where civil liberty and privacy groups went ballistic—but also around the world, creating diplomatic headaches for the White House.

The bad news: Bill Binney, the high-level NSA veteran who was actually the brains behind the agency's surveillance brawn—the guy who forged the future for massive data spy technology—said in a December 2013 shocker of an interview that America had already turned into a police state.[1]

The good news: Edward Snowden and the accompanying fallout from all the document dumps made us forget about the Internal Revenue scandal for a bit.

That the IRS was targeting conservative groups was probably not a huge surprise to those in the conservative camp, especially Tea Partiers, who felt the government under President Obama—along with a complicit media—already had bull's-eyes drawn on their backs. But what was dramatic was hearing Lois Lerner, head of the IRS unit that oversees tax-exempt groups, admit in May 2013 congressional testimony to singling out Tea Party and patriot organizations during the previous election cycle. Still, the confession was short-lived. She also blamed the targeting on lower-level operatives, absent political motivation—a quasi-apology that left legal minds howling.

And then there was Eric Holder.

Exactly which clause of the Constitution gives the US attorney general the right to send in the snoopers on journalists he deems conspirators, just because they write reports that are related to intelligence?

Holder apparently found one, because he obtained a warrant to track Fox News correspondent James Rosen's movements in and out of the State Department, and to access his private e-mails and telephone records. Coming to light in May 2013, too, was the Justice Department scandal involving the Associated Press. That's when it was revealed that the feds had been collecting telephone records on several reporters and editors who worked for the wire service for the previous two months. Meanwhile, Sharyl Attkisson, an investigative reporter with CBS News who regularly produced reports that the White House perceived as negative, came forward with the claim that same month: "My computer has been compromised by a sophisticated hacking system."

Even liberal and mainstream media didn't like that one.

But that's just the tip of the iceberg of constitutional grievances that have hit our nation in recent times. It's also just the tip of a long line of abuses that Americans, accustomed in previous generations to enjoying a limited government more rooted in regard for natural law, have been forced to endure. Think back to the 1776 Virginia Convention that stated in clear and unfettered language: "All men . . . have certain inherent natural rights."[2] It would seem that message has been corrupted.

In June 2013, the director of the Federal Bureau of Investigations, Robert Mueller, admitted to the Senate Intelligence Committee that the agency sometimes flies unmanned drones on US soil for surveillance reasons, to aid with criminal cases. That's about the same time a Freedom of Information Act request from the Electronic Frontier Foundation—a nonprofit that seeks to balance privacy and civil rights with emerging technology—revealed that the Department of Homeland Security in 2010 suggested using armed drones at the nation's borders.

Another federal agency that wants to use drones for surveillance? The Environmental Protection Agency.

In 2012, the mainstream media and liberal talking heads hit back at emerging reports of the EPA's use of drones to monitor compliance with environmental regulations, denouncing the reports as untrue and even mocking the claims in late-night comedy news shows. But the EPA itself admitted on its official website to a 2000–2009 project in collaboration with NASA to develop unmanned aerial vehicles—drones—to provide "next generation environmental monitoring capability."[3]

In March 2013, meanwhile, media reports surfaced of a possible

White House plan to give the Central Intelligence Agency the ability to track and access financial data on Americans.[4] The proposal—a substantial inroad to Americans' privacy rights for a spy group that's supposed to operate primarily on foreign soil—was promptly shot down by legal analysts, who called it an expansion of police state powers that would forever degrade the Bill of Rights. The FBI already has access to this information. Why give yet another federal group—and a secretive one, no less—such substantial power over our banks?

But that's the alarming trend in America—ceding power to the government. And such stories are becoming commonplace across the entire nation. The danger, of course, is that we're losing our constitutionally guaranteed rights.

But the deeper danger is that these rights, based on the idea that God is the true leader and provider, will soon be subject to government doling—like entitlements. Our future generations won't be equipped with the awareness that, since America's freedoms are based on natural law, they aren't rightly in the control of elected officials. How then to slow the tide of government encroachment?

In August 2012, a former Marine living in Virginia was taken into custody, thrown in jail, and forcibly transferred to a hospital located nearly three hours from his home and family to undergo a psychiatric evaluation, all at the order of law enforcement officials—and absent the normal court process.[5] His crime? He posted on his private Facebook page messages that painted the government in a poor light. Within days, a judge dismissed the case, finding no factual basis to jail him. He's turned the tables on the government and launched a lawsuit—but he's hardly the only American to be thrown behind bars for online messages deemed criminal by government entities. A Texas teen was locked in jail in February 2013 for making what he claimed were sarcastic comments on his Facebook page in an argument with a friend about an online video game, but which authorities said were genuine threats to kill kindergartners.[6]

Move over, First Amendment freedom of speech. Hello, George Orwell and the thought-crime scenarios described in his *1984*.

In July 2013, a University of Virginia student was swarmed by state Alcoholic Beverage Control agents who thought the carton of bottled water she was carrying across the parking lot of a grocery store was really a twelve-pack of beer and she was an underage buyer.[7] She said one drew her gun, another jumped on the hood of her SUV, and still others shouted conflicting orders and flashed badges she couldn't read. Terrified, she tried to flee in her SUV, but agents halted and arrested her, charging her with two counts of assault—for reportedly brushing two officials with her vehicle when she pulled from the parking lot—and one count of eluding police. Even the commonwealth's attorney who investigated the incident found the case ridiculous and refused to prosecute. But the twenty-year-old still spent a night in jail—for the crime of purchasing water.

Look to Arizona for a textbook example of ridiculous government action that's even worse.

In July 2012, Scottsdale City Council members approved the $1.87 million purchase of an office-warehouse building that spans 17,827 square feet for its police investigative unit—but refused to disclose the facility's location. Adding insult to taxpayer injury was the fact that council members approved the purchase as a consent agenda item, a fast-track means of giving simple thumbs-up or thumbs-down to proposals that are generally considered noncontroversial in nature, unworthy of public discussion.

The reason for the council's secretive action? They wanted to protect the lives of the police officers, many of whom were working undercover.[8] Given the well-publicized locations of the Central Intelligence Agency; the Federal Bureau of Investigation; the Bureau of Alcohol, Tobacco, Firearms and Explosives; and other federal agencies with officers who work sensitive cases that require undercover missions, that's hardly an excuse. Even America's top-secret federal data centers that serve as collection centers and clearinghouses for classified information have known locations. Wikipedia, for instance, publishes a photograph of the Utah data center along with a map of the facility's layout, and that's a project of the National Security

Agency. So, really, Scottsdale City Council members—really?

As counter as Scottsdale's City Council runs to the notion of America's of, by, and for the people form of governance, it's still not as egregious in terms of inflicting tyrannical rule on the populace as New York City, where the administration under Mayor Michael Bloomberg—who served for twelve years in that role, through 2013—became a laughingstock of nanny government.

His list of bans and mandates were great:

- Ban supersize sodas.

- Ban trans fats.

- Ban cigarettes from being displayed for sale in stores.

- Ban baby formula from automatic distribution to mothers who give birth in city hospitals.

- Ban Styrofoam.

- Mandate trash composting.

- Mandate that buildings push visitors off the elevators and escalators and onto the stairs.

- Mandate calorie counts on fast-food menus.

And that's all in addition to his biggest pet project, the one he's funded from his own pocket to the tune of millions of dollars—ban guns. He's the co-chair of Mayors Against Illegal Guns, a nonprofit he helped found in 2006 to clamp down on Second Amendment rights around the nation, all in the name of safety and security.[9]

It's head-spinning.

Add to that the private-sector abuses—retail stores that track customers' movements using their cell phones, and mannequins that watch you while you shop—and the future of America's freedoms looks dire.

Meanwhile, at the same time we're ramping up government, we're backing off of God.

In late 2013, an Ohio school district agreed to pay a $95,000 fine to stop the American Civil Liberties Union from pursuing a lawsuit about a painting of Jesus Christ that had hung for decades in one of its buildings.[10] The painting, a gift from one of the school's youth clubs, was part of the school's "Hall of Honor" display of great historical figures.[11] But a couple of students complained, and in came the ACLU to sue. The school was not only pressured to take the painting off the wall, but when administrators moved it into a closet for storage, the ACLU said that wasn't good enough. The group's civil rights attorneys said somebody might still see the painting—so the school had to move it completely off school grounds.[12]

Such attacks on all public shows of God have only increased in recent years. Yet our nation's greatest asset is etched in the Declaration of Independence, as well as other Founding Father writings, as hailing from the Almighty.

Our rights come from God, not government.

That was the root of our greatness—the key facet that separated our country from all others. But that principle is slowly fading. If we aren't careful, the next generation of Americans won't have an inkling of what the Founding Fathers intended when they signed off on those most powerful of words: "We hold these truths to be self-evident, that all men are created equal, that they are endowed by their Creator with certain unalienable rights."

1

THE FOUNDING FATHERS' INTENT VERSUS TWENTY-FIRST-CENTURY REALITIES

We hold these truths to be self-evident, that all men are created equal, that they are endowed by their Creator with certain unalienable Rights, that among these are Life, Liberty and the pursuit of Happiness—that to secure these rights, Governments are instituted among Men, deriving their just powers from the consent of the governed . . .

—*Declaration of Independence*

Anthony Mitchell of Henderson, Nevada, was sitting in his home on July 10, 2011, when the phone rang. It was police, asking for permission to use his house to conduct a surveillance operation on one of his neighbors, named as a suspect in a domestic violence call. Mr. Mitchell refused—he didn't want to get involved.

And why should he? It's his home, and his right to refuse. But police weren't happy with that response and, minutes later, five of them allegedly stood on his front door demanding to be let in, and ultimately forced entry with a metal ram.[1] Once inside the home, the police reportedly ordered him to the floor and began issuing conflicting orders: Crawl over here. Lay down. Stay still.[2]

They pointed a gun at his body and terrified him into a prostrate position on the floor, various media outlets reported.[3]

They also allegedly shot his dog with pepperball projectiles, shot Mitchell with pepperball rounds, and all the while kept cursing at him. Finally—and unbelievably—they arrested him for obstruction of a police officer, searched through his house, and moved his furniture around to create the strategic lookout for their domestic abuse investigation. The criminal charges against Mitchell were later dropped, but only after he had spent nine hours in jail.[4]

Talk about tyranny. Sounds more like a covert KGB mission from old-timey Soviet Union days.

Mitchell, as might be expected, filed a lawsuit against the City of Henderson, the Henderson police chief and five officers, the City of North Las Vegas, and that city's police chief.

Obviously Mitchell alleged his Fourth Amendment protections against unreasonable searches and seizures were abused. But what is perhaps unexpected is Mitchell's claim that his Third Amendment rights were also violated. That's the clause that prohibits the government from quartering soldiers in residential homes during times of peace, without permission of the owner. While that is a rare accusation in modern-day America, in Founding Father times, such threats were real and commonplace.[5]

The creators of America's constitutional system of governance recalled in the lead-up to the Revolutionary War, when tensions were at all-time highs, how colonists were forced to endure the occupation of the enemy—the king's soldiers—in their very own homes. The founders wanted to prevent the new government from ever wielding or exercising such power, and thus, the Third Amendment was born: "No soldier shall, in time of peace be quartered in any house, without the consent of the Owner, nor in time of war, but in a manner to be prescribed by law."

Mitchell's attorney argued in court documents that the Third

Amendment applies to police and law enforcement acting in militaristic manner too.

And why wouldn't it? After all, a government official storming a private home is a threat to that homeowner, whether that official is wearing a military uniform or police garb. Moreover, both draw salaries from taxpayers; both are representatives of the government.

Do we really want a country where police are free to operate absent recognition of a core American principle—that of a home being one's castle? Chaos could result.

For an extreme example, one need only look back to April 2013 to Boston, Massachusetts, when police were combing the area for marathon bombing suspects Tamerlan and Dzhokhar Tsarnaev. Scores of police sealed off entire neighborhoods, scouring streets and mapping out a crime grid, collecting evidence and analyzing thousands of pieces of items for clues to the bombers' whereabouts. They ultimately tracked the suspects' stolen black SUV to a Greater Boston area town, Watertown, and a shootout soon ensued.

Police and the Tsarnaev brothers reportedly traded more than 250 bullets in a dramatic street shootout near midnight that spanned more than four minutes.[6] Tamerlan was killed—hit and dragged thirty feet by the SUV his brother drove. Dzhokhar fled into the dark. And after tending to their shot and wounded, police officers pursued.

According to local media, one resident who heard the commotion and speeding cars stepped onto his porch, just in time to see a black SUV speed down the road. Forty-five seconds later, police cruisers slowed in front of his home, and he directed them to continue up the road, pointing the way of the SUV. Within minutes, police officers, SWAT teams, and National Guard soldiers swarmed into the neighborhood, sending dogs to sniff the grounds and pulling residents from their homes to perform room-by-room searches. One resident recounted how officers scoured through backyards, basements, and garages as neighbors were forced into the streets, clutching cell phones and wearing sweatpants, bathrobes, and other nighttime attire.[7]

Police, meanwhile, set up a command post at a nearby mall. Various media reported that anyone who walked the streets in the early morning was automatically stopped and searched.[8] The Boston police chief said that hundreds of homes in the area—a twenty-block grid that was mapped around the black SUV that Tsarnaev drove, after it was discovered abandoned—were entered and searched. Around 1:10 a.m., officers patrolling the streets saw what they characterized as a suspicious-looking man, and stripped him and cuffed him. They let him go a few minutes later after learning that he actually lived on the street they were patrolling.[9]

Overnight, Watertown was transformed into a military war zone. Hundreds of uniformed tactical teams patrolled the streets, heavily armed officers scurried back and forth from the nearby shopping mall–turned-command post, and armored trucks navigated through the neighborhoods.[10] The city was most definitely under lockdown. Agents and dogs went door-to-door, asking residents for information, reportedly requesting permission to search their homes, while patrolling their backyards and peering into garages and combing for any bit of evidence that would lead to the discovery of Tsarnaev.[11]

Not all the home searches were conducted with residential permission, however.

A YouTube video shows several armed and uniformed agents on the porch of one purported Watertown home, pounding on the door, brandishing weapons, and ordering the residents—with arms raised—onto the streets. Agents enter the home, guns drawn, while several others stand in strategic street locations, weapons trained on the door.[12]

In another incident recounted to the media, a Watertown woman in her seventies, named Karolyn Kurkjian Jones, was in her living room and heard a knock at her door. Simultaneously, her phone rang and the voice on the other end of the line ordered her to open her door. She did—and was immediately confronted by a sea of SWAT team agents with guns pointed her way. In the street was an armored vehicle, surrounded by snipers. And across the road, in a church parking lot, were another sixty or seventy armed and uniformed officers and National Guard troops, all training shotguns and rifles at her front door.[13]

Within thirty minutes, police had cuffed, taken into custody, and transported the woman to a nearby hospital for a physical and psychological evaluation. She was told only that authorities had received a text from someone in the house who was supposedly being held hostage. Police, meanwhile, entered her home and searched it. They found nothing—no hostage, no signs of struggle, no intruder.[14]

Two months later, after making inquiries and enlisting the help of the Boston police commissioner, Kurkjian Jones learned the truth of what happened that day: SWAT teams miscommunicated and went to the wrong home. Oops. Police later apologized, and even the woman's family recognized that their search and seizure—while alarming and unsettling at best—was actually conducted in a manner that showed restraint, considering the harrowing circumstances in Watertown at that time.[15]

But taken collectively, these stories do give rise to a crucial debate: Police overkill? Or proper response, given the terroristic nature of the Boston bombing?

That's definitely a question for the civil rights case books. But the larger point is this: America is not immune to a police state. Pressed, government will take actions that smack more of dictatorship-type rule than constitutional law. That's not a criticism of police reaction to the Boston bombing and search for suspects. That's just a detached reflection on the facts: when danger dawns, safety trumps civil rights.

Our Founding Fathers knew and warned of this very thing. Recall Benjamin Franklin's caveat: "Those who surrender freedom for security will not have, nor do they deserve, either one."

The difficulty, of course, is applying that caveat in a pragmatic manner. And it doesn't get more pragmatic than this: If you were a police officer in Watertown and watched Dzhokhar Tsarnaev shoot and wound your partner, would you think twice about ordering residents from their homes if you thought the suspect had run into the basement? How about if you were standing at the finish line of the Boston Marathon and an explosion occurred, and suddenly the streets were filled with bodies and body parts, or if you were one moment from finishing the running race of your life and then your leg was gone—would you give a flip about police barging into a home and ousting the residents because they were trying to locate the bomber?

It's easy to talk civil rights and constitutional privacy protections from the safety of an office or in the confines of a courtroom. But faced with a bomber who's sending scores of bullets your way, civil rights looks a bit different. And in the case of Boston, that's an anomaly. It's not often in America that law enforcement is tasked to respond to a citywide lockdown.

But here's the thing: Commonsense Americans may see Boston's response to a most distressing event as chaotic, yet necessary, and be willing to excuse any civil rights infractions as a distasteful casualty in the pursuit of evil. But these same commonsense Americans know the difference between extreme circumstances that call for extreme responses and a police-state mentality that's run amok.

Storming a home in a furious pursuit of a terrorist who stands accused of a horrific aggression on America's own soil is one thing. Storming a home and firing pepperball rounds at a property owner and his dog in order to set up spy shop for a neighbor's domestic complaint is quite another.

The war on terrorism that took off September 11, 2001, may have been a necessary response to an egregious attack that killed thousands of innocent Americans. But much of what's ensued since, in the name of keeping America safe, has crossed the line from commonsense action to civil rights atrocity. Much of America's fight for security nowadays is driven by personal agendas, special rights, unequally applied laws, political considerations—to include a great deal of political correctness—and the complete forgetfulness of and disregard for what really made this nation great in the first place: our rights come from God, not government.

"We hold these truths to be self-evident, that all men are created equal, that they are endowed by their Creator with certain unalienable Rights," and that governments are supposed to secure these rights—not grant them.

Nowadays, that founding premise is considered radical. Heck, even our Founding Fathers are often regarded as radicals—terrorists, even, by some.

In 2012, reports surfaced that some Texas schools were teaching students that the Boston Tea Party was not as much a warranted act of rebellion, undertaken by American colonists as a last-straw message to the king of England to quit the overtaxing, as it was an example of terrorism. The lesson, compliments of the nonprofit CSCOPE Curriculum Management System, drew widespread outrage, and in May 2013, Texas lawmakers passed a measure that banned teachers from using that particular course material.[16] But can you imagine such a notion sailing in America's schools one hundred years ago?

It was the colonists' rebellion against burdensome English taxes, after all, that ultimately led to the inclusion of the Fourth Amendment—the one that guards Americans against unlawful searches and seizures and protects against government-sponsored privacy infringements.[17] In founding times, the British government saw colonial America as a pure moneymaking investment, and imposed taxes and fees at whim. Colonists grew angry with the treatment and tried to bypass the burdensome tax system with smuggling operations. The British government responded with "writs of assistance," legal documents that granted officers of the king broad search and seizure powers that let them enter colonists' homes and scour through their properties for almost any reason at all.[18] The writs resulted in the random confiscations of colonists' properties on a widespread basis.

Massachusetts was the first to put a damper on the Brits' general warrant system, passing a ban on their use in 1756. Then in 1776, George Mason included prohibitions against general warrants in his Virginia Declaration of Rights—a document Thomas Jefferson used later as a stepping-stone when writing the Declaration of Independence.

In hashing out the Constitution, anti-Federalists and Federalists finally reached a consensus to include a Bill of Rights, limiting the federal government's powers and upholding the rights of the individual—and abolishing the hated writs system.

Originally intended as a rein on the federal government, the Fourth Amendment has since been applied to the state and local governments via various Supreme Court and lesser court rulings as well. It reads: "The right of the people to be secure in their persons, houses, papers, and effects, against unreasonable searches and seizure, shall not be violated, and no Warrants shall issue, but upon probable cause, supported by Oath or affirmation, and particularly describing the place to be searched, and the persons or things to be seized."

Seems pretty clear-cut.

It's curious, then, to read of cases like *Barnes v. Indiana, where the state's highest court ruled in May 2011 that a homeowner has "no right to reasonably resist unlawful entry by police officers."*[19] That would seem in direct conflict with the Fourth Amendment—and the "writs of assistance" system the founders worked so hard to annul.

The case focused on a November 2007 incident involving an Indiana homeowner, Richard Barnes; his wife, Mary; and police who responded to a call of domestic violence. Richard and Mary argued in their apartment, then outside in the parking lot, and that's where an officer met them and followed them back to the front door of their home. Mary entered the apartment and Richard followed, but he then turned and stood in the doorway to prevent the officer's entrance. Richard told the officer he couldn't enter, and while Mary didn't expressly forbid him from entering, she never gave verbal permission either. The officer pushed into the home, however, and Richard shoved him against the wall.[20] They struggled, and the officer ultimately used a Taser and choke hold to subdue and arrest Richard.[21]

Richard was found guilty in court of battery against a police officer, resisting law enforcement, and disorderly conduct.[22] Richard appealed, though, saying the court did not advise the jury of a citizen's reasonable right to resist unlawful entry into a home as part of the pre-deliberative process.[23]

The case ultimately ended up in Indiana Supreme Court—but for Fourth Amendment defenders it probably would have been better if it had stayed at a lower court level, where it wouldn't have received national attention. What if other courts see this case as cause for similar rulings?

This is part of the Indiana Supreme Court's finding: "We believe... that a right to resist an unlawful police entry into a home is against public policy and is incompatible with modern Fourth Amendment jurisprudence. . . . Further, we note that a warrant is not necessary for every entry into a home. For example, officers may enter the home if they are in 'hot pursuit' of the arrestee." The court also said that police are often called on to investigate crimes that are rapidly changing, and should therefore be given the latitude to take swift action to adjust to events that are in progress. The court ruling continues: "It is unrealistic to expect officers to wait for threats to escalate" as cause to intervene. "In sum, we hold that [in] Indiana, the right to reasonably resist an unlawful police entry into a home is no longer recognized under Indiana law."[24]

That's a marked morphing from Founding Father intent.

It's certainly a dark cloud that hovers over America's Constitution, the right of an individual to hold private property, and the centuries-old guarantee against unlawful government searches and seizures.

By itself, the court's ruling is troubling. Even a legal layman can read the court's logic and understand how that stroke of pen cut deep into individual rights and simultaneously opened the door to government oppression. But viewed in a wider prism—as a reflection of where we are in America, circa twenty-first century, and where our collective thought process lies in terms of respecting the principles upon which our government was founded—it's downright scary.

Here's why: The road to tyranny isn't always lit by in-your-face, direct offenses to freedom. It sometimes winds down narrow, indirect paths that are paved with good intentions that are actually dramatic trouncings of freedom—sometimes revealed years later, when the damage is already done. So if we as a nation can't put a stop to the direct steps toward tyrannical rule or police-state governance, if we have advanced to the point where rulings like what came from Indiana's highest court can actually stand as law, then how can we stop the more insidious threats to freedom?

How will we even be able to recognize them?

2

BIG GREEN TAKES THE WHEEL

The moment the idea is admitted into society that property is not as sacred as the laws of God, and that there is not a force of law and public justice to protect it, anarchy and tyranny commence. If "Thou shalt not covet" and "Thou shalt not steal" were not commandments of Heaven, they must be made inviolable precepts in every society before it can be civilized or made free.

—John Adams

n March 2013, Admiral Samuel Locklear, commander of US forces in the Pacific, said our nation's greatest long-term security threat in the region was climate change, not China and that nation's growing military. Not North Korea and nuclear threats. Climate change.[1]

Chuck Hagel, senator from Nebraska between 1997 and 2009 and secretary of defense since 2013, once called on authors of a leading government report, the National Intelligence Estimate, to look deeper at what he characterized as the global risks of climate change.[2] Later, Hagel also labeled climate change in a report by the American

Security Project a long-term and unpredictable threat for twenty-first-century nations.[3] And John Kerry, during his confirmation hearings for secretary of state in January 2013, vowed to then fellow senators that he would use his global platform to press for crucial climate change policy reforms, calling the issue a threat to humanity.[4]

Meanwhile, Congress and the White House under President Obama ratcheted up their orders for all branches of the military to find ways to lessen reliance on overseas oil, in part to reduce national security threats. But exploiting untapped American oil sources by drilling on domestic land was not an option for this administration. Rather, the military was told to find ways to expand its clean energy program.

So our soldiers stationed in Djibouti began using tents topped with solar panels. And troops stationed at Fort Irwin, California, began experimenting with "smart" generators, small power grids (microgrids) that can stand alone or work in tandem with commercial power grids and that monitor and regulate energy using computer technology.[5]

The Pentagon deployed the microgrid technology to an even more tactical environment, sending it to the battlegrounds of Camp Sabalu-Harrison in Parwan, Afghanistan.[6] Standard military transport vehicles like the Humvee were outfitted with solar panels near their rear hatches. The US Navy and US Air Force tried out fifty-fifty mixes of biofuel and standard fuel in their fighter jets. And even assault ships went green, as the US Navy switched its amphibious USS *Makin Island* to hybrid-electric propulsion.[7]

By itself, the military's push for cleaner energy is sound policy in the sense that no sane person actually comes out in support of more pollution, and also in the sense that the less America has to rely on foreign—and sometimes enemy—nations for energy, the better. Besides, the military has often served as a technological leader for change. President Theodore Roosevelt's early 1900s Great White Fleet was a coal-powered collection of steel ships that made a historic journey around the world that solidified further the decades-long shift from sail to steam.[8] Even today, the four squadrons that set off for the fourteen-month, round-the-world trip—the first of its kind for steam-powered, steel battleships—are still the pride of the Navy, regarded as one of America's greatest peacetime military achievements. Roosevelt in part commissioned the sixteen vessels to make the journey as a show of force to the Japanese, and as an assurance to the American people that the nation was well prepared for war.[9]

But what if America's modern-day national security decisions are being driven more by an environmental agenda and less by security concerns? What if the Big Green switch in the military is being flipped by radicals who care only about reversing so-called climate change?

In June 2013, a top Department of Defense official suggested that the military might be headed down just that path. Daniel Chiu, the deputy assistant secretary of DOD strategy, told a Woodrow Wilson International Center for Scholars crowd that climate change impacts the world's food and water supplies, which in turn impacts where people around the world want to live—which in turn can fuel clashes and wars. Therefore, he said, defense officials were taking climate change very seriously and were on board with taking preemptive actions. What kind of preemptive action?

He said America in general, and the Department of Defense in particular, needed to work with other nations and nongovernmental groups to do whatever could be done to offset climate change.

It's a global security priority, said Chiu.[10]

Sounds like an Al Gore dream come true. Chiu not only suggested climate change was a top issue but in essence recommended that America cede some sovereignty in the process by collaborating with other nations to formulate a global policy.

The US military devoted to the global common good—that's a dramatic departure from upholding the Constitution and protecting America's freedoms. America's military should not be more concerned with social justice, as environmentalism and climate change have now been defined, than with national security.

Yet Chiu's remarks have only gathered steam.

A study published in the online journal *Science* in August 2013 and picked up by press around the world reported a direct correlation between climate change and acts of violence. The report, titled "Quantifying the Influence of Climate on Human Conflict," claimed that even the smallest fluctuations in temperature or rainfall levels brought on an increase in crime, worldwide.[11] For example, the researchers found, cases of domestic violence rose in India during times of drought, while rapes, murders, and assaults spiked in the United States during heat waves.[12]

Interestingly, the study was conducted by researchers at Princeton University; the National Bureau of Economic Research in Cambridge, Massachusetts; and the University of California at Berkeley—one of the most noted liberal institutions of higher learning in the nation. And not to be flippant, but isn't it common knowledge that tempers flare in high heat? But to suggest that warmer temperatures—versus government corruption, or religious differences, or human greed and aspiration, or any number of other reasons people bicker, fight, and wage war—actually lead to ethnic clashes in Europe and civil wars in Africa is a major jump.[13] The report actually concluded that if weather patterns continue, and climate change is not properly addressed, then conflicts among humans could dramatically increase in the coming years.[14]

That just seems a tad too much to believe. Citing hot weather as a contributing factor for lost tempers during traffic jams is one thing, but blaming the politically charged subject of global warming for causing worldwide violence and ethnic wars is most definitely another—a liberal elitist line of thinking that should be nipped, then ignored. It outright dismisses the root reasons for violence and war, and instead inserts a theory that can be used to infiltrate and control nearly every aspect of human life and activity, from military missions to car emissions to what types of bags may be distributed at grocers.

But this is where environmentalism is these days.

Environmentalism is not so much about commonsense measures—

recycling, say, or keeping chemical companies from dumping toxic waste into waterways—but about control. The entire environmentalism mantra has been turned into a social justice debate. It's all about ensuring each and every human being is afforded the same playing field as his or her neighbor.

This is how the Environmental Protection Agency puts it on its website:

> Environmental Justice is the fair treatment and meaningful involvement of all people regardless of race, color, national origin or income with respect to the development, implementation, and enforcement of environmental laws, regulations and policies. EPA has this goal for all communities and persons across this Nation. It will be achieved when everyone enjoys the same degree of protection from environmental and health hazards and equal access to the decision-making process to have a healthy environment in which to live, learn, and work.[15]

What a picture of bliss. Everybody, everywhere, equally protected from all types of health hazards. That may be a worthy goal. But how the EPA tries to realize this nirvana is often via burdensome, costly federal overreaches that seem more in line with padding the pocketbooks of the government and of key environmental policy players, than with bringing about a pollution-free world.

Think carbon dioxide.

In 2009, the EPA decided that carbon dioxide—the same gas humans emit while breathing—is a pollutant because some scientists claimed that it could negatively impact ocean levels, fuel the size and ferocity of damaging wildfires, and contribute to climate change.[16] But that whole decision was based on a push from a special-agenda crowd.

The EPA's entire ruling stemmed from a 1999 suit brought by environmental activists who wanted the agency to implement new limits on carbon dioxide emissions from vehicles.[17] That activist-driven case eventually ended at the Supreme Court's door, and in 2007, the justices said that, yes, "greenhouse gases are covered by the Clean Air Act's definition of air pollution and that EPA must determine whether or not emissions of greenhouse gases from new motor vehicles cause or contribute to air pollution which may reasonably be anticipated to endanger public health or welfare."[18] That gave the EPA the open door to issue its endangerment finding and treat carbon dioxide—and other gases, if it chose—as a pollutant.[19]

But what's notable is that the pollutant label was assessed even though the EPA admits carbon dioxide doesn't directly impact human health—it only leads to changes in the environment that some scientists allege could bring about adverse health conditions on humans.

Interestingly, there's a whole crowd of independent scientists—those unaffiliated with the government—who say the research used to justify this endangerment ruling was bunk. Led in part by atmospheric physicist Dr. S. Fred Singer, this Nongovernmental International Panel on Climate Change (NIPCC) serves as the fact-checker for the global Intergovernmental Panel on Climate Change, a UN body with a base mission of saving the environment by generating worldwide regulations and policies that limit human activities.[20] Unlike the IPCC, the NIPCC doesn't begin its scientific research with the premise that all negative environmental impacts are due to human activity.[21]

As one might imagine, this more open-eyed and scientific approach often leads to sharp differences between the two groups' findings. While the IPCC issues report after report stressing the need for immediate government action to offset the devastating impacts of climate change, the NIPCC issues statements like this, signed by 31,478 US scientists: "There is no convincing scientific evidence that human release of carbon dioxide, methane or other greenhouse gases is causing or will, in the foreseeable future, cause catastrophic heating of the Earth's atmosphere and disruption of the Earth's climate."[22]

Of course, the EPA largely ignores the NIPCC view.

So what Americans face is a future of dramatically higher energy costs, including fuel and electricity, because producers will have to change how they do business in order to comply with new EPA emission mandates.[23] One energy consulting group, ICF International, estimates that by 2020, about 20 percent of the nation's coal plants will be shuttered, unable to afford all the overhauls and upgrades demanded by the EPA's clean air laws.[24] In fact, the closings have already started; they began shortly after the EPA issued its endangerment rule. In Ohio in 2012, authorities announced the closure of six coal-fired power plants.[25] In Georgia that same year, a utility company backtracked on its permit application for a new energy facility.[26] The common denominator for both examples was the EPA's ruling and the inability to pay compliance costs. That means consumers are not only going to be paying the costs the companies have to bear to comply with the EPA's new mandates, but consumers are also going to pay higher costs because of a simple economic principle: while energy demand remains high, energy sources are dwindling.

And what's it all for? As independent science says, regulating carbon dioxide emissions won't dramatically impact the state of climate change.[27] What's worse, Congress didn't even have a say in this matter—the entire endangerment finding came solely from environmental activists pushing the EPA to act.

That's a significant power shift that removes the duly elected from the regulatory picture and hands the policy reins to a select few in a federal agency. Moreover, the EPA's entire environmental justice policy that undercuts its easy acceptance of IPCC science over NIPCC findings, and its quick embrace of the human-induced climate-change theory, come from an even narrower viewpoint than that espoused by environmentalists—the Congressional Black Caucus, and the fewer than fifty lawmakers who make up its membership.

The entire concept of environmental justice is rooted in 1960s-era civil rights struggles, "primarily [by] people of color" who found it unfair that their communities seemed to be harder hit by pollution than others—particularly ones with wealthier residents—the EPA states on its government website.[28]

In 1990, the Congressional Black Caucus seized the issue. In partnership with EPA officials, the group developed a report that accused that "racial minority and low-income populations bear a higher environmental risk burden than the general population." Then President Clinton jumped in the mix, and in February 1994 he signed an executive order that directed all federal agencies to put in place environmental justice policies that would help minorities and lower-income earners escape health problems stemming from pollution.[29]

Environmental rules that protect those least able to defend themselves from the likes of businesses that want to sidestep law and cut cost corners with illegal chemical dumps, for instance, are both sensible and worthy. But basing an entire federal agency's environmental policy on a civil rights struggle, and equating a push for clean air and water to a fight for equality and justice for all, is a skewed line of logic that seems ripe for abuse. It truly paints a picture that anyone who stands against new environmental laws or new EPA mandates for whatever reason is a selfish profiteer—or worse, racist.

But a decade later, and the environmental justice mantra has only dug in deeper at the EPA. For instance, the agency's regulatory "roadmap," Plan EJ 2014, advances the need for the EPA to dig deeper into the community levels of government. Expect the coming years to see more federal encroachment—disguised as assistance and guidance—onto state and local boards and commissions, with the EPA taking a direct hand in how permitting applications are processed so they're in line with the federal vision of environmental justice.[30]

At the risk of understating, this is not good news.

In July 2012, the pastor of a small congregation of between twenty and forty people faced the prospect of closing his Good Shepherd Community Church because the Ohio Environmental Protection Agency said the building's septic system didn't meet standard. It's not as if the system was leaking, or broken. Rather, the agency said that because the church building was capable of holding more than the forty people who attended the worship services, the septic system had to be upgraded to provide for the maximum number of individuals the building could hold.[31] The pastor said those upgrades could cost up to $60,000—and the church didn't have the money to pay.[32]

In April 2011, the EPA stepped into Fairfax County, Virginia, politics by regulating the level of stormwater that could flow into the Accotink Creek, a tributary that feeds into the Potomac River. The EPA justified its action by saying it had authority under the Clean Water Act to limit stormwater and sediment runoff, to protect living organisms within the water. But Virginia's attorney general, Ken Cuccinelli, claimed otherwise, arguing the EPA had power only to regulate pollutants—and that stormwater wasn't a pollutant.[33] The issue was divisive and went to court. But a federal court ruled in January 2013 in the commonwealth's favor, with the judge finding that the EPA does not, as it alleged, have the power to regulate stormwater because it's a non-pollutant.[34] As Cuccinelli had queried: how can the EPA consider water itself a pollutant? The ruling handed builders and those in the construction trade—as well as Virginia taxpayers—a huge victory. Had the EPA won, the county would have faced a $300 million cost to reduce stormwater flow into Accotink Creek by the agency's demand of almost 50 percent.[35]

A few months later, and the EPA was at it again—this time, citing the Clean Air Act as justification for banning wood-burning stoves in private homes.

The EPA issued regulations limiting the level of "airborne fine-particle matter" to twelve micrograms per cubic meter of air in late 2013—a revamp of its old policy that allowed for emission levels of fifteen micrograms per cubic meter of air.[36] One immediate effect of the new regulation was that it made illegal an estimated 80 percent of woodstoves located in homes and cabins around the nation.[37] The ever-helpful EPA set up a partnership program, Burn Wise, to help Americans discern whether their particular models violated the new regulation and touting the "importance of burning the right wood, the right way, in the right wood-burning appliance to protect your home, health and the air we breathe."[38]

Seven states—Connecticut, Maryland, Massachusetts, New York, Oregon, Rhode Island, and Vermont—quickly jumped aboard the EPA "ban-wagon" and in October 2013 started a suit to demand the EPA extend its crackdown on woodstoves to wood-burning water heaters.[39] Some local governments have taken up the cause, too, banning not just the purchase of the EPA's banned stoves, but also the use of old stoves that haven't been replaced, and in some cases, of fireplaces that haven't received the federal agency's environmental stamp of approval.[40]

Such scenarios give rise to former president Ronald Reagan's warning: "The nine most terrifying words in the English language are, 'I'm from the government and I'm here to help.'"[41] Do we really need more federal environmental regulation breathing down the backs of state and local governments—entities that are hard enough to control as it is?

But EPA environmental justice policy is just one hammer the agency has at its disposal to compel new law. Think what happens when it gets a hand in enforcement from other federal entities—like the Department of Justice.

Remember Gibson Guitars? In 2011, the company's factories in Tennessee were raided by federal agents over alleged violations of the Lacey Act, which was amended in 2008 to prohibit wood obtained in breach of foreign or domestic laws from being imported into the United States.[42]

The Department of Justice under attorney general Eric Holder accused Gibson of importing ebony from Madagascar and both rosewood and ebony from India, in violation of harvesting and export laws those countries put in place to protect environmentally sensitive forestry.[43] Madagascar, for instance, issued a report in 2008 that the harvest and export of ebony was illegal, leading Gibson a year later to turn to a middleman to provide ebony via a circuitous route—a route that it still believed was legal.[44] The Department of Justice accused Gibson of knowingly breaking the countries' harvest and export laws, though. So in August 2011, roughly thirty armed federal agents swooped in and seized the wood—a move CEO Henry Juszkiewicz said cost the company millions of dollars.[45]

In August 2012, Gibson reached a settlement with the Justice Department. It agreed to pay a $300,000 fine, contribute $50,000 to the National Fish and Wildlife Foundation, and forfeit wood it had purchased from Madagascar at the price of $261,844. Gibson was also stuck with the $2.4 million in legal fees it spent to fight the government.[46]

The feds were to return wood it seized in 2011, valued at $155,000.[47]

The message the federal raid sent the American people was clear and foreboding: don't mess with us.

Even Speaker of the House John Boehner, a quasi-conservative who irks Tea Party types with his frequent concessions to the Obama administration, saw the Justice Department's shakedown as a government overreach. In media reports, Boehner characterized the federal government's targeting of the respected Gibson company as an unnecessary fiasco that wasted company resources.[48] Other members of Congress demanded the White House explain why on one hand President Obama wanted "Made in America" stamps on products all over the world, but on the other, squelched small business in the United States with a regulatory atmosphere that hinted of despotism.[49]

Nearly two years later, Congress was still awaiting its reply. On May 29, 2013, Rep. Marsha Blackburn once again asked the White House, the Justice Department, and the Interior Department to explain the necessity of the raids on Gibson Guitar and to account for the atmosphere of fear that ensued.[50]

We'll never hear from the Obama administration on this.

Meanwhile, the radical environmental agenda that's taken root in this nation continues to grow. And the federal government is hardly the lone taker of individual rights in this regard.

Former New York City mayor Michael Bloomberg—also known

as the nanny of New York—pledged in February 2013 to do away with all vestiges of plastic foam cups and Styrofoam containers within city limits, characterizing them as environmental hazards that pollute both streets and waterways.[51] He proposed in his final State of the City address a new rule that schools stop serving food on plastic foam trays, that restaurants and fast-food establishments quit using the packaging, and that all take-out trays, cups, and carry items use materials other than Styrofoam. Several city council members saw the proposed ban in a favorable light, calling it the natural next step in bolstering recycling in the city.[52]

Meanwhile, cities and counties around the nation, from Los Angeles to the District of Columbia, have been debating the merits of banning plastic bags in stores for the same reasons—to keep the streets and waterways free of the trash. Some cities have passed bans on the bags, some have tried but failed, and still others have imposed fees on shoppers who choose plastic bags.

In the District of Columbia, for example, the 2010 Anacostia River Clean Up and Protection Act, so-dubbed the Bag Law, requires that all businesses that sell food or alcohol pay five cents for each plastic or paper bag.[53] The fee, of course, is generally passed on to the customer.

Just a nickel; no big deal?

That's one way of looking at it. Another is that it's just one more government regulation in the name of the environment, and all in the name of the "greater good."

That doesn't even touch on the more widely publicized topic of regulatory takings or private property infringements that have occurred in recent years due to environmental arguments. The federal government pretty much controls every aspect of human activity that could pollute the nation's air and water, disturb a protected animal or plant, ruin a decreed wetland, or damage a labeled historic area or building—and where the feds haven't legislated, the states and localities have taken up the slack. It's gotten to the point now where some homeowners can't build a backyard shed without first obtaining permission from a local board to ensure compliance with floodplain laws, burn wood in their own fireplaces, or pave a new driveway and erect a property fence without paying massive permitting costs to abide by arbitrary stormwater runoff regulations.

With today's radical environmental regulatory atmosphere, the state of private property rights is this: You get to keep the property and pay its taxes. But the government gets to tell you what you can do on it.

Meanwhile, Americans are fielding ever more fire against freedom from the private sector.

3

WHEN BUSINESS TURNS BIG BROTHER

The right to be left alone—the most comprehensive of rights and the right most valued by civilized men.

—Supreme Court Justice Louis D. Brandeis

We've all been through it. You buy a new puzzle for your nephew at an online store, like Amazon. Then, while you are searching the web for the name of that novel a friend told you about, an advertisement for a child's toy pops up. All because it recognized your recent purchase. Or, you go to the checkout counter at a local retail store and suffer the third degree for personal information: "May I have your phone number? Your e-mail address? Your zip code, please? "

"Why do you need all that?" you ask.

"Oh, it's just routine," explains the clerk.

It's not all harmless store routine. Collecting and processing personal data is big business, and the private sector is among the worst offenders when it comes to asking citizens to relinquish their personal information. Moreover, plenty of privacy advocates agree: Americans generally don't know how much information businesses are collecting, what they're doing with it, or even why the concern is so great.

Take zip codes, for instance. Why does a store need this information to complete a purchase? Well in part, for planning purposes. Stores like to know where the majority of their customers live so they can best strategize where to build the next shop. But stores also covet the zip code in order to mail out flyers, store advertisements, coupons, and other marketing materials.[1] Thanks to the age of Big Data, stores don't need full names and addresses to target customers with mailers. One swipe of the credit card, one zip code entry, and voilà—the name and address are captured.

That may not sound like a big deal. But the problem is that stores aren't honest with customers about the reason for the data request—and moreover, there aren't many laws limiting what stores can do with the information once it's obtained. Refusing to give the information is always an option. After all, stores don't need a zip code to process payment. But some shoppers might feel pressured into providing the information—or tricked. The clothing retailer Urban Outfitters was recently sued in Washington, DC, for falsely informing shoppers that to pay by credit card, they had to provide their zip codes.[2] The company actually wanted the zip codes to expand its snail mail advertising campaign.

It's not as if that's the only ethical lapse on record for a store, either.

Making media rounds in June 2013 was the horror story of one customer in a California beauty product store who was trying to return an item with her receipt, but refused to provide the requested zip code—and the situation turned ugly. The cashier halted the return, told the woman she couldn't complete the refund, and called the store manager. The cashier refused to give the receipt back to the customer, so she grabbed it. An argument ensued between the customer and the manager. The manager ended up locking the doors and demanded the woman return the receipt. The shop ultimately issued an apology to the customer.[3] But so much for the old adage "The customer is always right."

Such horror tales are likely few and far between. And no doubt just as many shoppers don't mind providing a zip code as do. But ratchet the technology up a bit. Those who care little about the zip code debate might take umbrage at stores that track their cell phones or mannequins that record their movements. How about facial technology that alerts management to big spenders or celebrity, high-profile shoppers? This is all part and parcel of modern-day mall technology. Clothing retailer American Apparel uses data collected by store cameras to determine peak shopping hours and plan staffing schedules accordingly.[4] In 2013 Nordstrom tested an analytics program to track customers' movements in stores via their smartphone WiFi pings, a move designed to help determine their shopping habits.[5] Outraged customers complained, calling the data collection an over-the-top privacy infringement, and executives quickly abandoned the program. But the technology exists and now shoppers have to wonder: do I leave my cell phone at home, or face the possibility of stores tracking my every movement?

Big Brotherish, no doubt. But worse is the idea of being watched by store mannequins. Italian company Almax produces for shops dummies with cameras in the eyes that record the gender, estimated age, and ethnicity of each shopper.[6] The software in the eye socket also notes how many shoppers enter the establishment each day and how many just pass by the window and how long they pause at certain displays. Each mannequin costs just over $5,000, and the mannequins are already in use in select markets in Europe—and the United States.[7] Next up: mannequins that can hear as well. Almax recently began testing technology that allowed the mannequins to report to retailers what customers *said* about the outfits that were arranged on their bodies.[8]

Talk about creepy. Store owners say they need every marketing edge they can get to survive in this uber-competitive, global market. But privacy rights advocates say such tactics cross an ethical line. Legally, too, the mannequins may present an issue. In the United States, stores are required to post notices that alert customers to the presence of security cameras. Mannequins that collect data on shoppers' habits and preferences may not fall under this umbrella of security, but rather be considered tools for commercialism. And regulations regarding private company surveillance of customers for revenue-raising purposes only—especially when the customer may not know of the data collection—are much murkier.

Meanwhile, stores continue to push the button.

Some high-end retailers in the United States, the United Kingdom, and select Asian countries have even begun testing facial recognition software in their store cameras to identify when celebrity shoppers enter their establishments. The technology analyzes videos of shoppers' faces and creates facial templates, then compares that data to mugs of famous people. Salespeople are alerted with a computerized message when a match is made—and the data even includes the celebrity's recent shopping habits and preferences.[9] The company that created the technology, NEC, says it works even when celebrities wear hats and sunglasses, gain weight, and alter their hair colors and ages, and—for men—grow beards and mustaches.[10] The purpose?

To help stores make money. After all, what good is a wealthy and well-connected customer who's treated the same as any other schmuck shopper by a salesclerk who fails to recognize a potential gold mine?

The problem with the technology, of course, is that it captures the data on each and every customer who walks through the door. Meanwhile, it's not known which stores in what markets have installed the technology.[11] That information is proprietary, or at least it was back in July 2013, when the test period was ongoing. The hush-hush only fuels the creepiness factor.

Interesting to note, too, is that NEC's background is technology to identify criminals. The company first supplied this facial-recognition software to security officials to aid with the identification and capture of criminals and would-be terrorists, before stretching wings into the retail industry.[12]

Of course, it's not always the bottom line that's driving this age of high-tech shopping surveillance. Some customers are consenting to the surveillance because they are willing to trade privacy for convenience. The option to leave a credit card at home and pay for purchases by face—another facial-recognition software program—is gaining steam in Finland, and retailers are banking on its popularity soon spreading to Australia. How it works is simple: just take your purchase to the checkout, look into a camera, and—*cha-ching*—your facial data is connected to your bank account and payment is immediately processed.[13]

The company responsible for the new shopping technology, Uniqul, promises its data is secured with top-of-the-line algorithms—the type used by military and government intelligence agencies.[14] But what else are they going to claim? That their system is mostly safe and few have complained? Unlike store-initiated surveillance and tracking technology, at least this product is customer driven. Shoppers have to sign up for it and input their personal and banking information.

People should pause before giving away such data. After all, credit and debit cards aren't that difficult to carry, and all come with various theft and security protections—though, with the 2013 holiday shopping data theft reported by retail giant Target of potentially more than 100 million customers, maybe the mantra going forward should be: cash is king. What was especially notable about that data breach is that hackers were able to access shoppers' credit and debit card numbers and steal personal information at the swiping machines in the check-out line—and Target didn't even catch the crime until Secret Service agents notified them about two weeks before Christmas.[15] That's a good example of how technology backfires—and think how much more devastating the backfiring could be with the more advanced technology that's emerging. Moving down the road of paying by facial recognition is a recipe for abuse when the technology behind it is placed in the hands of the wrong people. End-time prophecies warn of accepting the mark of the beast in order to buy and sell. That alone seems like a good enough reason to avoid this payment option.

Retailers, meanwhile, stand to make big bucks from all this technology. So do data brokers, people who mine myriad online and offline sources for information about individuals and groups to pass along—for a price—to marketers, businesses, and others with interest. On top of that the data mining industry is plagued by secrecy.

The Federal Trade Commission issued a report in March 2012, "Protecting Consumer Privacy in an Era of Rapid Change," that recommended more regulatory control on data brokers.[16] Congress, too, has recently taken up proposals to compel data brokers and the companies that sell to them to let customers know where their information is going, as well as where and why it was collected.[17]

What little that leaks out in this regard is a bit shocking.

Researchers at the University of California–Berkeley recently learned that family-friendly Walt Disney is a big-time trader on the information market, supplying subsidiary companies ABC and ESPN and outside corporations like Honda, Almay cosmetics, and Dannon yogurt with adult theme park visitors' names, ages, occupations, and personal details about their children.[18]

Meanwhile, data broker TLO announced in June 2013 that it was going to offer a new service to its core customer base of attorneys, insurance companies, law enforcement companies, and private investigators. TLO now provides information on automobiles that tells where they parked and for how long. They obtain the data by tracking license plate numbers through various surveillance technologies, and then charge ten bucks per license plate number you want to look up.[19]

That technology isn't all-knowing; cameras that record license plates aren't in all areas of the country. But it won't be long before that technological advance catches up with another that tracks every mile a motorist drives—and even if those in the vehicle use seatbelts. Think little black box. In use since the 1990s, these tiny recording devices are now standard inclusions on 96 percent of cars coming off the assembly line, and mounted in about 150 million older-model vehicles. The devices, about the size of a deck of cards, monitor and record everything from speed and steering to braking habits and about a dozen other driving-related factors.[20] Insurance companies love them, because they help determine who's at fault in accidents—and if you're a habitual speeder, deserving of a higher premium.[21] But governments love them too. Cash-strapped states, for instance, have been drooling at their moneymaking potential, seeing the mile-tracking aspect of the technology as a new source of revenue. By 2025, California is likely to be tracking all drivers' trips, issuing taxes based on the number of miles each car's black box records as traveled, ostensibly to pay for road work.[22]

It won't be long before Americans are so accustomed to their every move being tracked, the question of privacy won't even crop up.

Almost every company that hits the Fortune 500 list maintains a data warehouse that includes high-tech analytical software that's used for marketing. Just swiping a credit card at Walmart feeds the information beast. One research company reported in 2012 that Walmart stores around the nation process a collective 1 million credit card purchases each hour, and that the retail giant stores enough data in its warehouse to surpass the amount of information found in all the books at the Library of Congress—by 170 times.[23]

That's mind-boggling!

In 2012, estimates were that Big Data could become a $55 billion industry in the next few years. Corporations are scrambling for their piece of that pie. Accel Partners invested $100 million into the field in November 2011. Around the same time, so did American Express.[24]

The government, meanwhile, is jumping aboard the data wagon—and that, in a nutshell, is why you should care.

It's one thing for Walmart to send flyers and e-mail coupons based on personal shopping preferences gleaned by mining past purchase histories. It's quite another for the federal government to have a look at private health records of American citizens or tap into data banks that reveal energy use and electricity consumption at individual homes.

Don't believe the government would intrude in this manner? On March 29, 2012, the White House announced a plan to spend $200 million for technology that could mine Big Data banks for information related to security, science, health, education, and energy, with an ultimate goal of shaping government policy.[25] The plan, the "Big Data Research and Development Initiative," called for the Department of Defense to research and develop artificial intelligence technology for machines, including a "Mind's Eye" program that lets machines detect and analyze information and actions captured on video. It also gave the Department of Energy money for its Biological and Environmental Research program to further a key facet of shaping climate change discussions and policies around the world: climate modeling. The Department of Veterans Affairs received funding to boost its Million Veteran Program, a government plan to obtain blood samples from a million veterans, on a voluntary basis, to perform genetic sequencing and learn more about disease.[26]

That's just a drop in the bucket.

The White House's "Big Data Research and Development Initiative" spans fourteen pages and lists more than one hundred data planned technology research projects across a dozen federal agencies. The nation, meanwhile, already has a textbook case of what can happen when government gets involved in the data collection business and why red flags should fly around any proposal to fund more government-based surveillance technologies.

The Federal Communications Commission reported in an April 13, 2012, letter that Google Inc. used its Street View project to collect scores of data from WiFi systems around the world that could be used to identify users' locations.[27] Google also collected other information that couldn't be claimed as necessary for its Street View project—e-mails, text messages, and other personal data, including evidence of adulterous affairs.[28] Mistake? Not really.

Google admitted the information collection was not a mistake, but rather a purposeful action on the part of one of its Street View workers.[29]

The FCC slapped the tech giant with a $25,000 fine for impeding the government investigation and also demanded a look at the information it collected in America, roughly 200 billion bytes of information stored in a company-owned data center in Oregon. Google refused. The FCC let the matter drop.[30]

Fast-forward to March 2013, and it's revealed: The Federal Bureau of Investigation has been spying on Google users. How? Via national security letters (NSLs), administrative orders that allow the FBI to obtain personal information, like telephone, e-mail, and financial records on those suspected of ties to terrorism.[31] The US Constitution largely prohibits the federal government and police forces from tapping into private citizens' information, absent a court warrant. But national security letters require only the FBI's stamp of approval for issuance. And what's more, the letters are typically issued with gag orders barring the recipients from releasing any information about what type of data was sought.[32]

The use of national security letters has expanded greatly since Right to Financial Privacy Act days, when the intelligence-gathering technique was first spelled out, circa 1978. For instance, the Congressional Research Service reported in December 2010 that the FBI through much of the 1980s and early 1990s used to merely request information via national security letters, while recipients maintained the right to refuse.[33] The FBI's issuance of the letters was more an exception, and the information the agency could receive was strictly limited. Then Congress, in the mid-1990s, added a few more teeth to the act for the FBI, giving agents the right to tap into credit agency records, as well as banking institutions. A few years later came the PATRIOT Act, and the balance of power completely shifted, allowing the government to demand—rather than request—

information and leaving recipients of the government's requests little recourse but to comply. One key change in the PATRIOT Act: the FBI could issue letters for almost any reason, so long as the information request was considered "relevant to an authorized investigation to protect against international terrorism or clandestine intelligence activities," the law stated in section 505(b).[34] Another key change: the PATRIOT Act expanded the right to issue national security letters beyond the FBI—to any federal agency investigating terrorism.[35]

That's pretty broad power. And the government took full advantage. The Electronic Frontier Foundation found that the FBI had been surreptitiously accessing and gathering information on Google users using just this power.[36]

In the end, the FBI wouldn't reveal how many national security letters it issued to Google, and the tech giant was barred from specifying. But Google could provide a range, and in a 2013 company transparency report, the company said that the FBI issued NSLs between 1,000 and 1,999 times on users and accounts over the previous four years.[37]

Then again, Google's reputation as a hotbed of activity for government snooping is well known.

The free-market, Chicago-based think tank the Heartland Institute profiled the company in a July 2013 paper aptly entitled "Google-Spy," citing the top ten reasons why privacy is hardly the company's middle name. Among the findings: Google maintains the largest behavioral profile data bank on individuals in the entire world, and Google executives are among some of the most politically connected people in Big Business.[38]

That opinion resonates across oceans, it would seem.

In July 2013—in the fallout from the National Security Agency information leaks from ex-NSA contractor Edward Snowden— Germany's then-head security honcho, former interior minister Hans-Peter Friedrich, warned his fellow countrymen against using social media sites that route through America. Bluntly, he said: if you don't want the United States to spy on your online communications, quit using Google and Facebook.[39]

And the hits keep on coming. Twitter in mid-2013 announced it, too, wanted to jump into the website tracking game and start recording via cookies what sites online users visit.[40]

Government by itself is a major threat to personal privacies. Government in cahoots with private business is an even greater risk—and what makes it worse, consumers in these cases often don't see the infringement coming.

Legal scholars have argued that the Constitution doesn't specifically mention the right of the individual to possess and maintain privacy. And that's true—the word *privacy* is nowhere to be found in the Bill of Rights or the remaining clauses of the Constitution. Neither is the word *spy*, or *surveillance*, or the direct reference to the government's right to track private individuals' personal correspondences. Moreover, the right of privacy is definitely suggested in several key sections of our nation's governing document, most notably in the Fourth Amendment and the guarantee for one and one's personal effects to be secure in one's home. Members of the US Supreme Court have found similarly.

Supreme Court Justice Louis Brandeis opined in the 1928 wiretapping case, *Olmstead v. United States*, that the government held the potential to invade privacy. In so doing Judge Brandeis implied that individuals do indeed possess legal and natural rights to privacy. His dissenting opinion stemmed from the Fourth Amendment's prohibition against unreasonable searches and seizures, and from considering what Founding Fathers might have thought of government's use of wiretapping technology to collect information and evidence. He wrote:

> The makers of our Constitution undertook to secure conditions favorable to the pursuit of happiness. They recognized the significance of man's spiritual nature, of his feelings and of his intellect. They knew that only part of the pain, pleasure and satisfactions of life are to be found in material things. They sought to protect

Americans in their beliefs, their thoughts, their emotions and their sensations. They conferred against the government, the right to be left alone—the most comprehensive of rights and the right most valued by civilized men.[41]

In this day and age of Big Data—with a business world that fights for any scrap of personal information that could give a marketing or revenue-raising edge, and a government that thinks nothing of casting aside civil liberties if safety and security are the stated goals, the fight to maintain privacy is rapidly becoming a losing battle. Yet if America cedes this right and tosses in the towel, then we may as well rip the Fourth Amendment from the Constitution. Where will the next generation learn that privacy is a cherished right that was bought with the lives of many brave revolutionaries and that exists only in the freest of nations?

We are for the most part willingly giving up our privacy and security in the name of commerce, but what about other aspects of our lives? In the next chapter we will look at the topic of banking and financial transactions and how deeply the government has sunk its claws into financial institutions, including your neighborhood bank—all in the name of security and rooting out terrorism.

4

THE PATRIOT ACT AND WHY YOU SHOULD CARE

Good intentions will always be pleaded for every assumption of authority. It is hardly too strong to say that the Constitution was made to guard the people against the dangers of good intentions. There are men in all ages who mean to govern well, but they mean to govern. They promise to be good masters, but they mean to be masters.

—Daniel Webster

On October 26, 2001, President George W. Bush signed into law the Uniting and Strengthening America by Providing Appropriate Tools Required to Intercept and Obstruct Terrorism Act. Most people know it as the PATRIOT Act.

The law was aimed at countering the tragic terrorist attack on American soil, September 11, 2001. It was supposed to be our safeguard against terrorists—a collaborative approach to law enforcement that sought to bolster the ability of police, security, and spy agencies to share information, with the ultimate goal of protecting

Americans. In Bush's own words, it was meant to "enhance the penalties that will fall on terrorists or anyone who helps them."[1]

Civil rights and privacy advocates hated it, fearing that the surveillance powers contained within its pages would lead to government infringements and intrusions that would never be turned back. Open government groups, too, criticized its passage.

Within the scope of a single month, the bill was introduced, sent through both sides of Congress, and signed by the president into law, a record-setting legislative success that left little time for members to discuss—never mind read—or debate its provisions. As Democrat Rep. Bobby Scott said upon receiving the bill in the House: "No one has really had an opportunity to look at the bill to see what is in it." Regardless, the bill made it to the full House floor for vote on October 23—the same day it was introduced—passed with a vote of 357–66 on October 24, and was sent over to the Senate for quick consideration. On October 26 the bill was passed through the Senate and sent to the president's desk for signing.[2]

That's fast—especially when you consider that on average only 10 percent of bills introduced into Congress are actually passed into law.[3] Most are weighted down by political bartering, lost or hidden in the committee process, bypassed or ignored, ultimately abandoned, or placed on congressional calendars for subsequent sessions. Not so with the PATRIOT Act.

America was under siege, and the political call was for action. So now we've got the PATRIOT Act, with all its various morphings, add-ons, reauthorizations, and reforms. It's a tremendous law with far-reaching impacts on average Americans, most of whom aren't even aware of just how deep the government can now dig into once-private affairs. Take banking, for instance.

As far back as September 2003, banks were alerting customers of the prying tendencies of the PATRIOT Act. Industry analysts warned people who wanted to open new accounts to be on guard for in-depth questions, deeper background checks, and more hoops to jump through. Banks now are required to collect even more information on account holders and account applicants, verifying identifies and cross-checking names with terrorist databases.

The information verification goes beyond what would be considered basic business practice. In addition to requesting name, date of birth, address, and social security or taxpayer identification number, banks now might also ask for employer information and the nature of the customer's line of business, the names and locations of the customer's financial accounts, all the sources of the customer's income, the customer's total wealth accumulation, and the customer's financial goals.[4] Moreover, it's not just banks, but all financial institutions—including credit agencies and broker dealers—that are subjected to the new information collection standards.

The reason for such questions? To get to know the customer better.

The PATRIOT Act doesn't spell out for banks what questions they must ask their customers in order to remain in good standing with the federal government. But what the act does do is put the responsibility for knowing customers in the hands of the banks, and then gives the financial institutions wide latitude in determining how they might meet that goal. And if they don't meet that goal to the satisfaction of the federal government?

Fines and punishments can result.

Congressional testimony in November 2004 by Herbert Biern, then a senior-level member of the Federal Reserve Board, said the PATRIOT Act gave the federal government tremendous oversight of banks and was "arguably the single most significant anti-money-laundering law" that Congress had approved since the 1970 Currency and Foreign Transactions Reporting Act, better known as the Bank Secrecy Act (BSA).[5] That's a startling statement, especially when one considers all the powers the federal government has at its disposal to control the financial sector. The BSA forces banks and other financial institutions to track and report both domestic and international transactions in excess of $10,000 to assist the government with criminal and tax investigations and prosecutions.

But there's also the Money Laundering Control Act of 1986,

which gave prosecutors the ability to go after financial institutions that knowingly circumvented the BSA and charge them with a criminal act. A few years later, Congress brought the Treasury Department into the action with the 1992 Annunzio-Wylie Anti-Money Laundering Act and the 1994 Money Laundering Suppression Act. Both gave the Treasury Department a stronger role in investigating and helping prosecute financial crimes, as well as in strengthening some of the punishments for banks that violate the BSA.[6]

Then came the PATRIOT Act, which expanded on all those previous laws.

In the first couple of years after it passed into law, the new statute:

- expanded the AML compliance program requirements to all financial institutions, including broker-dealers and casinos;

- increased the civil and criminal penalties for money laundering;

- facilitated access to records and required banks to respond to requests for information within 120 hours;

- required regulatory agencies to evaluate an institution's AML record when considering bank mergers, acquisitions, and other applications for business combinations; and

- provided the secretary of the Treasury with the authority to impose "Special Measures" on jurisdictions, institutions, or transactions that are of "primary money-laundering concern."[7]

Treasury has since designated many of its oversight powers to a unit within its agency, FinCEN.[8] The bureau of FinCEN, in turn, has farmed out some of its regulatory authority to other federal agencies—including the various factions of the Federal Reserve—and in so doing, tangled the web of bureaucracy even further.

That's just a brief background glimpse at how deep the federal government has plunged into the financial sector. But even that quick glance serves to shatter any notion of an individual's finances remaining private.

Why care?

Remember the days when banks would entice customers with free toasters or appliances for opening accounts? The PATRIOT Act's amendment to the BSA now means banks must instead play Big Brother, and generate what's called a Customer Identification Program (CIP) that lays out account-opening procedures and tells employees what information to collect from each and every potential client—including a list of all the personal information that must be gathered and stored.[9] The CIP is so banks can show federal authorities that, yes indeed, they've established a personal relationship with each customer, and they've done due diligence to make sure none of their clients are criminals—or worse, terrorists.

But is it sound security policy or regulatory overkill? The Bank Secrecy Act already required banks to report suspicious activity to the federal government by filing the aptly named Suspicious Activity Report, or SAR. The PATRIOT Act ratchets up the motivation for banks to perform thorough customer checks.

As Biern testified, "Today, it is abundantly clear that banking organizations face legal, reputational and operational risks when they do not perform appropriate due diligence and safeguard their institutions with adequate internal controls to mitigate risks."[10]

Banks now establish profiles of customers to determine their normal level of banking activity and then monitor them to assess if there is ever deviation. That's called Customer Due Diligence, or CDD, and if you've ever been asked for some highly sensitive information while applying for a new account or conducting a financial transaction—information that maybe struck you as a bit random or overly intrusive—now you know why.[11] The financial institution was just doing its CDD on you—and you don't even get a free toaster in return.

Banking institutions are under so much pressure to comply with the demands of the PATRIOT Act and all its regulatory expansions that they're even trying to review transactions that are conducted by other banks, mainly in the international market. The line of logic is this: know and vet even those institutions that may one day do business with your own customers. That's a tall order for most banks. Just where in the eye of the federal government does an individual bank's responsibility for a customer's actions end?

But maybe the bigger question: how much are all these mandates going to cost?

One anti-money-laundering expert estimated in 2003—before the regulations were tightened even further—that the costs for banks to comply with the PATRIOT Act would hit around $200 million each year. The banks, of course, would pass these costs on to the customer in the form of higher fees. It was predicted the average charge per customer would rise nearly 300 percent, from about $7.50 a year to $22 a year.[12]

Fast-forward a few years and the costs have only grown.

In 2011, banks were still wrestling with the costs of compliance with the PATRIOT Act. In a survey conducted by financial services giant Deloitte, nearly half of the more than thirteen hundred respondents to the web-based poll "Global Fraud and Corruption: A Decade of Change" cited the costs of complying with PATRIOT Act-related regulations as their greatest concern.[13] That concern, coupled with the sluggish economy that hit lenders hard, has led most small- to mid-size financial institutions to grapple with the unsavory choice of cutting corners on compliance to keep afloat or abide by all the mandates and hope the bank won't be forced to sell to one of the giant banks.

Choosing the former, and bypassing federal mandates, carries significant risks.

When the PATRIOT Act first went into effect, the Federal Reserve was somewhat slow to take enforcement action. For instance, between 2001 and 2004, the Federal Reserve issued only about two dozen public enforcement citations of varying degrees—from imposing civil penalties to issuing cease-and-desist orders—on small and large institutions that were deemed to have violated money-laundering and bank secrecy laws.[14] But the agency has stepped up its enforcement and, in recent years, shown a more aggressive side.

Between January and August 2013, the Federal Reserve issued about forty of these violation orders, almost twice the amount it sent in the entire first three years of the PATRIOT Act's passage.[15]

This isn't really to say banks deserve pity. Institutions that engage in criminal activity or aid with the spread of terrorism should be prosecuted to the fullest extent of the law. But the way the federal government uses banks to create profiles on every American with a bank account smacks of police state policy. The government invades the privacy of these Americans by demanding banks ask for and collect personal information. Yet the government doesn't specify what the banks must ask. When people get upset for the intrusion, they blame the banks, not the government, which hovers in the background all the while, wielding the power to impose punishments for banks that don't meet standards that aren't even clearly spelled out. If you're applying for a credit card and the questions get a bit too personal, whom are you going to blame? The PATRIOT Act? That's doubtful. More likely, you'll blame the financial institution. And that's how the federal government avoids massive consumer criticisms in this regard. It shields its regulatory actions behind the banks, so most consumers see the financial sector, rather than the government, as the enemy. Talk about a win-win for the federal government.

That's not the only fallout from the PATRIOT Act, however.

Thanks to the PATRIOT Act, the Central Intelligence Agency can now deviate from its founding mission of rooting out international espionage and turn its spying eyes on American citizens. Of course, the CIA already had a history of putting Americans under surveillance—but doing so was illegal and scandalous. Agents involved in Operation CHAOS, for example, tracked and collected information on Vietnam War dissenters and student activists between 1967 and 1973. The Rockefeller Commission exposed the program, ruling it an egregious violation of the CIA's charter.[16]

While that probably didn't stop the CIA's information-collection game, now the agency is legally able to grab everything from a citizen's telephone conversations and Internet activity to school records and financial transactions. Moreover, it can share the information with other law enforcement agencies. It's a quid pro quo. Other law enforcement agencies previously banned by law from sharing information on Americans with the CIA can now send it right along to the agency. Thanks to the PATRIOT Act, the gathered information can also be given to the National Security Agency, the Secret Service, the Department of Defense, and the Immigration and Naturalization Service—no court order needed.[17]

When the PATRIOT Act first passed in 2001, the American Civil Liberties Union warned of its section 203, saying it would serve as a means for law enforcement agencies to give the CIA information related to foreign intelligence or counterintelligence that's released during grand jury proceedings. And why should you care? As the ACLU warned, the definition of "foreign intelligence information" was pretty broad. As written, the CIA could ostensibly collect information on American citizens that had little to do with counterintelligence or with protecting the nation from a terrorist attack.[18]

Years later, much of that section still stands. Even though the ACLU has been joined by others voicing similar concerns, the controversial section 203 has withstood several sunsets and lived past previously set automatic expiration dates.

Another hotly contested section of the PATRIOT Act—section 215—has also withstood the effects of time. Section 215 guides how the federal government can access records and information through the Foreign Intelligence Surveillance Act (FISA) of 1978. The FISA set up a special court that was supposed to hear requests from the government to conduct electronic surveillance operations. Under the act, the chief justice of the United States Supreme Court holds the power to name seven judges from the nation's seven federal judicial court circuits to serve on the special court and field the requests from government. Originally FISA allowed only an agency—say, the FBI—the ability to petition the court for business records related to hotels, motels, and vehicle rentals. Section 215 of the PATRIOT Act expanded the authority of government agencies to obtain records from nearly all types of businesses. Further, the section gave the FBI the ability to obtain more than records. Under section 215, law enforcement agents could also acquire "any tangible thing" related to the investigation, including books, papers, and documents.[19]

That's pretty broad. But that's not all.

Section 215 also relaxed the requirements on government to show how these record seizures were necessary to its investigation. Previously, FISA mandated that FBI agents show "specific articulable facts" to the judge that would prove the records were related to an investigation about a "foreign power or the agent of a foreign power," the text of the act states.[20] But post–section 215, the government only has to say that the records or documents are necessary to conduct a foreign intelligence investigation, or to protect Americans against terrorism. If the information provided in court meets the broad standards set forth in section 215, the judge must approve the application. The judge doesn't even have much discretion with the requests.[21]

That's how you get to a scenario like the private telecommunications company Verizon being forced to give up telephone records of millions of American citizens. It's all in the name of national security. Moreover, under the PATRIOT Act and section 215, even third-party record holders, like libraries, churches, medical providers, and video rental establishments, can be compelled to divulge private information on individual Americans.[22]

The PATRIOT Act was reauthorized in 2005, and in that version section 215 required that requesters of information provide a list of "tangible things" to the FISA court that are relevant to an ongoing investigation—such as what a grand jury would allow. The reauthorization also put Congress in charge of overseeing FISA and tasked the Department of Justice with auditing and rating the effectiveness of section 215. But to opponents, that wasn't good enough. Many claimed the definition of tangible things was overly broad and would pretty much grant any government agency going through FISA whatever information was desired. Moreover, the requests could be made in complete secret.

The privacy protection group Electronic Frontier Foundation warned that targets of section 215 surveillance would never know they were under watch because the FISA court affixed gag orders to all its approved applications.[23]

In 2009, Sen. Russell Feingold, a Democrat from Wisconsin, criticized section 215 as an overly secretive spy program that should be explained in greater detail to the American people. In 2011, Sen. Mark Udall, a Democrat from Colorado, said the government was wrongfully collecting information from individuals who were not even connected to terrorism or espionage investigations.[24]

But in 2011, President Obama signed an extension to keep section 215, in its 2005 form, intact until June 1, 2015. And Senator Wyden, once again, expressed dismay. In an August 2013 letter, he called the FISA court the "most one-sided court in the nation" and said the need for section 215 reform or outright repeal was immediate.[25]

The section 215 fight is pitting Democrat against Democrat, legislative branch against executive branch. But for the average American, the underlying concerns with section 215 are pretty simple: Does the federal government have the right to demand via a secret court petition that a local library release an individual's book borrowing records? Or that a privately held company release personal information on an unaware customer—an American citizen who may not even be part of an official criminal or terrorist investigation?

One of the leading authors of the PATRIOT Act, Rep. Jim Sensenbrenner, Republican from Wisconsin, apparently didn't think so.

In a letter to US attorney general Eric Holder dated June 6, 2013, Representative Sensenbrenner expressed concern about "what appears to be an overbroad interpretation of the Act" and suggested the FBI went above and beyond the law by citing section 215 to the FISA court to obtain telephone records on millions of Verizon clients. From

his letter: "I do not believe [this] . . . is consistent with the requirements of the Patriot Act. How could the phone records of so many
innocent Americans be relevant to an unauthorized investigation?"[26]

Good question. And one that rocked the nation.

Which brings us to PRISM, and the whole National Security
Agency debacle.

5

WHAT'S A PRISM? THE LONG HISTORY OF GOVERNMENT ABUSES

The whole art of government consists in the art of being honest.
—*Thomas Jefferson,* **Rights of British America,** *1774*

eny, deny, deny. Through June 2013, that was pretty much the standard answer for tech giants tapped to explain their part in the National Security Agency's so-dubbed PRISM program.

PRISM/US-984XN was the agency's official name for the computer network it used to access data processed by nine of the nation's leading Internet corporations: Google, Apple, Facebook, Microsoft, Paltalk, Yahoo, YouTube, AOL, and Skype. Specifically, PRISM let the NSA collect users' search histories, e-mail content, file transfers, and even live chats.[1] The data collection went on behind closed doors for six years. And the law that allowed NSA to conduct the spy work was the Foreign Intelligence Surveillance Act (FISA) of 1978 Amendments Act of 2008, which amended FISA. More specifically, it was section 702 of the Amendments Act, which allowed foreign intelligence operations on non-US individuals whom agents "reasonably believe" are dwelling outside America's borders.[2] Of course, it is difficult for agents to know where their target is dwelling, since most of the information being collected stems from online or cellular communications.

Nevertheless—the NSA was able to gather data between 2006 and 2013, largely without the American people's awareness. Then came Edward Snowden and the globe-rocking news stories in the UK newspaper the *Guardian*. Snowden, a former computer technician for the Central Intelligence Agency and contractor for the NSA, leaked details of the PRISM program to the press—and soon after, fled from US authorities, who wanted to try him as a traitor, to the comparative safety of Russia. But what his leaks revealed about the NSA's surveillance program reverberated around the world.

First off, FISA's section 702 doesn't require the government to obtain surveillance permission from the court. It only mandates the court issue procedures to the requesting government entity so the information that's collected on innocent Americans is kept to a minimum.[3]

Section 702 also doesn't allow for the government to intentionally put Americans under surveillance—but since the court can't deny surveillance activities that are sought under section 702, the doors are thrown wide open to abuse. The records of private, innocent Americans have been tapped, and frequently. The prohibitions in section 702 against spying on Americans are so easily tossed to the side because the court, under the same section 702, can't deny the government's request to spy—the court can't challenge the request on Fourth Amendment grounds. So what happens in this fox-in-charge-of-the-henhouse scenario is that the government conducts surveillance operations on unsuspecting and innocent Americans, completely absent warrant, all under guise of rooting out terrorism.[4]

And thus, the PRISM scandal is born.

The US government through the FISA court ordered tech companies to comply with the data interception and collection. Technically, the companies could challenge the order, but if they did, those proceedings would take place in secret in the same FISA court that authorized the orders in the first place. In other words, why bother?[5]

What the involved companies did instead was deny their participation in the data collection. As late as June 2013, Google denied knowledge of PRISM and said only in the blandest of statements that it allowed the government to access data in accordance with law. Specifically, Google said it did not grant the federal government any backdoor access to private user information. A spokesman for Apple also said he'd never heard of PRISM. And Microsoft—a PRISM participant beginning in 2007—was still blasting forth its company slogan in 2013: "Your privacy is our priority."[6]

Still, the companies can't be held 100 percent accountable. They were prohibited by a gag order from revealing the government's information collection activities.[7]

But much of what the NSA was doing was illegal.

The FISA court ruled—albeit behind closed doors—in October 2011 that the NSA was not able to completely separate domestic communications from foreign communications, and that companies that intercepted communications after hitting US soil were in violation of the Fourth Amendment.[8]

That ruling stayed largely secret until the Obama administration declassified it in mid-August 2013. And while the ruling did not directly speak to the PRISM program, what it did do was force the NSA to scramble to bring its surveillance practices into compliance with the court's finding.

As leaked information from Edward Snowden indicated, those costs of compliance hit into the millions of dollars.[9]

The technology giants participating in PRISM were supposed to pay, but what really happened is the NSA tapped a special fund called Special Source Operations to help the companies meet the costs of compliance and obtain the legal certifications the court required. And Special Source Operations, it was revealed in a December 2012 document provided the press by Edward Snowden, are ultimately funded by the taxpayer.[10]

When asked about this influx of tax dollars, tech giants initially denied knowledge of the funding program and said they only provided specific information to authorities, as required by law. But after more information leaked, it became harder for the companies to deny their participation in collecting data on US citizens or their receipt of tax dollars to cover the cost of compliance. Yahoo finally issued a statement that the company had indeed requested reimbursement for costs incurred from compulsory legal requests from the government—and that they were allowed to request the reimbursement under federal law.[11]

Not only were Americans outraged at the extent of NSA surveillance—and the FISA court finding that the agency broke constitutional laws—but so were our overseas allies.

In early August 2013, German chancellor Angela Merkel canceled a surveillance agreement with the United States and Britain that dated back to the Cold War years, citing concerns about NSA eavesdropping and privacy breaches.[12] The European Union stuttered on the creation of the world's largest free-trade zone with the United States, as France nearly blocked the first round of talks solely because of the PRISM scandal; Germany was forced to intercede.[13] Britain and Ireland, both American allies with close ties to US intelligence, took heat from the government heads of the other EU countries who wanted them to tighten up their own security and intelligence operations in order to keep at bay another PRISM-type controversy.[14] Germany's interior minister, Hans-Peter Friedrich, gave a press conference in Berlin during which he outright told citizens who feared their communications could be intercepted to avoid any technology services that route through the United States.[15]

Ouch.

The scandal only deepened when in late August 2013 it was confirmed that NSA staffers were using their intelligence positions to look into the pasts of love interests. The operation was dubbed "Love-int," short for the act of gathering intelligence information on love interests and partners. The NSA in response issued a statement saying its leadership has a zero-tolerance policy for such infractions of workplace rules.[16]

Facing rising outrage and a public relations disaster, President Obama faced the issue of government spying head-on, in a January 2014 speech, insisting that the United States doesn't conduct surveillance operations on anyone who isn't deemed a threat to national security.[17] Obama also spelled out a handful of reforms, first promising that the United States would not conduct surveillance operations of some of its overseas allies and then tasking key administration officials to come up with a plan to curb section 702 data collection powers.[18] But Obama's vows of reform were vague – political pandering and public relations.

Really, what's more shocking than these surveillance infractions is the fact that Americans could even be surprised an intelligence organization would violate their right to privacy. It's not as if US government agencies are keepers of the civil rights flame. Rather, throughout American history, federal spy agencies have violated with some regularity the right of individuals to maintain privacy—or worse.

Part of the problem is that the business of security got a lot more critical post-9/11. But part of it, too, is that America's intelligence community is just such a bureaucratic web with an underlying mission of secrecy that constantly butts heads with the notion of individual privacy rights. The intelligence community spans seventeen different agencies, all under the oversight of one national director, and it's difficult to weed through the individual missions of each unit, never mind delve below the surface to gain a truer understanding of how the member agencies operate on a day-to-day basis. But briefly, there are three separate categories for the agencies:

1. the services, which include intelligence for the military forces;

2. the departmental, which deal with government agencies and include offices within the Treasury Department and the Department of Homeland Security; and

3. the program managers, like the NSA, the FBI National Security Branch, and the CIA.[19]

That doesn't include the dozens of other tactical subunits that deal with specific cyber warfare, covert operations, narcotics investigations, international organized crime, and a slew of other special operations.[20]

But the common denominator for all of this is that their mission statements blare patriotic and honorable dogma—to support the president and policy makers with decisions of national security. But some have been involved in such decidedly unpatriotic, financially wasteful, and even outright criminal activities in past decades that the larger question arises: who's watching the fox?

On January 27, 1975, after media reports revealed the CIA's illegal intelligence operations against thousands of American citizens, the US Senate created a special body to investigate, taking inspiration and subtle guidance from the Watergate Committee that had just wrapped up its work. Idaho senator Frank Church was appointed to head the committee and tasked with reporting back to the full Senate his findings within nine months.[21] What resulted was the now-famous Church Committee reports, a fourteen-volume investigative work that detailed a range of US intelligence agency abuses, from illegal attempts to assassinate various heads of state, like Cuba's Fidel Castro and the Congo's Patrice Lumumba, to the CIA's stockpiling of enough shellfish toxin to kill thousands.[22]

The report shook America's faith in government at a sensitive moment in history.

Just a few months earlier, the seven-member Senate Watergate Committee had informed the American public of the intimate details of President Nixon's full role in the hotel break-in, as well as other political campaign scandals dating back to 1972.[23] Just weeks earlier, the Rockefeller Commission had released its findings of CIA abuses, including that agency's mail opening operations and surveillance of organizations on US soil that were nonetheless suspected of dissident political activities.[24] Then came Senator Church and his proof of the FBI's harassment of the Reverend Martin Luther King Jr., and his committee's findings that the NSA placed seventy-five Americans—some of whom were only guilty of taking part in antiwar protests—on a special watch list.[25]

The Church Committee ultimately led to the passage of the Foreign Intelligence Surveillance Act, which established the FISA court, and to the creation of Senate and House Intelligence Committees, both of which were supposed to serve as America's watchdogs. As we've seen, the FISA court has not exactly proven itself as the bastion of individual privacy rights, has it? Meanwhile, congressional committees have proven largely inefficient in reining in some of the abuses that have occurred at the hands of intelligence agencies in recent months.

Once again, it's not as if America hasn't been duly warned.

The CIA from 1953 to 1964 conducted secret LSD experiments on hundreds of subjects, some of whom were completely unwitting, as part of its MK-ULTRA program to beat major communist nations—Russia, North Korea, and China—in the development of brainwashing drugs and truth serums.[26] Agents under the direction of American chemist and CIA technical division head Dr. Sidney Gottlieb sometimes conducted the experiments in controlled office settings—but sometimes not.

Declassified documents revealed that CIA agents were sometimes slipping the hallucinogenic into the drinks of unsuspecting Americans in bars. They were luring heroin addicts to participate in the study by paying them in heroin.[27] The program grew so out of control that a small band of agents actually held LSD parties at home, observing the effects of the secretly drugged from a covert distance.[28]

George Hunter White, a man with a colorful law enforcement and intelligence agency background who went by the alias Morgan Hall, indicated in his diaries that the covert operation may have ratcheted to an entirely new level that included prostitutes, their clients, and a staged CIA viewing area.[29] Reportedly, the prostitutes would surreptitiously slip LSD into their clients' drinks while CIA agents sat in secret in the background, scribbling on notepads and watching the show.[30]

In late 2012, the American public got a glimpse of how very dark the CIA's LSD mission turned when the family of a military biological warfare scientist, Frank Olson, launched a lawsuit against the federal government over the MK-ULTRA program.

Olson worked with the CIA on its LSD experiments, but ended up committing suicide—at least, according to official government statements. The CIA told his wife he jumped out of a hotel room in New York City. In the 1970s, congressional testimony revealed that Olson had actually been an unwitting recipient of LSD, a test subject in the very hallucinogenic experimental program he was helping the CIA develop. His family demanded answers, and the CIA admitted giving Olson LSD. The CIA apologized for giving him the drug, which played a role in his sudden suicide, while the federal government paid a settlement to the family. But subsequent investigations into the MK-ULTRA program showed that Olson may have actually have been thrown from the hotel window by CIA operatives angry with his attempt to speak out about internal agency secrets. The whole suicide story from the CIA was actually a reported cover-up. So in November 2012 the Olson family sued, accusing the CIA of the outright murder of their loved one.[31]

With stories like that, it's almost hard to believe we're talking about an American agency.

Also in the 1950s, the CIA was reportedly responsible for sending three thousand agents into America's major press operations in hopes of gaining editorial control.[32] The *New York Times* and *Time* and *Newsweek* magazines all were unknowing players in the agency's

Operation Mockingbird, one of the largest propaganda campaigns in history, the existence and extent of which are still the subject of much dispute today.[33] The Church Committee revealed that the operation stretched across the world, and gave the CIA access to a multitude of press services and radio and television stations to influence international discourse with covert propaganda.[34] The most egregious aspect of this program was the cost: it's estimated taxpayers were shelling out about $265 million a year just so the CIA could influence politics and policy and sway public discourse domestically and abroad.[35]

That's the CIA.

The Department of Defense conducted thousands of experiments on what it termed "soldier volunteers" who helped discern the effects of various chemical weapons. By the end of World War II, an estimated sixty thousand US military members had participated in the testing program, serving as human subjects for mostly mustard and Lewisite agents. About four thousand of them were heavily exposed to the agents. Meanwhile, thousands more US military members took part in experiments at the US Army Laboratories at Edgewood Arsenal in Maryland that tested more than two hundred different substances—from LSD to derivatives of THC, the active ingredient in marijuana—to determine the chemicals' effect on human function. Researchers also wanted to ascertain whether any of the substances could be used for riot control, as weapons, or for other military and security reasons.[36]

All these tests were halted in 1975. Higher-ups were concerned that the soldiers faced unknown health complications from the testing. They were also troubled by the fact that the soldiers hadn't been handed the information they needed to give a fully informed consent.[37] So much for the validity of the "soldier volunteer."

Invading the privacy of US citizens is not limited to the intelligence agencies. Other government agencies throughout US history have perpetrated questionable deeds on an unwitting American public.

In 1932, the Public Health Service partnered with Tuskegee

Institute for a project called "Tuskegee Study of Untreated Syphilis in the Negro Male." The test involved 600 black men, 201 of whom weren't infected with the disease. And the testing went forth without their consent. Testers only told the men they were being treated for a generic "bad blood" symptom, and failed to properly treat those with syphilis with the best known treatments of the time—or to provide them with penicillin, which became available in 1947.[38]

In 1990, the Centers for Disease Control partnered with Johns Hopkins University medical professionals to give thousands of Third World infants an experimental measles vaccine. Kaiser Permanente jumped on board and helped administer the experimental vaccine to more than fifteen hundred black and Hispanic babies at a hospital in Los Angeles. A few months later, and after receiving reports that female babies in Africa who were given the vaccine were experiencing high death rates, the program was halted.[39] But then CDC director David Satcher subsequently admitted that the parents of the babies in Los Angeles had never given medical professionals informed consent to participate in the program—because they had never been told their babies were going to be given an experimental vaccine that hadn't received Food and Drug Administration approval for US use.[40]

This is all to make one major point: should Americans really place their trust in government?

From spy agencies to defense offices to medical researchers, history speaks volumes: the US government won't hesitate to cross ethical boundaries and upset the moral compass if the justification of "for the common good" speaks loud enough.

And what better common good than the need to protect the nation from another terrorist attack of the size and devastation of September 11?

6

THE WAR ON TERRORISM AND THE RISE OF MILITARIZED POLICE

The very definition of tyranny is when all powers are gathered under one place.

—James Madison

On September 20, 2001, then president George W. Bush laid out his vision for America's response to the terrorist attacks on US soil, defining the parameters of the so-dubbed War on Terror during a nationally televised speech before Congress. Here is part of what he said:

Americans are asking: How will we fight and win this war? We will direct every resource at our command—every means of diplomacy, every tool of intelligence, every instrument of law enforcement, every financial influence, and every necessary weapon of war—to the disruption and to the defeat of the global terror network. . . . Our response involves far more than instant retaliation and isolated strikes. Americans should not expect one battle, but a lengthy campaign, unlike any other we have ever seen. It may include dramatic strikes, visible on TV, and covert operations, secret even in success. We will starve terrorists of funding, turn them one against another, drive them from place to place, until there is no refuge or rest. And we will pursue nations that provide aid or safe haven to terrorism. Every nation, in every region, now has a decision to make. Either you are with us, or you are with the terrorists. From this day forward, any nation that continues to harbor or support terrorism will be regarded by the United States as a hostile regime.[1]

Tough words, and years later his promise still holds true: the war against terrorism has most certainly been a lengthy campaign. Moreover, it's one that's resulted in much head-butting among the branches of government, with the judiciary slapping back the perceived constitutional encroachments by the executive, and the legislative mired in political infighting, trying to strike balance with laws that secure the nation yet uphold God-given individual rights.

In the 2004 case *Hamdi v. Rumsfeld*, the Bush administration went to battle with the court system over the classification of a US citizen as an "enemy combatant" when the Louisiana-born Yaser Hamdi was accused of fighting for the Taliban in Afghanistan. The US military captured him in Afghanistan and the government subsequently kept him imprisoned for about three years without charge, mostly at the Guantánamo Bay, Cuba, camp. Civil rights activists rallied and attorneys filed motions on Hamdi's behalf, arguing he was entitled to his constitutional birthright protections.

The US District Court for the Eastern District of Virginia ruled that Hamdi was entitled to due process under the Constitution, and that the US government was wrong in holding him without charge and without access to his attorney. The US Court of Appeals for the Fourth Circuit reversed that ruling and sided with the government—that the president has constitutional war powers and that part of those powers allows for the imprisonment of those deemed dangerous "enemy combatants" to the United States. The case then moved to the US Supreme Court, where the majority reversed the Fourth Circuit.[2]

In the end, the government and Hamdi struck a deal. He would renounce his US citizenship and the United States would deport him to Saudi Arabia, the country where he was raised. But the case highlighted a growing unrest among liberals and libertarians over the War on Terror. Gone were the days of Democrats joining Republicans on the steps of the Capitol to sing "God Bless America." Roughly three years into the PATRIOT Act, with the War on Terror's end nowhere in sight, Democrats and antiwar activists were finding their voice again. The Hamdi case, to many, was a pure example of government run amok and of executive overreach, and liberals ran with it as proof positive of the Bush administration's saber-rattling love for war.

Rumsfeld v. Padilla, also 2004, was no less contentious. That's the case where FBI agents arrested Brooklyn resident José Padilla in 2002 at Chicago O'Hare International Airport on charges of plotting a dirty bomb attack.[3] The government then deemed him a material witness, a classification that let them get by with detaining him for further questioning. A month later, President Bush stepped in and declared him an enemy combatant, and Padilla was whisked away to a naval station in South Carolina and held behind military bars for the next three-plus years, largely without benefit of legal representation.[4]

Again, civil rights groups rallied for his release from military custody, accusing authorities of illegally torturing and interrogating him and demanding he be given his constitutional right to a civilian court trial and to an attorney. The government finally acquiesced, and in 2006, Padilla was sent to a Florida jail on conspiracy charges.[5] He was ultimately convicted of waging a jihad overseas and of aiding in overseas terrorism—but never of the dirty bomb charges that set his arrest in motion.[6] Nevertheless, in 2008, Padilla was sentenced to more than seventeen years in prison—a term that was later deemed too short and landed him back in court.[7]

The question loomed: does the president of the United States have the lawful authority to detain an American citizen on US soil, miles away from the actual combat field?

The Court of Appeals for the Second Circuit said no. The US Supreme Court reversed that decision, but only because it decided that the named defendant—Rumsfeld—wasn't the proper respondent. Unlike in *Hamdi*, the Supreme Court didn't clarify the president's powers of using military rather than police force to detain US citizens on US soil.

For Americans concerned about the state of our nation's Constitution, the bigger issue is this: Padilla may very well deserve the treatment he received. But did the Founding Fathers envision a president with power to throw a civilian citizen behind military bars without benefit of charge, attorney, or trial? Years later that same question still nags at our conscience.

Hamdi, at least, was captured in Afghanistan, allegedly in the throes of fighting American forces alongside the Taliban. Padilla was grabbed at a US airport and was accused only of plotting a bomb attack on American interests. Both were American citizens, both were declared illegal enemy combatants, both were tossed into military prisons, and both were denied normal constitutional legal processes—the rights to an attorney, to be informed of the charges, and to a speedy trial. Is this the American way?

Bereft of the behind-scenes intelligence investigations and revelations that would lead a president and his administration to make such a call, the American public has been forced to adopt a more "trust me" approach of government when addressing that question. No wonder the head-butting among the branches of government—and with the American public—never ends. At present the issues over the War on Terror are still pitting entire branches of government against each other.

In May 2013, it was Congress and the White House—rather than the executive and judiciary branches—that were hitting at each other's brick walls. The issue? The fate of the 2001 Authorization for Use of Military Force (AUMF) joint resolution and the War on Terror that the document essentially declared.

The AUMF, approved just a few days after the September 11, 2001, terrorist assault on America, gives the president the congressional stamp of approval to take all "necessary and appropriate force" against any and all "nations, organizations, or persons" he finds who have "planned, authorized, committed, or aided" in the attack.[8] One pertinent section of the document makes clear that the president can take action against even those who are believed to have "harbored such organizations or persons."[9] It was this AUMF that gave President Bush the power to declare and detain Hamdi as an illegal enemy combatant. After a court ruled that Bush in that case did indeed utilize "necessary and appropriate force" by declaring him an enemy combatant—that the label and ensuing detention were legal and congressionally authorized—then the AUMF also became the justification for future detainments of prisoners at Guantánamo Bay.[10]

But the AUMF grants government broad powers.

It was this same AUMF that was cited as justification for the executive branch to use electronic surveillance absent FISA court authorization.[11]

In 2001, President Bush authorized the National Security Agency to conduct a top-secret operation with other intelligence agencies to uncover and halt terrorist attacks in the country—a general directive that included a range of spy activities, all under the dubbed umbrella of the President's Surveillance Program. The President's Surveillance Program eventually gave the NSA the authority to tap into all communications flowing in and out of the United States believed to be tied to al Qaeda or a similar terrorist group. This part of the program was called the Terrorist Surveillance Program, and in 2005, it became the talk of the media town.[12]

The then-ranking Democrat on the Senate Intelligence Committee, John D. Rockefeller, expressed concerns that these surveillance activities were unlawful. The *New York Times*, meanwhile, said it had known about the NSA spy program for a year, but declined to publish a story about it because the administration had asked for media silence, citing national security reasons.[13]

From there, national outcry only grew.

Answering critics of the government program of spying on US citizens, President Bush and his attorney general, Alberto Gonzales, claimed the joint resolution AUMF gave the White House the authority to conduct the surveillance. However, in 2006 the Congressional Research Service—the nonpartisan investigative arm of Congress—said the AUMF did not give the president the power to secretly spy on Americans.[14] And the Senate introduced a resolution to clarify that the original AUMF from 2001 did not authorize any warrantless government surveillance of American citizens.[15]

Predictably, privacy advocates were outraged.

Yet in 2013, this highly contested AUMF for the War on Terror was still in use. And it was still setting up a significant stumbling block between Congress (primarily the Republicans) and the White House.

In May 2013, President Obama wanted to outright declare an end to the War on Terror, repeal the 2001 joint resolution AUMF, and finally make good on his campaign promise to close down Guantánamo Bay.[16] But many in Congress, especially conservatives, saw the president's push to call off the War on Terror as premature and balked at the repeal of the AUMF.[17]

Meanwhile, Sen. Saxby Chambliss, R-GA, summed up the conservative response to the idea of closing Gitmo with a statement that characterized the president's plan as an irresponsible notion that would unleash 166 of the world's most violent criminals onto innocent Americans. Other Republicans in the House agreed.[18]

So did the Pentagon, setting the stage for an interesting division between the president and commander in chief and the military forces he supposedly leads. In testimony before the US Senate Committee on Armed Forces in May, a top Pentagon official suggested that America's best course of action would be to keep the AUMF intact for ten or twenty more years, as a solid means of continuing to root out terrorism and battle suspected terrorists.[19]

Doubtless, the fate of the national war on terror will take twists and turns in the coming years, based on political winds and directed largely by which party happens to hold White House and congressional control. But there's a darker side to the fight for freedom, one that's not going to lighten anytime soon. Undercutting all this political bickering is the fact that this perpetual War on Terror has created a trickle-down effect with significant impact on average Americans—the serious militarization of civilian police forces.

Before September 11, small-town police were more often than not armed with pump-action shotguns and high-powered rifles. Some were lucky enough to scrounge a stray M16 or two, but for the most part, the weaponry was of a decidedly civilian make and model. A decade later, and these same small police stations are often outfitted with top-of-the-line, military-grade assault weapons, the very type used on the battlefields of Iraq and Afghanistan.[20]

Officers, meanwhile, now don full-battle dress—from Kevlar helmets to body armor to high-tech bulletproof vests—for routine beat patrol. They ride Humvees and scour for suspects from their helicopters. And even small-town police departments house fully trained special weapons and tactics (SWAT) teams—the kind who used to work primarily at big, inner-city police units on violent and dangerous investigations.[21] Moreover, these SWAT teams aren't just responding to terrorist-related investigations. Some now perform the most routine of police duties, like serving warrants or making minor drug arrests.

The outcomes are not always peaceful.

In May 2011, Jose Guerena, a twenty-six-year-old Marine and Iraq war veteran, was killed in a hail of gunfire from SWAT officers who broke into his Pima County, Arizona, home on the belief he was a key player in an ongoing marijuana and drug investigation. Guerena thought he was being robbed, or worse, and moved to protect his wife and four-year-old son by hiding them in a closet and grabbing his rifle. Authorities saw the rifle and fired, ultimately shooting him between sixty and seventy times. Guerena didn't even get a shot off, and police found his rifle on the floor next to his body, with the safety still in the on position.[22]

Guerena's family subsequently filed a $20 million lawsuit against the county, seeking redress to a key question that undercut the entire fiasco: why would the county send SWAT agents to serve a warrant in the first place?[23]

That's hardly the only case of police overkill.

In August 2013, a Florida couple told a local newspaper they were awakened by the sound of their barking pit bulls and gunshots. They said they opened the bedroom door and were startled to find six officers pointing guns and flashlights, ordering them to the floor.[24]

What was going on?

The police said they had been investigating an aggravated assault complaint and saw an open window on a house near where they last saw their suspect, so they entered the home. After climbing through the window, the officers encountered two pit bulls coming at them, defending the home against the intruders. After a brief scuffle with the dogs, one of the officers shot them. The police said they then searched the rest of the house and found the couple in bed. They handcuffed and interviewed them, but as it turned out, the couple had nothing to do with the assault incident. The police had stormed the wrong home.[25]

Head north to Virginia, where former Marine Brandon Raub was arrested in August 2012 by a swarm of federal agents and Chesterfield police and forcibly sent to a psychiatric ward for a mental health evaluation. His crime? Posting antigovernment messages and controversial song lyrics on his private Facebook page. While Raub sat in a mental hospital, his family scrambled to find legal representation. The circuit court judge who finally heard his case called the government's claims 100 percent folly and totally unjustified, and ruled for his immediate release. Raub was let go and shortly after filed a civil rights suit for wrongful arrest.[26]

Cases like these are becoming all too commonplace. And given the military-type training that's becoming normal for police around the nation, it's more than likely that civilian law enforcement is only going to get more hard-charging, more "arrest first, ask questions later."

The New York Police Department now has officers "stationed in London working with New Scotland Yard; in Lyons at the headquarters of Interpol; and in Hamburg, Tel Aviv, and Toronto." The department has also sent its detectives to Afghanistan, Egypt, Yemen, Pakistan, and Guantánamo Bay, Cuba, to learn how to properly interrogate a prisoner.[27]

The technology police now receive as part of their crime-fighting tools of the trade is the stuff of science fiction. Police departments across the country are trying out guns that fire darts equipped with GPS technology. The darts are capable of attaching to bumpers and are supposed to be used by police involved in high-speed vehicle chases. Instead of endangering residents and other drivers, police simply take the data from the attached GPS device, plot the suspects' travels via a digital mapping system, and intervene at a choice location or follow them home.[28] Other high-tech gadgets include surveillance cameras that mount on officers' ears and special cameras on patrol vehicles that scan license plates and search a database for outstanding violations.[29]

In September 2013, police were treated to even more high-tech gear at the annual Police Innovation Conference in Cambridge, Massachusetts. Amid the glitz of developing surveillance gear and the technological wizardry of iPad and iPhone tracking apps was information about a shocking new data program: a system to help law enforcement predict crimes before they even occur and identify suspects before they're even suspected—a sort of community policing to the tenth degree.[30] This latest trend in law enforcement is a potential civil liberties nightmare that twists traditional policing by sending cops to crime scenes before, not after, incidents occur. The software takes past crime statistics, analyzes them, and uses them to predict the direction crime is moving.[31] By mid-2013, police in Los Angeles had incorporated the technology into their department to help with community policy efforts.[32] Around the same time, law enforcement in Seattle wanted to test out the software's ability to stave off gun-related violence.[33]

Think about the repercussions of that software for a minute. What will be law enforcement's new boundary line, in terms of questioning, detaining, or even outright arresting citizens who may not even be suspected of a crime? It's sometimes hard enough to strike an agreeable balance between police work and constitutional rights—as seen in the mad law enforcement swoop in Watertown, Massachusetts, to root out the two Boston Marathon terrorist suspects. But armed with software and technological data that could actually lead to the prevention of a crime, police may soon run roughshod over the Fourth and Fifth amendments with both regularity and abandon. After all, if you thought you could prevent a crime before it happened, wouldn't you try?

Add to that software the likes of drones, and suddenly it's like Hollywood out there.[34]

Drones are the new, to-die-for police tool, seen as cost-efficient, safe, and dependable ways of conducting surveillance operations in dangerous and life-threatening situations. They can help locate stranded mountain climbers or forest hikers just as easily as they track and monitor violent offenders who break out of jail, or armed suspects trying to flee police. But the creepiness factor of a law enforcement eye in the sky can't be disregarded. City council members in Charlottesville, Virginia, disturbed by the prospect of police trolling the airspace with small, unmanned data recorders, actually voted in February 2013 to ban local law enforcement from using drones for criminal investigations—the first local government body in the nation to do so.[35]

But the technology isn't going away. Police in Seattle considered drones for surveillance, and went so far as to purchase two in early 2013. But the mayor's office was besieged with complaints from residents concerned about their privacies, and the local government banned their use.[36] In Oakland, California, meanwhile, police pressured the board of supervisors to accept federal dollars and buy a four-pound drone to use to fight crime in the community. The public rallied in outrage, and the American Civil Liberties Union mounted a protest.[37] Such shows of opposition aren't so successful elsewhere in the nation, however. By June 2013 the Mesa County Sheriff's Department in Arizona had embraced drone technology so tightly that officials had sent its two aircraft into skies to help with police chases and crime scene investigations a total of 171 hours over the course of three years. One sheriff reportedly said that the drones had been originally purchased to help with search-and-rescue missions, but that law enforcement basically used them however they wanted.[38]

It's that attitude that's a recipe for disaster for the fate of our Constitution. Good intentions—rooting out crime—often go awry when the government and police are involved. For a stark example, look at Fort Worth, Texas, and the partnership police forged with the National Highway Transportation Safety Administration, all in the name of maintaining a safe environment for drivers.

In November 2013, police in that community set up a roadblock and directed select drivers to a staged area, in a nearby parking lot. Once the motorists pulled into the lot, they were asked to provide a Breathalyzer reading, or give up samples of their saliva or blood—$10 for a cheek swab or $50 for a bit of blood. The reason? The NHTSA, in conjunction with a research company and partnering law enforcement agencies, was trying to collect data on drivers who operated vehicles under the influence of drugs and alcohol. Ostensibly, the DNA requests were just that—requests. And the NHTSA itself put out that all participation was voluntary, and that all DNA samples would be processed by an independent lab, anonymously. But some drivers said they felt intimidated by the whole affair. Others, including at least one local lawyer schooled in civil rights law, questioned the constitutional right of police to randomly select drivers and delay their travels for what amounted to a data collection drive.[39]

In the end, Fort Worth's police chief actually apologized for pulling over motorists and promised that his force would not take part in any similar DNA collections in the future.[40]

But here's the kicker: the NHTSA has conducted this same survey about every ten years for the past four decades at select spots around the nation.[41] Its last drug and alcohol survey reined in about nine thousand drivers to participate.[42] The latest leg that included Fort Worth was only a small part of a three-year effort to collect the same DNA data in sixty cities around the nation.

Is this really where we want our nation to head?

Armed with data and provided with the best technological advancements taxpayer money can buy, the government will eventually become the master and the individual, the servant. And when those government agents take the form of uniformed police, the intimidation factor on innocent civilians will be chilling.

Moreover, saying it's all for our security or claiming it's for the good of our nation is hardly a comfort—especially once it's realized how much policing nowadays is done for profit, not protection.

7

THE DOJ AND CIVIL FORFEITURES

Among the natural rights of the Colonists are these: First, a right to life; secondly, to liberty; thirdly, to property; together with the right to support and defend them in the best manner they can. These are evident branches of, rather than deductions from, the duty of self-preservation, commonly called the first law of nature.

—Samuel Adams

In America, suspects are considered innocent until proven guilty, right?

Wrong.

Consider the case of a Maryland man named Dale Agostini, who was driving with his fiancée; their sixteen-month-old son, Amir; and an employee of Agostini's restaurant, through East Texas a few years ago, on their way to buy some new equipment for their business. Agostini carried $50,291 in the car—a large sum, but one which he said spoke volumes among restaurant equipment sellers, who would slash prices if the buyer paid in cash.[1]

The four, all black, were approaching the Texas town of Tenaha, about an hour from Shreveport, Louisiana, when a police officer pulled them over. The road they traveled was a known drug-trafficking route, and the officer made them wait while he sent a drug-sniffing dog to scour their car. The officer then told them the presence of the dog actually served as a warrant, so he could legally search their vehicle. He found the cash, accused them of money laundering, arrested the adults, and sent the infant to child protective services.[2] Police also confiscated six cell phones, an iPod, and the car Agostini was driving.[3] That was in September 2007.

Agostini was never charged with a crime. But he was finally released, along with his fiancée and employee, was given his child back, and was able to win back his cash—that last only after months of fighting in court to prove he had rightfully earned it through his restaurant business.[4]

What the heck happened?

Turns out, Agostini was the victim of a long-running police power play to use asset forfeiture laws to seize properties.

In September 2012, the American Civil Liberties Union and an East Texas attorney reached a settlement with Tenaha authorities in a class action suit that revealed Agostini was one of about a thousand black or Hispanic motorists who had been pulled over between 2006 and 2008 in that same Shelby County area, for no apparent reason except for officers to strip them of cash and property. The judge called the police action a classic case of highway robbery, agreeing with plaintiffs that law enforcement had engaged in racial profiling to target their victims.[5] But what gave police the right to confiscate the properties of those they pulled over was actually based on Texas law—an asset forfeiture right that lets law enforcement take money and other items from those suspected of engaging in illegal drug-related activity. The police can seize the properties without waiting for a conviction or admission of guilt.

Another caught up in the Tenaha police snare in August 2007 was thirty-two-year-old James Morrow, a black man en route to visit his brother in Houston, pulled over for driving too close to the white line. Morrow didn't commit any crime; police had no warrant for his arrest. Yet they ordered him out of the car and began interrogating him, demanding he explain why he was driving through the small town. As with Agostini, the police brought out the drug-sniffing dog and searched Morrow's car. They found, and confiscated, $3,969 in cash and two cell phones. Morrow was never charged with a crime, but was transported to the police department and jailed nonetheless. The district attorney gave him a choice: forfeit the cash to the police or face prosecution for money laundering. Morrow chose the former, but then hired an attorney—for $3,500—to win back his money. He was left with $400 and an attitude of utter shock. He told the ACLU who fought his case as part of the class suit against Tenaha that he couldn't believe police could act that way in modern days.[6]

Once again, blame Texas asset forfeiture laws.

It sounds like a scenario right out of the eighteenth century, when England's system of "writs of assistance" permitted the king's soldiers to enter any home and take whatever they determined to be contraband. That untenable situation is what led in part to the American Revolution—but apparently, we have come full circle. The federal and state civil forfeiture laws are exactly what the Founding Fathers feared, which is why they wrote the Fifth Amendment to the Constitution:

> No person shall be held to answer for a capital, or otherwise infamous crime, unless on a presentment or indictment of a Grand Jury, except in cases arising in the land or naval forces, or in the Militia, when in actual service in time of War or public danger; nor shall any person be subject for the same offense to be twice put in jeopardy of life or limb; nor shall be compelled in any criminal case to be a witness against himself, nor be deprived of life, liberty, or property, without due process of law; *nor shall private property be taken for public use, without just compensation.* (emphasis added)

The Department of Justice defines its Asset Forfeiture Program as a means of obtaining properties that were used during the commission or facilitation of a federal crime. Its main purpose, the department claims, is to bolster public safety, specifically by taking away the tools criminals use to commit their crimes. For instance, if a drug dealer depends on a vehicle to ply his wares, law enforcement can take away his car and in so doing "disrupt or dismantle" the criminal operation and organization, as the Justice Department puts it.[7] The US Marshals Service oversees the program, and is in charge basically of disposing of all the properties seized by law enforcement agents around the nation.[8]

On the surface the idea seems sound. Why not let law enforcement seize items that criminals use to commit crimes? Certainly, the fear of losing one's valuables might serve as a deterrent to some criminals, and perhaps public safety really does come out the winner.

The problem, of course, is that the program is rife with abuse. Federal, state, and local law enforcement often use the asset forfeiture power more for personal gain than for genuine protection of the community. It's common sense, really. Take one small, cash-strapped town with a police force on a tight budget. Then give the police a means of adding to their coffers via on-the-job busts that don't have to meet high standards of probable cause. The tea leaves aren't hard to read. As the National Bureau of Economic Research found, when policy gives police the ability to keep what they seize, they seize more, and not always with justification.[9]

The genesis for this widespread system of abuse was the Comprehensive Drug Abuse Prevention and Control Act of 1970, which was enacted to fight the rising drug-trafficking epidemic and gave federal authorities the power to forfeit properties in drug-related cases. The law allows for criminal asset confiscation, where the property used in a crime could be seized and confiscated only after a criminal was convicted. But federal and state statutes recognize two other types of asset forfeitures too—civil and administrative.[10] This is where the standard of conviction falls to the wayside. Police and government agents can seize properties from those suspected of certain crimes without waiting for a guilty plea or verdict, and without having to obtain a court order or warrant.

In 2000, President Clinton signed the Civil Asset Forfeiture Reform Act, aimed at giving victims a few more rights in the fight to regain their seized properties.[11] But in the end, the basic gist of the power still stands: civil forfeiture gives police the legal right to seize cash and properties from suspects, while property owners are put in the sticky situation of having to prove their innocence to win back their properties.

Meanwhile, the draw of big money from asset forfeiture is a temptation that's hard for government to resist. Put bluntly: asset forfeiture is big business.

In 1984, Congress passed the Comprehensive Crime Control Act, which, among other things, created a new Department of Justice Assets Forfeiture Fund. That's where all the monies from asset forfeitures go, awaiting disbursement and allotment.[12]

State and local law enforcement agencies share in this pot, thanks to what the federal government created—an Equitable Sharing Program—that lets all the participants of a criminal or civil investigation receive a share of the asset forfeitures.[13]

For localities with cash flow issues, the Equitable Sharing Program is a budget dream come true. The US Marshals Service reported that between 1985 and 2012 the amount of Equitable Sharing Program proceeds that were distributed among all the players amounted to $5.8 billion. Another $2.4 billion in assets was still in the US Marshals' coffers, awaiting distribution.[14] The Department of Justice figures break it down with more specificity, by state and even jurisdiction.

For instance, during fiscal year 2012, the asset forfeiture program resulted in authorities confiscating a 2008 Viking Sport Fisherman-Cacique vessel valued at nearly $3.1 million from a Bayfield, Wisconsin, owner; $2.9 million in real property in Austin, Texas; $2.7 million in Chinese collectible coins and cash in Chesterfield,

Missouri; $2.8 million in silver coins, bars, and scrap metal in Coeur D'Alene, Idaho; $5 million in jewelry in Latrobe, Pennsylvania; a Cessna Citation 93 airplane valued at $1.7 million from Palm Springs, California; more than $25 million in artwork in New York; and 5,540 iPods valued at almost $1.2 million in Miami, Florida.[15]

That's just a drop in the bucket for fiscal year 2012 asset forfeitures reported by the Department of Justice. It doesn't even account for the millions of dollars in cash that agents seized during that twelve-month period. In one particularly lucrative bust, law enforcement netted almost $78 million in cash from a single operation in New York; in another, also in New York, they seized almost $75 million. Agents seized another $54 million in an asset forfeiture in Denver, Colorado.[16]

Not a bad haul for the civil servant sector.

As you can imagine, a US General Accountability Office investigation found the asset forfeiture program is in need of reform. The GAO reported in July 2012 that annual revenues from the Assets Forfeiture Fund increased significantly between 2003 and 2011, from $500 million to $1.8 billion. Part of the reason was an increase in prosecutions in cases of financial fraud—meaning some of that seized money was due to valid property seizures carried out in line with the full spirit of the law. But the GAO also said that the Department of Justice didn't properly document how it carried over undisbursed seizure funds into the next budget year, opening the doors to fiscal mismanagement—especially since the funds can be used for any expenses, as long as they relate to agency operations. And, the GAO said, the Department of Justice failed to expressly state how disbursements of seizure dollars are made, and what type of formulas are used to give money to one agency instead of another. In other words, the GAO said that those determination factors could be a lot more consistent and transparent.[17]

What the GAO report failed to address, however, was the core constitutional concern with the program: how is it legal for government to take private property without just cause?

While many Americans may see the sensibility of criminal asset forfeitures, or those that take place after a suspect has been tried and convicted of an actual crime, it's distressing that civil asset forfeitures allow for property seizures absent any crime or guilt. Here's an example of forfeiture law in motion that's easy to stomach: In December 2013, Virginia attorney general Ken Cuccinelli announced a cash award of $245,000 for a few local police departments in the state to buy bulletproof vests. The money didn't come from taxpayers, though. It came from asset forfeiture money Virginia earned by serving as a lead investigator in a massive Medicaid fraud case that settled for $1.5 billion. Virginia's asset forfeiture share from that case? It was $115 million. The $245,000 was one of the first drops in the bucket of asset forfeiture money Cuccinelli promised to share with local and state police agencies.[18] That's a criminal asset forfeiture and subsequent cash disbursement that many would applaud.

But the darker side of these powers completely obliterates any constitutional notion of innocent until proven guilty.

Civil asset forfeiture laws are much more lax and let government entities and their local police partners seize properties—including homes, cars, and cash—without due process of law, without a court guilty verdict or plea, and really, without very much probable cause. In essence, all police need according to the law is a "suspicion of guilt," and then they can take property.[19] Moreover, the third leg of asset forfeitures—the administrative forfeiture—is where law becomes even more loosey-goosey in terms of favoring the police over the individual. Administrative forfeitures give law enforcement officers the right to outright take properties valued below $500,000 based on what the FBI defines as "a reasonable ground for belief of guilt." As if that weren't unconstitutional enough, the law allows for an exemption for cash—meaning, police can confiscate any amount of cash at all, as long as they think someone might be breaking a law.[20]

Innocent? Guilty? With civil forfeitures, that's a moot point—an unnecessary consideration. And those who want their properties back have an uphill battle. The law puts the onus on those whose properties have been taken to prove their innocence, rather than on the police or government agency to prove their guilt. It's a topsy-turvy scenario that's not only difficult for victims to argue and prove in court, but expensive. Fact is, most asset forfeiture laws favor police, not property owners.

Convoluting the issue further is that states are free to determine what standard of proof they will use to carry out an asset forfeiture on a suspect or property owner—and those standards might differ from the standard the federal government uses.

Only a handful of states require police to meet the higher standard of "beyond a reasonable doubt" when faced with a question of asset forfeiture. The federal government and most states use the more relaxed standards—and in most cases, the evidence needed to seize property is actually lower than the proof needed to show that the individual was guilty of any criminal act that allowed for the seizure in the first place.[21] What results is that asset forfeitures are carried out with alarming frequency on the truly innocent.

It's almost as if the government has a license to steal—but sometimes, justice does prevail.

A sixty-nine-year-old man in Tewksbury, Massachusetts, nearly lost his family-owned business, Motel Caswell, after federal prosecutors seized it and claimed it was commonly used to facilitate illegal drug sales. The owner, Russell Caswell, denied that claim but was nonetheless forced to take his fight with federal authorities to court. In January 2013, a judge found in Caswell's favor, homing in on testimony that showed the motel had actually given police free reign to scope out the property and investigate suspected drug deals—belying any claim from police that motel management tolerated illegal activity and, therefore, facilitated crime. Caswell won his case and won back his motel. But his win is somewhat tempered by this realization: Caswell was forced into a legal brouhaha over his property rights that never should have been waged. He was never even charged with a crime.[22]

That's the insidious evil of asset forfeitures, though. And abuses of the power aren't exactly few and far between.

The nonprofit Institute for Justice tracked and graded asset forfeiture trends at the state level and found, with the exception of Maine, North Dakota, and Vermont, all ranked average or subpar in terms of upholding the individual's constitutional rights versus the ability of police to confiscate. The organization determined rankings based on the percentage of forfeited assets that agencies in the state were allowed to keep and the level of difficulty for property owners to win back their assets. Maine received an A–, and two other states, North Dakota and Vermont, received B+ and B, respectively. Eighteen other states fell in the average and low-average category, the C range. The remaining were rated between D+ and D–, near failing.[23]

GRADING THE STATES[24]

Forfeiture Law Grade: This grade indicates how rewarding and easy civil forfeiture is in a state.

State Law Evasion Grade: This grade indicates the use of equitable sharing as a measure of the extent to which state and local law enforcement agencies attempt to circumvent limits in state law. Higher grades indicate lower levels of equitable sharing.

STATE	FORFEITURE LAW GRADE	STATE LAW EVASION GRADE	FINAL GRADE
AL	D–	C	D
AK	F	B	D+
AZ	D–	C	D
AR	D–	C	D
CA	C+	F	D
CO	C+	C	C
CT	C+	B	C+
DE	F	A	C
FL	D+	D	D
GA	D–	F	D–
HI	D–	C	D

STATE	FORFEITURE LAW GRADE	STATE LAW EVASION GRADE	FINAL GRADE
ID	D–	A	C
IL	D	D	D
IN	B+	C	C+
IA	D–	C	D
KS	D–	C	D
KY	D–	C	D
LA	D	B	C–
ME	B+	A	A–
MD	B	C	C+
MA	F	C	D
MI	D–	D	D–
MN	D	B	C
MS	D	C	D+
MO	B	C	C+
MT	F	B	D+
NE	C	C	C
NV	D–	C	D+
NH	D	C	D+
NJ	D–	C	D
NM	D–	C	D+
NY	C–	F	D
NC	A–	D	C+
ND	D–	C	D
OH	B+	F	C–
OK	D–	C	D
OR	C	B	C+
PA	D–	C	D
RI	D	B	C–
SC	F	B	D+
SD	D–	A	C
TN	D–	C	D
TX	D	F	D–
UT	D–	B	C–
VT	B+	B	B
VA	D–	D	D–
WA	D–	C	D
WV	D–	D	D–
WI	C	C	C
WY	F	A	C

That's a dim showing, at best. And it's led to some egregious police abuses over the years that seem more in line with KGB tactics than American founding law. An elderly couple who had lived in their West Philadelphia home for nearly fifty years were practically tossed into the streets in August 2012 after their son, thirty-one, allegedly bought a small amount of marijuana from undercover police on the front porch of the house.[25] After the son was arrested, police told the parents—the mother was sixty-eight and the father, seventy, and in poor health from pancreatic cancer—the state was going to take their home and sell it at auction. The proceeds would be split between the district attorney's office and the local police department. Here's the real kicker: The asset seizure was due to go forth whether the son was acquitted of an illegal drug buy or not. In fact, the auction was likely to take place before the son's case even wrapped up in court.

How is that constitutional?

Ultimately, the elderly couple was granted a reprieve. The officer who showed up to evict them took pity on the man's health condition and said he'd delay serving the notice to give them time to mount a defense and fight the forfeiture proceedings. But the fact that they had to fight for their own home is egregious. In essence, the couple suddenly found themselves having to *thank* the government for letting them keep the home that rightfully belonged to them in the first place.

In what alternate universe does the government have the right to boot innocent Americans from their rightfully owned properties? Let's not forget: Our rights come from God, not government, and so do our properties. And that concept is backed by our legal system.

Private property rights are enshrined in the Constitution in several key amendments—the Fourth speaks to search and seizures; the Fifth speaks to due process; the Fourteenth speaks to the right of life, liberty, and property and denies the state the power to take them without due process. As John Adams made clear: "The moment the idea is admitted into society that property is not as sacred as the laws of God . . . anarchy and tyranny commence. Property must be secured or liberty cannot exist."

How right he was. Adams would be shocked to hear some of the private property infringements that go forth at the hands of our government these days.

Traffic officers in one of the busiest drug-smuggling regions in the world, the border area of South Texas, have a history of regularly using moving violations as the jumping point for asset forfeitures. In Kleberg County, Texas, home to about twenty-five thousand residents, the police drive high-performance Dodge Chargers as patrol vehicles and use digital ticket writers that are priced around $40,000 each. The police were able to pay for these high-ticket items because of the $7 million or so they seized in asset forfeitures stemming from various traffic stops conducted over a four-year period. In 2008, one section of Highway 77 roadway proved so lucrative for Kleberg County police that an area sheriff dubbed it a "piggy bank" for the community.[26]

The big question is, do you feel safer because of asset forfeiture?

Ask Nelly Moreira, an El Salvadorian woman who worked two cleaning jobs at a university in Washington, DC, and at the US Treasury Department. In March 2012, she loaned her car to her son, who was later pulled over by a police officer for a traffic violation. The officer ended up patting him down and found a gun in his clothing. The son was arrested and the officer confiscated Moreira's car.

A few weeks later, she received a letter in the mail advising that she owed $1,020 in bond money. She thought the money was to get her car back and borrowed the sum from friends. But the bill was actually a "penal sum," a fee that had to be paid to keep police from sending her car to auction. Worse, paying the fee only secured her the right to contest the seizure of her car. The civil forfeiture appeal process took months—and all along she still had to make payments on her car loan. Meanwhile she took costly public transportation to her jobs.

She finally won back her vehicle, but the public defender who argued her case said another 375 car owners faced the same situation—where their main modes of transportation were seized over minor infractions and stored at locked lots until they paid huge penal sums. The attorney blamed the situation on loose civil asset forfeiture standards that gave the city and police too much power to seize properties.[27]

Just a couple of months earlier, a man named Victor Ramos Guzman was traveling Interstate 95 by Emporia, Virginia, with his brother-in-law. A police cruiser drove up to them on the highway, peered into their window, and pulled them to the side of the road. The officer said Guzman was driving sixteen miles over the speed limit, but he didn't issue a ticket. What the officer did do, however, was confiscate $28,500 in cash that was in the car. The officer said the two were acting suspiciously and gave conflicting accounts of why they had the money. But the unclear statements and misunderstandings could just as easily have been due to the men's inability to speak fluent English. Turns out, Guzman was carrying the cash because the church where he serves as secretary commissioned him to go to Atlanta to conduct a real estate transaction to build a worship center in El Salvador. The church confirmed that to police, but the Virginia State Police called Immigration and Customs Enforcement to check on the men's legal status—they were lawful US residents—and then confiscated the cash, turning it over to the immigration authorities for safekeeping.[28] It took two months, but Guzman and his church finally won back their money. In March 2012, US Customs and Border Patrol cut a check for $28,500 and presented it to Guzman. The law firm that defended Guzman suggested that the police were so willing to break the law to grab the cash because the state's asset forfeiture law would have allowed Virginia State Police to keep 80 percent of the pot.[29]

Where's the due process there?

It seems one easy fix for asset forfeiture abuses would be to reform the system so that properties can be seized only when the owner is convicted of a crime. In truth, that's not really a reform. That's simply what the Constitution already says—that property may not be removed or taken without due process of law.

As it stands now, asset forfeitures are cash cows for law enforcement—little more than government-approved theft that adds insult to injury when its proponents audaciously proclaim that such action promotes safer communities.

But these cases of constitutional atrocity often fall under the radar of American consciousness. Why? Most asset forfeitures are reported as one-liners in newspaper crime stories—if at all. The insidious nature of the program often escapes local press scrutiny. Truly, this is an area where the Fourth Estate, the press, could really step up and do some due diligence, uncover and report on how the entire practice is leading our nation further down the road to Big Government and deeper into the pit of a police state.

But with the state of media as it is, don't hold your breath.

8

WHERE ARE THE WATCHDOGS?

If a nation expects to be ignorant and free in a state of civilization, it expects what never was and never will be.

—Thomas Jefferson to Charles Yancey, 1816

The October 16, 2012, town hall debate between former governor Mitt Romney and President Obama over the fight for the White House will go down in history as one of media's big moments of bias—a breathtaking show of liberal slant that was nonetheless vigorously defended by its protagonist, CNN's Candy Crowley, and those in her cheerleading camp.

In the middle of a tense moment in which Romney reminded Obama that he did not label the September 11, 2012, attacks on America's consulate in Benghazi, Libya, an act of terror for fully two weeks after the incident, and while Obama was fending off that claim with uncomfortable smiles and verbal denials, Crowley stepped in to calm the arena. Her famous proclamation: Obama did in fact call it an act of terror. He did so, she said, the day after the attacks, during a televised speech from the White House.[1]

Except—he didn't. Obama only said during Rose Garden remarks on September 12 that "no acts of terror will ever shake the resolve of this great nation, alter that character, or eclipse the light of the values we stand for." He didn't specifically label Benghazi a terrorist attack or an act of terror. He spoke only in the broadest of terms about acts of terror, to say that no terror attack could ever shake our nation's foundation.[2]

The president must have breathed a sigh of relief over Crowley's save. Not only did she violate previously agreed-upon debate rules between Romney and Obama campaign camps that mandated a more hands-off moderator role and strict limits on follow-up questioning—a pact she outright denied making.[3] She also jumped in at one of the debate's most pivotal moments, right when Romney was exposing Obama's lie and insisting on his accountability. And if her intervention weren't bad enough, Crowley obscured the truth from the American people by shutting down Romney's questioning. She then quickly moved the conversation to a softball sell for Obama, segueing into his crackdown on assault weapons at a time when the nation was emotionally drained over the July 2012 mass shooting at an Aurora, Colorado, movie theater.[4]

With media bias like that, it's no wonder Obama won reelection. But that's just one example of how the media turns a blind eye for leaders they favor to get away with dodging issues and skewing truths.

Remember, for days the American public was sold the line that the Benghazi attack was sparked by a California man who made a movie, *Innocence of Muslims*, with a twelve-minute YouTube trailer that mocked the prophet Muhammad and incensed the Middle East. The media should have been all over this story, investigating at all levels of the government. They should have worked tirelessly to expose who knew what and when, asking how the most powerful country on earth could be caught so off guard.

But the media completely dropped the ball.

And such overt bias flies in the face of the intent of the Founding Fathers when they created the First Amendment's freedom of the press—that an independent body was needed to hold the three branches of government accountable and to shed bright and continuous light on its doings for the benefit of the people. Thomas Jefferson spoke specifically of the power of the press, and raved of its ability to bring about societal changes in a peaceful manner, absent armed revolution. In a letter dated October 31, 1823, he wrote that the press is "the best instrument for enlightening the mind of man, and improving him as a rational moral and social being."

But the media is hardly living up to that honorable description.

Pew Research Center reported in July 2013 that only 28 percent of Americans see the media as contributing a great deal to society—a 10 percent drop in just four years, which is about the same percentage of Americans who think journalists contribute nothing at all.[5]

Pulitzer Prize–winning journalist Seymour Hersh—the bane of presidents as far back as the 1960s—thinks he has the answer: Fire the majority of editors and promote the few who can't be controlled.[6] Maybe then the press will stop carting water for the politicians they're actually supposed to vet. With the type of bias that strikes the heart of much in the media these days, that's not really a bad idea. As former secretary of defense Donald Rumsfeld said in an analysis he wrote about the media's role in the war on terrorism, when the press is complicit in not revealing the truth, they are in essence supporting the enemy. Only half of the fight takes place on the physical battlefield, he said. The other half plays out in the press, a constant war to win the hearts and minds of individuals.[7]

Which side does the US press serve?

On February 27, 1968, that dynamic became a little bit muddled, when Walter Cronkite signed off his broadcast with the pure opinion that the bloody violence in Vietnam was fated to end in a draw. Nowadays, television news watchers are used to having talking heads and pundits, along with hosts and anchors, deliver an even mix of opinion and fact. But Cronkite's words dropped with a thud into living rooms across the nation. President Johnson reportedly said, after hearing the anchor's assessment of the conflict, that since he'd lost Cronkite, he'd also lost heartland America.

Had Cronkite uttered those words today, nobody would have thought twice. His finger-wagging would fit right in with today's press coverage of war and warlike situations—at least when a Republican is in charge.

In August 2002, the media was filled with reports about President George W. Bush's "rush to war" in the months leading up to America's attack on Baghdad. And when America did drop bombs on a targeted government building in Iraq in March 2003, it was as if the Bush administration had committed an act of aggression the size and scope of Hiroshima. MSNBC said the US bombing was akin to the firebombing of cities in Japan during World War II years. The *New York Times* penned a piece that compared it to the September 11, 2001, terrorist hit on American soil, reminiscing of the time that New York was under attack. And NBC/MSNBC's Peter Arnett—already caught lying about America's use of cluster bombs against Iraqi civilians—then condemned the United States on a video, saying American forces were taken off guard by Iraq's military might and compelled to reevaluate war plans.[8]

Arnett was later fired for putting forth his personal view on television—but not for the anti-American views he held.[9]

Meanwhile, when the Bush administration rooted out and captured Iraqi dictator Saddam Hussein, the media outlet ABC described the situation as unhappy for Iraqis, because now the country was even more unstable. CBS took a slightly different tack, saying that Saddam's fall was tantamount to a slap in the face of all proud Iraqis, and that his humiliation at being captured was shared by the entire nation.[10]

Now go forward a few years to the Obama administration and the hunt for al Qaeda leader Osama bin Laden. The media fawned as President Obama announced in a dramatic May 2011 announcement outside the White House that "justice has been done."[11] Reports of the White House's real-time monitoring of the Navy SEAL and CIA operative raid of the Pakistani compound where bin Laden was holed up flew across the wires and permeated the network coverage. White House counterterrorism adviser John Brennan described it on CBS as an anxiety-filled moment, during which the president was constantly monitoring, constantly concerned.[12] On the one-year anniversary of the raid, NBC host Brian Williams spent considerable airtime discussing with *Today's* Ann Curry the president's tense time in a lengthy segment entitled, "Looking Back, Looking Ahead: Politics and the Osama bin Laden Raid." The segment—no small surprise—was little more than a way of singing the president's praises.[13] Meanwhile, the White House and media sell of Obama as an active and caring monitor of the mission as it unfolded turned out to be a total farce.

Former presidential body man Reggie Love came out in August 2013 at an event at UCLA and said that Obama had avoided the Situation Room like the plague at the time of the SEAL raid. Rather, Love said he and Obama were actually playing cards—during which the president remarked in a tense manner that he couldn't possibly watch the operation.[14]

The White House later responded to these comments, saying that Obama had actually stepped out of the Situation Room several times during the raid, but did not miss the key parts of the raid, including the part where the helicopter flew American forces to safety.[15] And once again, Seymour Hersh has weighed in, calling the entire White House mantra on the bin Laden raid—and the accompanying media coverage—a fiasco, a fake, and an utter lie. In late 2013, Hersh said he was so disgusted with what he slammed as the pathetic and biased press coverage of Obama's much-ballyhooed bin Laden win, that he was dedicating an entire chapter in a new book to telling the true narrative.[16]

The more malleable the press, the more chances for a dictator to emerge, and the more tyrannical a government, the more repressed and propagandistic the press. An informed citizenry is necessary for the proper function of our republic. When the press doesn't demand accountability from America's officials, it's a lot harder for the citizenry to stay informed. Perhaps that's part of the reason why months go by and the Benghazi terrorist attacks continue to be shrouded in mystery.

The biased press weaves into more than just military coverage, however.

Remember in 2008, when MSNBC's Chris Matthews, of *Hardball* fame, made mention on national television that Obama's oratory style sent thrills up his leg?[17] This attempt at a compliment earned him the nickname "Tingles" from conservative outlets.[18]

Or, when the press was so desperate to paint the Tea Party in a poor light that mainstream media resorted to flat-out lies?

The *New York Times* was actually forced to issue a correction for falsely reporting that a member of the Tea Party shouted racial epithets at Rep. John Lewis, a Georgia lawmaker with a storied civil rights past.[19] Lewis said he was called the slurs while crossing through the crowds of Obamacare protesters at Capitol Hill in March 2010. Despite the lack of any corroborating proof, the *Times* ran with the completely irresponsible headline "Spitting and Slurs Directed at Lawmakers," leaving no doubt that they intended for the reader to assume that the slurs and spitting did, in fact, occur. It only shows how little regard the press has for the Tea Party.[20]

And why? The Tea Party, after all, is all about lower taxation— about rooting out waste and abuse in Washington, DC. That used to be something the press also tried to do. On top of that, the press might at least be interested in digging into the real motivations behind the Tea Party message, and finding out why so many across America seem so outraged and frustrated with politicians. But instead, we get CNN's Suzanne Malveaux, who referred to Tea Party activists in the vulgar "teabagger" term during a November 2009 nationally televised Situation Room broadcast.[21]

This same Malveaux, however, had a completely different—and fawning—read on the Occupy movement. In a November 2011 broadcast on CNN, she told noted leftist and former Obama administration environmental czar Van Jones that he'd make a terrific spokesman for the Occupiers.[22] A month later, she asked Jones back on her show to explain how squatting, the illegal practice of taking over a property absent title or deed or payment or rent or mortgage, might actually help the Occupy movement.[23]

When you read through the coverage of the Tea Party activism versus the Occupy movement, you clearly see that the mainstream press for Occupy is by and large more sympathetic, willing to dismiss or gloss over the many instances of real crime committed by those who camped at public parks in various spots of the nation—and outright ignore that the camping activities were in themselves often illegal, absent permit and local approval. Yet let a Tea Party protester litter, and it's as noted media bias author and commentator Bernie Goldberg said: The media's line is, Tea Party people are racists—terrorists, even.[24]

Simply put, the media hands the Occupy activists a free pass, even when their movement is connected to a variety of crimes, from property destruction to assault to rape.[25] Why? Just as simply put: many in mainstream press are just too deep in the ideological camp of the Occupy movement to see with clear eyes.

And what an ideological camp it is.

Occupy supporters included the likes of the Communist Party USA, the American Nazi Party, the Socialist Party, Venezuela's former president Hugo Chavez, Nation of Islam leader Louis Farrakhan, the Ayatollah Khameini of Iran,[26] and the Communist Party in China.[27] Many members of the media—lured by Hollywood influences or revisionist histories—view these same organizations and individuals through rose-colored glasses. Others perhaps grab at a bit of 1960s-style rebel factor with the idealized support of dictators and radicals.

With ideology like that, it's perhaps easier to see how the press can spin and skew with such disregard for truth and still sleep at night.

Remember George Zimmerman? He was the Florida homeowner who shot and killed seventeen-year-old Trayvon Martin in what he claimed was an act of self-defense, in line with the state's stand-your-ground gun laws. Mainstream media hate the stand-your-ground law because they want more gun control, and they hated Zimmerman because they thought he was a white man who had killed a black teenager. Some news outlets painted Zimmerman, who had Hispanic roots, as simply white. Others labeled him a "white Hispanic."[28] And still others, like *Salon*, dedicated entire stories to unearthing the mystery with full-length pieces topped by blunt headlines: "Is George Zimmerman white or Hispanic? That depends."[29]

Truly, many in the media were slanting even the earliest stories of Zimmerman's shooting death of Martin as an act of racism, a clear-cut unwarranted killing, before the case went to trial. Zimmerman was ultimately acquitted of murder charges, after his attorney successfully proved he acted in self-defense in line with state laws. But not before the media had its run of racist rants, fueled in part by noted black activists Al Sharpton and Jesse Jackson, who worked hard to portray Zimmerman's act, and Florida's self-defense gun laws, as unlawful.[30]

Sharpton and Jackson ran to Florida in the weeks after Martin's killing and held prayer vigils, protests, and marches, attended by thousands and dutifully covered by both local and national media. And their marches didn't stop after Zimmerman was acquitted of second-degree murder. Within days of the jury decision, Jackson and Sharpton were back in Florida, addressing the NAACP convention and pushing for one million to sign on to their petition for the US Justice Department to go after Zimmerman for civil rights violations and other federal charges.[31]

Sharpton, in fact, called the not-guilty ruling a travesty of justice, likening it to the Rodney King police brutality case in Los Angeles, 1991–1992, and vowing to push for the same outcome—that the Justice Department file federal civil rights charges.[32]

The mainstream media, meanwhile, continued to refer to Jackson and Sharpton as simple civil rights activists, drumming forth a message of peace.[33] Conservative news commentator Tucker Carlson finally exploded on Fox News and decried the favor being shown Sharpton and Jackson during the Zimmerman trial, saying the two don't deserve to be characterized as civil rights leaders. On national television Carlson called the pair "hustlers and pimps" who earn their livings by inciting fear and racial strife.[34]

The favor shown Jackson and Sharpton wasn't the only media bias taking place during the Zimmerman trial, however. Other instances were far more blatant.

NBC News was perhaps the worst. They creatively edited the tape of Zimmerman's 911 call to give the impression that he was telling the operator that Martin appeared to be a seedy character and seemed to be "up to no good," because of his skin color. Then they played the altered tape on television—and not just once.[35]

What really transpired during the 911 call, however, was that Zimmerman only mentioned Martin's skin color in response to a direct question of ethnicity from the operator—she asked if he was black, white, or Hispanic, and Zimmerman, of course, answered black.[36]

NBC ultimately fired one of its Miami reporter-producers for that shameful show of bias. The network also fired a national NBC producer after the same altered clip was aired on *The Today Show*.[37] Meanwhile, the network president released a statement that NBC was conducting an internal investigation but that the edit was done only to fit the network's time schedule and was not a purposeful move to portray Zimmerman in a negative light.[38]

NBC's broadcast of its tampered version of the 911 call was a pure propaganda move to further the story line that Zimmerman was white and racist. And NBC's explanation—that the tape was creatively edited only to fit the time allotted for broadcast—is bunk and a slap in the face to America's intelligence.

But then again, when it comes to some agendas that the media has claimed as its own—specifically those related to the Second

Amendment and clamping gun-ownership rights—many in the press seem to adopt the attitude that all means are justified as long as the desired end is achieved.

In May 2013, a Pew Research Center poll found that 56 percent of Americans were under the impression that gun-related violence has been on a steady rise, despite crime statistics that showed such crimes have actually dropped by nearly half since 1993.[39]

Why is that?

The only clear answer is that the media—pushed on by anti–Second Amendment politicians, personal agendas, and gun control activists—dismiss facts, either out of disbelief or with intent to influence policy. Either way, instead of being a watchdog for the little guy and helping him make informed decisions, the press keeps up a steady drumbeat of the ever-increasing need for more gun control. It's the expected reporting package nowadays: acts of gun violence followed by stories of the need to curb access to guns, especially assault-style weapons. In April 2009, Michael Lindenberger wrote in *Time* magazine a ten-year anniversary piece on the Columbine shootings by Dylan Klebold and Eric Harris, calling the mass shootings that left twelve students and one teacher dead an act of "carnage" that sadly showcased America as a "nation of shooters." The headline for this piece? "Ten Years After Columbine, It's Easier to Bear Arms."[40]

In June 2013, *Slate* blared forth the headline "After Newtown, We Vowed to Take Gun Control Seriously. Why Has Nothing Changed?"[41] The piece's conclusion: because America as a whole has chosen to disregard the plight of gun-violence victims and their loved ones and turned a blind eye to their cause.

The message from the media is clear: if you don't support more gun control, then you don't care about victims of gun violence.

The Fourth Estate is crumbling, preferring to serve as a mouthpiece for politicians rather than as a watchdog for the people, and as an active participant in the advancement of select social justice causes rather than as an arbiter of the truth. Even that wouldn't be so bad, though, if only the bias were admitted. But a press that claims nonpartisanship, while secretly pushing partisanship, is contemptible.

The Founding Fathers put such stock in the need for a free and vibrant press, in part to help curtail and control government's activities, they enshrined it in the very first amendment, guaranteeing its life so long as the republic remains. Before the passage of the Stamp Act of 1765, American colonies regarded newspapers in the same vein as books and pamphlets. But then came Samuel Adams, the hard-charging journalist who used words and publishing power to change the shape of policy, to stage somewhat of a revolution against taxes and sway the people to fight back against the Stamp Act. Due in part to his influence, the act was repealed. He wrote of the success to the colonial people: "But YOUR Press has sounded the alarm. YOUR Press has spoken to us the words of truth. It has pointed to this people their danger and their remedy. It has set before them liberty and slavery."[42]

Unfortunately, today's press is falling far short of this calling, leaving Americans vulnerable to the advances of government and encroachments into private rights.

9

THE BATTLE AGAINST ZONING ZEALOTS

Find out just what the people will submit to and you will have found out the exact amount of injustice and wrong which will be imposed upon them; and these will continue until they are resisted with either words or blows, or both. The limits of tyrants are prescribed by the endurance of those whom they oppress.

—Frederick Douglass

Sun City Shadow Hills is a gated community for adults ages fifty-five and higher in Indio, California, just outside Palm Springs. The website for the housing development bills it as a cultural and recreational mecca with plenty of nearby offerings for the active senior, including theater, golf, hiking trails, hot air ballooning, and resorts and spas.[1]

Residents, at least some of them, have a different take.

They say the homeowner's association (HOA) has grown so out of control that living there is like living under a monarchy.[2] The rules, they charge, are aimed more at generating money for the property managers than at providing the promised amenities for the residents.

Here's an example: One rule at the community, called the "Conduct Code," put the responsibility for visitors' behavior in the residents' hands. Likely, the regulation was in part aimed at curbing outrageous behaviors, such as drunken visitors who then destroyed neighbors' properties. But the code went further than that. It even made residents responsible for vendors and contractors. So when the Home Depot contractor who went to work at several homes in the community was caught driving seven miles over the speed limit and issued a ticket by the HOA's private police force, the unlucky resident who happened to be named at the guard gate as the worker's first visit of the day was also fined $50.[3]

That resident wasn't driving. It wasn't her car. But because the contractor was her visitor, the "Conduct Code" deemed her responsible.

Fair?

That doesn't really figure into the equation. The fact is, HOAs are legal entities created to maintain and regulate the properties within a residential community, run by board members who often wield considerable power. Once you sign on the dotted line and agree to move into an HOA community, you're committed to abiding by the rules and regulations, and to paying the monthly dues.

And it's a large number of homeowners in the United States who have signed that dotted line. In 2012, roughly 63 million Americans were living in HOA communities.[4]

By comparison, in 1970, only about 2.1 million Americans lived in HOA-run housing. In 1980, it was 9.6 million. The big boom occurred between 1990 and 2012, when that statistic rose from 29.6 million to 63.4 million.[5]

Industry experts predict the growth will continue. Part of the reason for HOA popularity is that homeowners believe the community oversight helps preserve and protect their property values, and they ultimately see a good return on their fees.[6]

But is the trade-off of freedom worth it?

Private property rights, after all, are etched into this nation's soul. HOA horror stories suggest that residents are frequently called upon to abide by the strictest of regulations, some of which seem to go far beyond what board members claim are aimed at preserving community safety or property values. Those who protest the rules have limited recourse. They can oust the board—but that requires an election. They can wage a legal battle—but that can prove both lengthy and expensive, because in the eyes of the courts HOAs are quasi-governments with legislative and judicial powers.

Option number three for HOA residents: they can pack up and move.

Or, they can choose to ignore the HOA rules. But that's a risky decision that opens the door to lawsuit.

In 2011, a Marine Corps veteran living in a Texas housing community was sued by his HOA over a flagpole that board members deemed as too tall. The resident, Mike Merola, said he wanted the twenty-foot pole to hang his American and Marine Corps flags, but was denied a permit by the HOA board.[7] He went ahead and erected it anyway, calling the HOA's 6-foot height limit for flagpoles a ridiculous policy.[8] The HOA, however, filed a complaint in the nearby district court to order the flagpole's removal and to fine the homeowner $10 each day his pole remained in place.[9] The HOA further petitioned to pass along its court costs to the homeowner.

Merola ultimately won his case and the right to keep his twenty-foot pole.[10]

Moreover, his case actually spawned a new state law that guarantees HOAs cannot prevent homeowners from flying US, Texas, or military branch flags on their properties, and that they may hang them from flagpoles that reach as high as twenty feet.[11]

Yet some HOAs refused to cede their power on this point, choosing instead to defy state law.

Just a couple of years after Merola's case was settled, another HOA in Texas demanded a community resident remove his American flag. The case involved a retiree in a northwest Houston housing development, Billy B. Martin, who said he was targeted by his HOA after he complained to them about a tattered flag that flew over the community clubhouse.[12] The HOA finally replaced it, but soon after demanded he take down his personal American flag, alleging its pole was improperly mounted on a common area and therefore impeded other residents' access to the area.[13] The HOA threatened a $200 fine for each day he refused to take down the flag. They would also go after him for an unspecified amount of civil damages and attorney fees, they warned.[14]

Martin did refuse to take down his flag. Furthermore, in an act of defiance, he turned his flag upside down—the national symbol of distress.[15]

The HOA sued, actually accusing Martin in court documents of jeopardizing the property values of the other two hundred community residents because of his flagpole.[16]

The same lawyer who successfully defended Merola took on Martin's case pro bono.[17] The case was set for initial court hearing in early 2014.[18]

But really, why are we even here?

It hardly seems American to dicker over the proper length of a flagpole that might fly a US flag on a homeowner's private property. Yet that's what HOAs in many instances do. And just because many don't—just because some HOAs are actually freer than others—doesn't take away from the main point.

HOAs are still regulatory bodies tasked with telling homeowners what they can and cannot do with their lawfully purchased properties. It's baffling, not to mention a sad commentary on the state of our national regard for private property rights, that so many Americans would embrace this regulatory system.

Celina, Texas, homeowners trying to repair roof damage after a hailstorm in 2012 were told to stop construction after their Carter Ranch HOA board members said the new shingle color didn't match the others in the community. The shingles were apparently tinged brown, while most of the other roofs in the community were gray. So the HOA started issuing fines to the homeowners, David and

Melinda Hawkes, first at $25 per day, then $50, then $500. When all was said and done, the Hawkeses accrued a total of $6,000 in fines—simply because their shingles weren't the right color.[19]

Not paying is not an option. HOAs maintain legal authority to place liens and to foreclose upon homeowners who don't pay their fees and fines.

In the Hawkeses' case, the HOA helpfully offered to set up an installment plan so the couple could pay over time.[20]

But this is just disastrous when looked at through the lens of the Constitution. How can we so easily cede something that's supposed to be a core American principle—the right to own and the right to control one's own property?

If only such HOA grievances were few and far between. It really doesn't even matter if the homeowner fights the HOA and wins or fights the HOA and loses. That any homeowner is forced to fight at all is the real offense. Why should a homeowner have to battle for a right that's already been won during the signing and ratification of our Constitution?

The answer is simple, really: because the homeowner agreed to the terms of the HOA policy before purchasing the home.

But that doesn't make the HOA regulatory system any easier to swallow. And its growth on American soil is just a disease, rooting out all that colonists, founders, and early Americans fought so hard to achieve—a form of government that held private property rights as sacred.

In June 2013, a Chesterfield County, Virginia, homeowner waged a war against his HOA when board members advised him his garden violated community code. Chris Gilson and his wife, Teresa Collier, maintained a sizable plot of herbs, vegetables, and flowers in the front of their home, and the HOA said its location was improper. Board members threatened to fine him $10 a day for ninety days if he didn't immediately remove the garden.[21]

In August 2013, the board and Gilson reached a compromise. He could keep his garden intact for four more months, at which time he would have to modify his plot and confine his vegetable growing to one side of his house. The HOA board also waived all the fees and fines.[22]

HOA members patted themselves on the back for achieving a successful compromise and avoiding a legal battle. Gilson, too, said he was happy with the decision.[23]

But just the idea that a homeowner has to obtain permission to grow vegetables in his front yard is an affront to the Constitution and to the freedoms forged by our Founding Fathers. It's a pure violation of our core American belief system.

Do our rights come from government? Or do they come from God?

When homeowners are happy when they only lose part of their private property rights, but get to keep a portion—even though they worked and paid for all—something is seriously wrong with our collective thought process. HOAs are just the tip of the iceberg. Modern-day government has far too many tools at its disposal to wrest control of property rights from businesses and homeowners— and to do it in what's touted as a lawful manner.

William and Marlene Pepin are Massachusetts residents who were forced into a court battle over their right to use their private property as they saw fit after somebody reported to state conservation authorities the presence of an Eastern box turtle on their land.[24] The Massachusetts Division of Fisheries and Wildlife then affixed a habitat label to their property, effectively preventing them from developing their land.[25] The curious aspect of this story is that the state statute guiding the use of the habitat label does not include that particular species.[26] In other words, seeing an Eastern box turtle does not automatically rain down a habitat label on the property where the turtle was seen.

It would seem, then, that the MDFW seriously overreached its lawful authority by tossing the habitat label onto the Pepins, given state law doesn't even recognize that label for turtles. And the label is far from simply honorific.

It brings some heavy-hitting private property regulations, requiring that every acre of proposed development be offset by three acres of open space and conservation.[27] That effectively derailed the homeowners' plans for the property, which were to construct a home where they could comfortably retire.[28]

The Pepins, facing hefty punishments and fines of $10,000—as well as imprisonment—if they violated the environmental order, took their case to court, alleging the state agency wasn't abiding by its own laws.[29] In late 2013, it wound up at the feet of the state's supreme judicial court, fully five years after the fight with the MDFW began and with an unknown decision date.[30]

Down the road in bucolic Fauquier County, Virginia, about forty-five miles southwest of our nation's capital, farmers in 2012 were fighting local governing officials for the right to sell their own farmed produce on their own privately owned farmland.

The battle kicked off when a homeowner complained that a neighbor—a farmer with sixty-eight acres—was selling her home-grown fruits and vegetables on her property in alleged violation of business laws. Local zoning officials got involved, and suddenly the farmer was fending off attacks from government bureaucrats who cited various permit rules and regulations and tried to fine her $5,000.[31] Virginia state law, meanwhile, includes a provision to prevent locals from infringing on a farmer's business—but it also leaves open the door for locals to regulate standards to protect citizens' health and safety.

Has this nation come so far that erecting a farm stand to sell one's own grown produce on one's own property is a violation of law? That's as bad as the many reports in recent years that have grabbed national headlines about local zoning zealots sending in police to clamp down on kids' lemonade stands.

In 2011, three girls in Midway, Georgia, ages fourteen, twelve, and ten, were trying to make a few dollars for a planned trip to Jekyll Island by selling lemonade at a homemade stand.[32] Local police swarmed and demanded proof of a permit. They didn't have one and couldn't afford the $50 per day per permit—called a peddler's and food permit—or the $50 per day business license fee to continue another twenty-four hours of operations.[33] So they closed shop at that location.

The same scenario befell a couple of sisters in Apple, Wisconsin, who had been selling lemonade at a makeshift stand for seven years in a row at an annual car show. But in 2011, city officials passed an ordinance that banned vendor food sales within two blocks of the event—effectively shutting down the sisters' lemonade shop.[34]

These are hardly anomalies.

Even the Girl Scouts and member cookie sales have come under fire.

In 2011, Girl Scouts of Savannah, Georgia, were booted from the same sidewalk peddling position they had maintained for years— in front of the home of the woman who had actually founded the Girl Scouts in 1912—after an anonymous source complained to city officials. The city, citing local ordinance, told them to move. The story made international headlines, and zoning officials finally caved and found a loophole to let the girls sell their cookies.[35]

But should we be thanking the local government officials for finally coming to their senses? Or voting them out of office for even thinking such a crackdown was sane?

In a nation where rights come from God, not government, such thanks aren't needed. But America's thought process on this point is upside down, and now citizens are expected to be grateful and express gratitude for being allowed to keep those very rights that are already guaranteed in the Constitution.

In August 2013, Pasco County, Florida, planning department officials dreamed up a new ordinance aimed at giving the region more roads in a most cost-efficient of manners—by taking the land from private owners for free.[36] They didn't describe it that way, of course.

In bureaucratic lingo, the planning department termed it the "Right of Way Preservation Ordinance." That gave local government officials the means of declaring certain properties necessary for the construction of roads as "right-of-way" properties—and of then compelling landowners to dedicate these properties for road construction. Landowners, in return, would get permits to develop the remainder of their properties as they see fit.[37]

It's a win-win, local officials declared.

Not really. The system is more like a robber stealing some property, returning part of it—and then expecting gratitude.

How is it constitutional for a local governing body to take control of private land and then decide that just compensation is a development permit? The Fifth Amendment speaks to the need for government to provide proper compensation when it takes land for public use.

A court finally did find in favor of landowners on that point— but the fact that the practice could even be seen as sensible policy in a country that's supposed to be run by a notion of God-given rights is outrageous.

Without private property rights, all other constitutional rights crumble.

In January 2013, the National Rifle Association won a lawsuit against the San Francisco Housing Authority over a rule that had been in effect since 2005 banning guns from public housing units.[38] The ban wasn't just for those with criminal or felony pasts. Rather, even lawful gun owners with valid permits who moved into the public housing had to relinquish their arms.

The government got away with that ban for so many years because the government, in that case, controlled the property. At least the courts sided with the NRA on that one.

But similar bans have popped up in other locales around the nation.

In Fernandina Beach, Florida, a seventy-three-year-old man living in public assistance housing was ordered in 2009 by the Housing Authority to give up his otherwise lawfully owned weapon or face eviction.[39]

Hundreds of miles away, in Warren County, Illinois, a disabled former police officer living in a government-subsidized home filed suit after the Warren County Housing Authority tried to ban him from owning a gun.[40]

These state actions all came on the heels of a mid-1990s effort from the federal Department of Housing and Urban Development, under secretary Henry Cisneros, to ban all firearms in all publicly funded housing as a means of lowering crime rates.[41]

The outcome of these cases isn't as important as the message they herald: private property rights are necessary to preserve all others. If the government thinks it owns your home, then it by logical extension thinks it has the right to control what occurs in your home. And it's not only guns that come under attack when private property rights are not held as sacrosanct.

In July 2012, a Phoenix, Arizona, pastor was tossed into jail for sixty days for holding prayer services in his home. His accusers, members of the local government, said his home-based worship violated a total of sixty-seven different zoning laws, and that he was wrongfully operating a church from his residence.[42]

In a separate case in 2010, the Alliance Defense Fund filed a legal petition against Gilbert, Arizona, government officials for banning church services, including Bible studies, from private residences. The nonprofit filed the court documents on behalf of a pastor who was targeted by zoning officials and ordered to stop holding religious services in his home—even if they were small and occurred only infrequently.[43]

Hartford, Connecticut, local zoning bureaucrats tried the same thing years earlier.

In 2000, the American Center for Law and Justice stepped in to defend a family who was ordered by the Town of New Milford Zoning Commission to stop holding home-based religious services. The town's line of argument: the family could not by law pray with anybody in their home except for other family members.[44]

How does this all fit with our declarative founding vision—that we are endowed by our Creator with life, liberty, and the pursuit of happiness? Or with our constitutional guarantee that we will not be deprived of life, liberty, or property, without due process of law?

The arrogance with which all levels of government violate these basic principles is shocking. But it gets worse. In some jurisdictions of the nation, local governing officials actually think it's quite proper policy to spend tens of thousands of dollars of taxpayer money to buy property—but then refuse to disclose the location of the property. The cited reason?

It's all for our safety and security.

10

THE DATA GRAB AND THE GROWTH OF SECRET GOVERNMENT CENTERS

Necessity is the plea for every infringement of human freedom. It is the argument of tyrants. It is the creed of slaves.

—William Pitt in the House of Commons, November 18, 1783

In September 2012, Scottsdale, Arizona, City Council members voted unanimously, 7-0, to spend $1.87 million to purchase a new facility for the Scottsdale Police Department's Investigative Service Bureau. The council agreed to the expenditure by consent agenda—a fast-track way for the governing body to approve items en masse that are generally mundane and noncontroversial in nature, and that don't warrant open discussion and citizen input.[1]

Spending $1.87 million should by itself require open discussion, open debate, and plenty of input from citizens who are footing the bill.

But that's not the worst part of this story.

The council also voted to keep secret the location of this facility. Why? It's a safety issue, they said. Undercover police enter and exit on a daily basis, and the council members felt keeping the building location a secret would prevent criminals from hiding on the outskirts of the facility and taking note of the officers' faces and identities.[2] But really, that justification just defies common sense. Scottsdale isn't that large a community. Wouldn't someone, somewhere, someday notice?

Moreover, the council did publicly announce the facility spanned 17,827 square feet—a sizable property that stands apart from other buildings in the community. And following that announcement, a local newspaper actually guessed—and printed for public view—the address of the only building that fit that size and description, after doing a little legwork through property appraisal information and real estate sales records.[3] So it just seems doubly ridiculous that the government body would try to hide the building location.

That's just an entirely new level of arrogance that makes a complete mockery of the idea of the citizenry as the boss and the government as the employee—the civil servant.

America's founders etched into our national belief system that the government is run by the people, and that it's the citizens' duty to ensure the government is kept in its proper place. Thomas Jefferson wrote of it in one of our country's foremost documents, the Declaration of Independence: "But when a long train of abuses and usurpations, pursuing invariably the same object evinces a design to reduce them under absolute despotism, it is their right, it is their duty, to throw off such government and to provide new guards for their future security."

That's a core American spirit—that of the government being run by the people, for the people. And that's why Scottsdale City Council members committed such a grave constitutional offense. The seven members of that voting body exemplified government at its worst: arrogant, dismissive, elitist, and willfully above the law.

Yet more and more in America, it's this attitude of government that prevails.

In mid-June 2013, national media jumped on reports of the National Security Agency's newest data center, a massive, top-secret facility just south of Salt Lake City, Utah.[4] Spanning one million square feet, it's one of six major data sites for the NSA and will serve as a backup for the other facilities and also as a central point of intelligence gathering with real-time access for analysts seeking the most up-to-date information.[5] Utah was reportedly the location of choice because of the state's provision of cheap electricity rates, a skilled workforce, and access to massive water supplies necessary for the cooling of computer servers.[6]

That's the official line, anyway.

Unofficially, Utah was the rumored site for the center because of the state's large Mormon population and the belief that this perceived closed, cloistered society could keep a secret. There's little proof of that aspect driving the government's choice of Utah, but it does keep the conspiracy wheels turning.[7]

The facility cost an estimated $1.5 billion to build. But reports varied on how much data the facility could collect and store, ranging from several terabytes to five zetabytes—the equivalent of the amount of information that can be gleaned from 62 billion stacked iPhone 5s.[8] Another estimate of what the facility could store in terms of data per minute equals the amount of printed material that's housed at the Library of Congress.[9]

Either way, the center is a massive data collection site—the NSA's largest computing facility in the entire world—and NSA deputy director John C. Inglis's offhand attempt to defray America's suspicions and fears in the early days of its announced construction fell on deaf ears.

In essence, Inglis told Americans not to worry, that the NSA was all-American, with heartfelt regard for the Constitution, and that analysts and agents were fully trained to uphold civil rights while rooting out national security threats.[10]

But it was only a few days later that Edward Snowden began leaking to the public previously undisclosed information about the NSA's spy operations on Americans.[11] So much for the "trust me" form of government. Suddenly, Inglis's remarks didn't seem to hold much water.

That's called bad timing.

Still, even after the Snowden leaks, the NSA continued to tout its openness, and Inglis continued to sing loud about his agency's transparency. On the NSA's website to promote its core values and mission statements, Inglis is quoted as saying: "I'm often asked the question, 'What's more important—civil liberties or national security?' It's a false question; it's a false choice. At the end of the day, we must do both, and they are not irreconcilable. We have to find a way to ensure that we support the entirety of the Constitution—that was the intention of the framers of the Constitution, and that's what we do on a daily basis at the National Security Agency." In a different section on the same website, Inglis also said the NSA worked hard to maintain transparency. He said: "We must remain transparent. And the way we do that is we ensure that there is external oversight that is rich—some might say pervasive—across the National Security Agency."[12]

But that's just bureaucratic speech.

In September 2013, the NSA wouldn't even give a local Salt Lake City newspaper a straight answer on whether or not the Utah Data Center had officially opened for business.[13] A spokeswoman would only say that each machine that's installed is immediately turned on—a bland statement without context.

Is that the type of "support [of] the entirety of the Constitution" Inglis meant? Or, is that more the type of transparency he claimed the NSA worked diligently, daily, to uphold?

The American public would have a lot more tolerance for government intelligence's need to keep its secrets if these same government intelligence agencies weren't so frequently caught breaking the law. That "trust me" mantra grows old fast. You know, the average

American citizen can't even drive into the parking lot of the new Utah Data Center, never mind set up a visit. Only a few dignitaries from the state were lucky enough to take the tour—and then they were mum on what they saw.[14]

On top of that, the one thousand or so workers the site had employed during its two-year construction phase have been sent packing.[15] In the end, the center is going to employ only about two hundred people—a small handful of the nation's best and brightest whose analytical skills and technological brilliance will no doubt be matched only by their ramped-up reticence. We'll never know what goes on there.

All we know is the NSA line, courtesy of Deputy Director Inglis—trust us. But (a) the Utah Data Center is equipped with supercomputers to monitor, collect, and disseminate mind-boggling amounts of data from e-mails, telephone calls, social media, and Internet search sites. And (b) the NSA has already been caught snooping in Americans' own private information, absent proper court permission.

In a much-awaited January 2014 speech about NSA surveillance, President Obama attempted to tamp down fears about government spying, telling Americans that he was ordering Congress to create a watchdog of sorts to help the surveillance court judges decide certain data and technology spy decisions—an advisory panel of independent individuals. Obama also said that he was tasking Attorney General Eric Holder and National Intelligence Director James Clapper to decide who has charge of Americans' phone records—metadata—and where those records will be stored.[16] But first off: The president can't order Congress to do anything. The executive branch doesn't control the legislative branch—and that's how Founding Fathers intended it. So Obama's so-called strong message of NSA reform was little more than damage control, dependent on lawmakers' decision to act. And second off: Who really cares which federal agency takes control of the phone collection data? In the end, the American individual is still the victim and the federal

government, the new owner of citizen data. Just because the metadata might be stored with the NSA instead of the CIA or the DOJ
doesn't really matter—they're all government entities.

The question Americans should be asking is why the government
needs to keep the information at all.

A mathematician, William Binney, who worked for the NSA
for forty years but quit in 2001 after blowing the whistle on the
NSA's domestic spying program, said it's really not that hard to
collect massive amounts of information that can then be stored for
hundreds of years.[17] Hundreds of years? What an uncomfortable
thought. In the meantime, Americans will just have to trust that
the NSA, the agency that collects and stores the data, will act in the
individual's best interests in securing it and keeping it private too.
It's worth noting that in December 2013, Binney came forward with
a shocking statement to the press: The NSA's spy program has progressed to the point where America has now become a police state.[18]

But wait, it gets worse. It seems the Utah Data Center where
much of the information is stored has experienced operational
problems—yet one more red flag about the government's ability to
keep information private and secure.

Let's hope the powers that be are better at keeping information
private than they are at building and running a usable facility. The
data center's opening was delayed in late 2013, after a series of meltdowns confounded system operators and led to the destruction of
tens of thousands of dollars' worth of equipment.[19] In the span of
just over a year, between August 2012 and October 2013, the site
suffered a total of ten major meltdowns—and investigators were
clueless about their cause.[20]

But it's not just the federal government and the NSA that are
in the data collection game. States have jumped into the fray, via
dozens of fusion centers located across the nation.

Billed as collection and dissemination points for any and all
information related to terrorist threats, fusion centers are supposed
to serve law enforcement on the local and state levels and help

pave the way for the smooth transmission of breaking intelligence news from federal authorities.[21] They're operated by state and local authorities, in partnership with federal entities, and are part of the Department of Homeland Security's program to fight terrorism. As their name suggests, they're supposed to fuse information from various sources and offer law enforcement a sort of one-stop shopping site to gather the latest on specific threats.

But what sounds good in theory doesn't always translate well in practice.

A 2012 Senate report from the Homeland Security and Governmental Affairs Permanent Subcommittee on Investigations found that the seventy-two state and local fusion centers around the nation produced subpar intelligence, "oftentimes shoddy, rarely timely." The information was of such poor quality that investigators reported it even "sometimes endanger[ed] citizens' civil liberties and Privacy Act protections."[22]

Ouch. But that's just the beginning. From the executive summary:

> Under the leadership of Senator Coburn, Ranking Subcommittee Member, the Subcommitee has spent two years examining federal support of fusion centers and evaluating the resulting counterterrorism intelligence. The Subcommittee's investigative efforts included interviewing dozens of current former federal state and local officials, reviewing more than a year's worth of intelligence reporting from centers, conducting a nationwide survey of fusion centers, and examining thousands of pages of financial records and grant documentation. The investigation identified problems with nearly every significant aspect of DHS' involvement with fusion centers. The Subcommittee investigation also determined that senior DHS officials were aware of the problems hampering effective counterterrorism work by the fusion centers, but did not always inform Congress of the issues, nor ensure the problems were fixed in a timely manner.[23]

On top of that, the report authors found the bulk of information the centers disseminated between April 2009 and April 2010 was more criminal in nature, focused on incidents or investigations involving drugs, illegal cash, or human smuggling—not terrorism, as the sites were supposed to target.[24] Senators reacting to the report wanted to know: Where are all the intelligence reports? Where is all the counterterrorism information? Where has the $289 million—or, as some estimates put it, $1.4 billion—that was spent on fusion center development over the course of a decade gone?[25]

Some of it, roughly $6,000, went to buy laptops and big-screen televisions for various centers. Another $45,000 went to buy a city official a new commuting car—a top-of-the-line SUV with all the bells and whistles of luxury add-ons.[26]

In the end, the report concluded: there was no evidence that fusion center intelligence led to the unveiling of any true terrorist threat.[27]

Wow! That's a lot of taxpayer money for so little return. But an independent assessment from the nonprofit Constitution Project that was released a month before the Senate's report came out forewarned of just that, concluding after extensive research that, absent reform and strict oversight, Americans weren't likely to get much for their fusion center tax dollars—except for civil rights infractions. One of the report's more shocking findings? Only 15 percent of fusion center operators cite their main mission as fighting terrorism. The majority say they exist to fight terrorism—but also to battle crime and assist with natural disasters and other hazards.[28]

Still, defenders of the Homeland Security's core antiterrorism program rushed to debunk the Senate report, calling the information outdated and suggesting authors played up the negatives in the report for political reasons.

Sen. Joe Lieberman, then chairman of the Homeland Security and Governmental Affairs Committee, admitted that while the centers had abused some grant funding, they nonetheless served an important purpose and were crucial components in the government's war on terrorism. His counterpart on the House side, Homeland Security Committee chairman Peter King, agreed and blamed the report authors for not taking into account more updated information that better highlighted the centers' usefulness.[29]

Okay—but then there was this, from the Government Accountability Office, in April 2013.

The GAO reported that federal, state, and local agencies actually operate five different types of fusion centers—the Joint Terrorism Task Forces, the Field Intelligence Groups, the Regional Information Sharing Systems, High Intensity Drug Trafficking Area Investigative Support Centers, and the state and major urban fusion centers.[30] Altogether, they total 268 different fusion-type facilities around the nation.[31] And the information they provide frequently overlaps.

From the GAO report: "GAO identified 91 instances of overlap in some analytical activities—such as producing intelligence reports—and 32 instances of overlap in investigative support activities, such as identifying links between criminal organizations. These entities conducted similar activities within the same mission area . . . [which] can lead to benefits . . . but may also burden customers with redundant information."[32]

The GAO suggested better coordination among the White House, the Justice Department, and the Department of Homeland Security to avoid confusion over intelligence reports generated among fusion centers. But the thing is—wasn't the entire reason for the Homeland Security Department's creation to stave off such conflicting intelligence, overlapping investigations, and confusing and time-wasting security reportage?

When President George W. Bush in 2002 folded twenty-two federal agencies under one massive law enforcement umbrella, thereby creating the Department of Homeland Security, he promised during a ceremonial signing of the enabling legislation that "state and local governments will be able to turn for help and information to one federal domestic security agency, instead of more than 20 that divide those responsibilities . . . and help our local governments work in concert with the federal government."[33] The Department of Homeland Security spelled it out even more explicitly, vowing that its mission was sound—a surefire means of "transforming and realigning the current confusing patchwork of government activities" into one unified department.[34]

Well, it didn't turn out quite as planned, did it?

All this collective, collaborative information sharing has really only led to confusing and overlapping intelligence that has little to do with terrorism. It's also fueled the local police drive for better technology, more militarized training, and more influence and reach with crime-fighting tools—including legislative and judicial leeway.

The Department of Homeland Security's 2013 success stories for fusion centers don't even predominantly speak to terrorism cases. They detail crime stories and how the fusion centers helped.

For instance, the Central Florida Intelligence Exchange, the Tennessee Fusion Center, and the Georgia Information Sharing and Analysis Center were credited on the DHS website's success story section with a joint investigation that led to the arrest of an individual for production of child pornography. A second success story spoke of another collaborative investigation—between the Southwest Texas Fusion Center, the Minnesota Fusion Center, two local police and sheriff departments in Minnesota, and both San Antonio's FBI Joint Terrorism Task Force and Minnesota Joint Terrorism Task Force—that ultimately led to the arrest of a militia group leader.[35] Authorities did report finding Molotov cocktails, suspected pipe bombs, and various types of firearms at this suspect's home—but that's hardly the type of terrorist threat fusion centers were touted as uprooting.

And that leads to a major problem with these fusion centers: they've branched out from their core mission of rooting out terrorism and have taken on a more militarized police role.

Now combine that need of fusion centers to keep busy—to justify their existence and continued funding—and their ensuing mission creep into criminal investigations, with the likes of the federal Nationwide Suspicious Activity Reporting Initiative, and it's a recipe for privacy rights disaster.

The NSI, Nationwide SAR Initiative, is a partnership program among federal, state, and local law enforcement to report and disseminate, as its name suggests, suspicious activities.[36] That information is then fed through the chain of fusion centers and up the ladder to federal law partners for analysis.[37] The aim, once again, is to root out terrorists before they attack. But the information provided is often shaky at best. The suspicious report can generate from a local police officer—or from a private citizen, completely unschooled in law enforcement techniques. Hopefully, if it is the latter, it's not a case of a private citizen taking revenge on a neighbor for some perceived slight.

Regardless, the local police department that fields the complaint of suspicious activity then forwards the information to the state fusion center.[38] Analysts at the fusion center log the data into a computer and then determine if the suspicious activity merits immediate investigation.

Either way, that data is shared with higher-ranking law enforcement officers, including the FBI.[39] Once information makes it to the fusion center, a file is created. But what happens to the information in that file is largely unknown.

The FBI maintains the information in its SAR database, eGuardian, often for years.[40] Civil rights groups say these files can stay in "open" mode, allowing law enforcement to add information as they collect it, or stumble upon it, or otherwise obtain it.[41] Suddenly, that file of the unidentified suspicious-looking guy seen snapping photos of an urban police station and jotting notes on a piece of paper becomes thicker, filled in and fleshed out with information collected over the years about his name, place of employment, marriage situation, and banking habits.

Sound too conspiracy theory to be true? Think again.

The Department of Justice has issued guidance on how law enforcement might vet suspicious activities. But these standards are broad. The Los Angeles Police Department, for example, once considered individuals caught peering through binoculars in public, or scribbling on notepads and drawing diagrams, suspicious characters, worthy of reporting up the fusion center chain.[42]

On top of that, the Department of Homeland Security works with the Department of Justice to further root out terrorists and criminals via the SAR, or NSI, program with a simple public relations campaign even a five-year-old can remember: "If you see something, say something."[43] On its website, DHS says it's looking to expand the campaign around the nation by "partnering with a variety of entities, including: transportation systems, universities, states, cities, sports leagues and local law enforcement."[44]

Be careful what you say; Big Brother has some pretty big ears. As DHS indicates, the trend is only for more data collection.

We've already seen a significant expansion in government powers based on the justification of battling terrorism in just the past few years. What used to be the domain of the federal authorities has now been taken up by state—and even local—law enforcement authorities.[45] And the danger of so much data collection by government at all levels is multifaceted: the more agencies that collect information, the harder it is to regulate how that information is used—and guarantee whether that information can be protected. Moreover, the harder it is to track what government does with that information years down the line as generation gives way to generation.

11

UNMANNED DRONES COMING TO A COMMUNITY NEAR YOU

Government is not reason; it is not eloquence. It is force. And force, like fire, is a dangerous servant and a fearful master.

—George Washington

n February 2013, a sixteen-page undated white paper from the Justice Department made a dramatic splash on the front pages of newspapers around the world: high-ranking Obama administration officials can order the killing of American citizens as long as they're believed to be "senior operational leader[s]" of the terrorist group al-Qa'ida or of an associated al-Qa'ida unit.[1] The memo, which had been provided to members of Congress in June 2012, was leaked to the press at a time when the White House had dramatically ratcheted up its use of unmanned aerial—drone—attacks against al-Qa'ida suspects on foreign soil.[2]

It also came on the heels of widespread controversy over the September 2011 drone kill of US citizen Anwar al-Awlaki, a suspected recruiter for al-Qa'ida, and his sixteen-year-old son, Abdulrahman al-Awlaki.

Still, it's not as if the assertions in the memo were completely new.

Then White House counterterrorism adviser John Brennan spoke similarly in an April 2012 speech at the Woodrow Wilson Center, maintaining that the American government certainly had the legal right to attack members of terrorist groups using drones. He also admitted publicly what was pretty much an open secret in the military and political worlds: "The United States is the first nation to regularly conduct strikes using remotely piloted aircraft in an armed conflict" against al-Qa'ida.[3]

A month earlier, in March 2012, Attorney General Eric Holder had also spoken of America's right to conduct fatal drone operations against suspected members of al-Qa'ida—only Holder also addressed the point of when American citizens were the accused terrorists and targets.

Speaking at the Northwestern University School of Law, Holder first affirmed the president's legal right to order the military to conduct fatal drone strikes on suspected al-Qa'ida operatives on foreign soil, clarifying that such attacks are acts of "self-defense," not "assassinations." He then confirmed that the United States has the right to target and kill absent federal court permission "a U.S. citizen who is a senior operational leader of al Qaeda or associated forces, and who is actively engaged in planning to kill Americans . . . [if] the individual poses an imminent threat of violent attack against the United States" and if capture is not an option.[4]

Civil rights groups howled, of course. The American Civil Liberties Union, for instance, called Holder's claim that the president could target and kill American civilians overseas absent judicial review a chilling development in the war on terror.[5]

But a year later, the United States affirmed that presidential power to kill at a new level.

In a letter to Sen. Rand Paul dated March 4, 2013, Holder

addressed a hypothetical and emerging concern: Does the president also have the right to authorize a fatal drone strike against an American, on American soil, under the same set of conditions—if the American was believed to be an al-Qa'ida operative planning to attack US citizens? In an explanation that reverberated around the nation, Holder replied: Yes.

Holder's exact words: "It is possible, I suppose, to imagine an extraordinary circumstance in which it would be necessary and appropriate under the Constitution and applicable laws of the United States for the president to authorize the military to use lethal force within the territory of the United States." He then cited December 7, 1941, the Japanese attack on Pearl Harbor, and September 11, 2001, the al-Qa'ida attack on the United States, as two examples of when that presidential power might be exercised.[6]

And just a few months later, America learned that the federal government had, in fact, already used drones on domestic soil to root out various criminal activities.

A July 19, 2013, letter from the FBI's director of legislative affairs, Stephen D. Kelly, to Senator Paul contained the shocking claim that the federal agency had dispatched unarmed, unmanned aerial craft to assist with ten different criminal investigations on domestic soil in the previous seven years—all without a court warrant. An excerpt:

> The FBI uses [Unmanned Aerial Vehicles] in very limited circumstances to conduct surveillance when there is a specific, operational need. UAVs have been used for surveillance to support missions related to kidnappings, search and rescue operations, drug interdictions and fugitive investigations. Since late 2006, the FBI has conducted surveillance using UAVs in eight criminal cases and two national security cases. . . . The FBI has no plans to use weapons with UAVs. The FBI does not use UAVs to conduct "bulk" surveillance or to conduct general surveillance not related to an investigation or assessment. . . .

In addition, every request to use UAVs for surveillance is reviewed by FBI legal counsel to ensure there are not potential Fourth Amendment or privacy concerns. . . . Every request to use UAVs for surveillance must be approved by senior FBI management at FBI Headquarters and in the relevant FBI Field Office.[7]

For example, the FBI said its management approved a drone surveillance operation for a criminal case in January 2013 involving sixty-five-year-old Vietnam veteran Jimmy Lee Dykes. The case grabbed the attention of the nation: Dykes was reported to have boarded a school bus in Alabama, shot the driver, abducted a five-year-old boy, and held him hostage for days in an underground bunker. Law enforcement officials ultimately rescued the boy and killed the suspect. The FBI said it used "UAV surveillance to support the successful rescue."[8]

On a practical level, nobody could fault the FBI for using a surveillance drone in this instance. But the long-term effects of law enforcement's warrantless use of drones on our constitutional form of governance is worrisome. At what point is a crime considered horrific enough to warrant the use of drones—and what's the guarantee that boundary line won't be moved? The issue of who determines those boundary lines is part and parcel of that long-term worry too.

The FBI in its letter to Senator Paul clarified and vowed that the agency would never use unarmed drones for surveillance on American soil without a warrant in those instances when "individuals have a reasonable expectation of privacy under the Fourth Amendment."[9]

But that's a rather broad phrase. In modern-day America, cameras are everywhere. So what would reasonably constitute an expectation of privacy nowadays?

The problem with drones is the technology is outpacing any policy that guides their lawful use. The regulations are being formed on a test-case basis, creating a horse-follows-the-cart scenario. Case in point: al-Awlaki.

Anwar al-Awlaki was born in New Mexico but became a radical

Muslim cleric and a senior al-Qa'ida operative for the terrorist group's Yemen branch. His fellow terrorist operative, Samir Khan—another American citizen, born in North Carolina—was the creative brains behind the al-Qa'ida Internet magazine, *Inspire.* In September 2011, drones operating out of the CIA's Saudi Arabia base located the pair in a convoy of trucks in the desert region of Jawf Province. Using a combination of Predator and Reaper drones, US pilots operating thousands of miles away shot and killed the two, putting to end a years-long intelligence investigation among the CIA, the White House, and the Pentagon. A month later, another US drone killed al-Awlaki's son, Abdulrahman, in what government officials said was an accidental shooting.[10]

All three were American citizens, killed without benefit of formal arrest and charge, trial, or jury conviction. Abdulrahman, born in America but moved to Yemen at age seven, wasn't even considered a terrorist—he wasn't on a White House "kill list" of high-ranking terrorist operatives—nor was he a member of al-Qa'ida. He hadn't even seen his father, who had gone into hiding, in two years.[11] On the night of his death, October 14, 2011, he was reportedly on a search to find his father.[12]

Their drone kills set off a constitutional firestorm, pitting civil libertarians, who waxed outrage, against politicians, who saw the attacks as justifiable parts and parcels of the War on Terror. Senator Paul called the killings assassinations; Rep. Peter King, then chairman of the House Homeland Security Committee, said they were entirely legal.[13]

Few would dispute that al-Awlaki was a dangerous terrorist, a traitor to America. US authorities believed he had a hand in the November 2009 fatal shootings by Muslim radical Nidal Hasan at Fort Hood, Texas, and in the December 25, 2009, failed underwear bombing attempt to bring down a plane en route from the Netherlands to Detroit.[14] But the idea of our US government killing American citizens by drone without even charging them with any crime—or, in the case of sixteen-year-old Abdulrahman, even suspecting them of any crime—should give pause.

The fact that the Obama administration was able to conduct these fatal attacks without later retribution is the silent thumbs-up to new US policy: apparently, the federal government doesn't need to submit to the Constitution when the perceived threat reaches a certain level.

If that's the standard, then we as a nation are in trouble. With a precedent like that, America's government can move this drone discussion off the battlefield and into law enforcement with ease—as the FBI has already admitted, to a limited degree. And here comes the slippery slope. First terrorism, then egregious crimes, then— what? High-speed chases down the highway?

The possibilities for drone uses are endless if the standard to determine their worthiness is to save or safeguard innocents. After all, isn't it safer for police and for residents to track a car thief hightailing it down the highway via a drone than a speeding cop cruiser? The eye of a drone camera could simply survey the driver's travel from a safe distance, and alert authorities to the location of the vehicle's stopping point. No high-speed chase through residential neighbor- hoods or on congested interstates. No need to endanger the lives of the police officers in the chasing vehicles or the residents and drivers they pass. Information from the surveillance drone could just tell police where to show up and make the arrest.

But the principle of unintended consequences kicks into high gear here. In February 2011, a high-profile criminal search for suspected cop killer Christopher Dorner led officials with the Los Angeles Police Department to dispatch surveillance drones to assist with his location—or did it? Initial media reports indicated the police force used borrowed drones from the US Customs and Border Protection agency to root out Dorner. But in subsequent media interviews, police spokespeople backtracked and said drones weren't used.[15] Yes, drones were used—no, they weren't.

The fact that citizens can't get a straight answer is a problem.

As in the case of the five-year-old boy who was held hostage in an Alabama bunker for days, the use of surveillance drones by law enforcement in the Dorner case might actually be understandable. But what's not is the secretive spirit that law enforcement adopts when it comes to drone use. That's just a step even further down the road to a government that holds itself higher than the average American—a bit smarter, a tad superior—and by logical extension, above the law, outside the confines of the Constitution. In a word, arrogant.

Either way, Dorner wouldn't have been the first criminal suspect placed under drone surveillance by a local police department. That honor belongs to a North Dakota family, the Brossarts, who in 2011 reportedly failed to return some cows that wandered onto their three thousand acres.[16] Police located the cattle and tried to remove them from the property, but the three Brossart sons allegedly pointed shotguns and rifles at the officers and refused to let them take the cows until they paid for the feed they ate.[17] So the sheriff, absent court warrant, sent into the air a Predator drone—a military-grade, $154 million MQ-9 Predator B borrowed from Grand Forks Air Force Base—to monitor the sixteen-hour armed standoff that ensued between police and family members, on the family's private property. As soon as the drone camera captured a moment when the family put down their weapons, agents dressed in SWAT gear stormed into their home and arrested them without incident.[18]

The family moved to dismiss the arrests, arguing through an attorney that law enforcement's use of a military-type unmanned surveillance aircraft without first obtaining a warrant was an egregious abuse of power.[19] But a judge in August 2012 shot down that request, denying that the use of the drone was improper—and in so doing, marked the first time in America that a court gave a judicial stamp of approval to an unmanned drone arrest of a US citizen.[20]

The law enforcement trend to use drones to capture suspected criminals is not going away anytime soon.

In September 2013, an audit from the Department of Justice's Office of Inspector General found taxpayers spent more than $5 million to buy drones for the Justice Department, the FBI, and the

Bureau of Alcohol, Tobacco, Firearms and Explosives, between 2004 and 2013.[21] The audit report also revealed that the Justice Department gave out $1.26 million in grants during that same period for several local police departments and nonprofit groups to buy their own drones.[22] In 2012 alone, the Department of Homeland Security had on hand $4 million in grant funds earmarked for small-town sheriff departments and local police units to obtain unmanned aerial craft to assist with criminal investigations and apprehensions.[23]

But law enforcement isn't the only interested segment of society. Local governments and private businesses are grabbing for the technology too.

A new list released by the Federal Aviation Administration in early 2013 indicated eighty-one different entities from around the nation—from colleges and universities to city governments and private businesses, as well as police departments—had petitioned the FAA for Certificates of Authorization to fly drones on domestic soil.[24] Among the petitioners: National Aeronautics & Space Administration; Ogden Police Department in Utah; the Department of Energy's Oak Ridge National Laboratory; Pennsylvania State University; all major branches of the US military—the Army, Air Force, Navy, and Marine Corps; the US Department of State; and the US Department of Agriculture.[25]

Farming, it seems, is a big draw for drone supporters.

Kansas State University agricultural experts said they asked the FAA for permission to fly drones in order to replace the existing means of checking on crop problems—walking by the fields and performing spot checks on plants—with a faster, fly-by method. Whereas it takes hours for an individual to walk and inspect a field, a camera-carting drone can swoop through in just minutes and relay pictures and problems back to the piloting station. Agriculture specialists can even pinpoint troubled crop areas with the drone technology and spray and treat just those areas, saving farmers money.[26]

Useful—true. But the dark side of agricultural-related drone use was highlighted by a congressional bill brought forward in June

2012 by West Virginia Republican Rep. Shelley Moore Capito.[27] Called the Farmer's Privacy Act, the measure was aimed at prohibiting the Environmental Protection Agency from conducting aerial surveillance on land to ensure owners were complying with the Clean Water Act.[28] The bill, had it passed, would have required the EPA to give public notice of its intent to conduct the air surveillance, to have reasonable suspicion that a violation had occurred, and to first obtain the property owner's permission in writing.[29]

Capito's legislation didn't specifically mention drones—but it was more than implied. The EPA already expressed interest in just that notion in a published study in the mid-2000s. In a summary document entitled "Landscape Characterization and Change Detection Methods Development Research" for 2005 to 2007, on how the EPA might meet its growing mission and keep pace with emerging technologies, the agency specified it was forming partnerships to develop Unmanned Aerial Vehicle missions.[30] The jargon, right from the EPA website, is this:

> EPA is collaborating with NASA to develop terrestrial, coastal ocean and surface-troposphere flux unmanned aerial vehicle (UAV) missions. These missions will combine advanced multi-sensor packages with the extended duration UAV platform capabilities to provide the Agency with a next generation environmental monitoring capability. The ultimate goal is to provide EPA staff with a new data rich environment to significantly increase productivity and enhance the scientific knowledge base to support environmental decision making.[31]

In layman's terms, that means the EPA has been mulling for years how to tap into drones for aerial surveillance of environmental law violators. And they partnered with NASA to get the technology.

What a nightmare of regulatory policing that will be for landowners around the nation. The solution, though, is so simple. Capito's bill, or a lookalike, would effectively squash those plans.

Unfortunately, though, it seems unlikely the drone genie will be put back in the bottle. Even the media wants them. The University of Missouri Drone Journalism Program was flying the unmanned aerial craft for months to take pictures and record video from afar. So was the Drone Journalism Lab at the University of Nebraska–Lincoln. The FAA shut them down in August 2013, prohibiting them from operating drones without first obtaining Certificates of Authorization.[32] But the fact that journalists see drone use as a potential career tool only highlights how deeply the technology's dug into the national consciousness.

Private companies want them too. The FAA in mid-2013 granted permission for the first time to a private company, Conoco Phillips, to fly unmanned aerial vehicles off the coast of Alaska to monitor oil-drilling activities. By 2015, the skies could be littered with commercially owned unmanned aircraft. That's the year the FAA is supposed to open the doors to private businesses to operate drones on American soil for commercial interests.[33] How to tell the difference between a privately owned drone and a government-operated UAV? And moreover, does it really matter?

In 2011, researchers announced the creation of the Nano Hummingbird, a technological advancement that's the size of a real hummingbird.[34] It can flit onto a windowsill, hover and snap photographs and shoot video—and fly away with barely a sound.

The Defense Advanced Research Projects Agency, or DARPA, spent years perfecting this technology. The latest version is able to fly forward, backward, and sideways, as well as turn completely in both directions, clockwise then counterclockwise. Its wingspan is just inches, allowing for close-up scrutiny and recording of subjects, in complete secrecy.[35]

And given the latest invention from Harvard University, it won't be long before even that drone technology has moved into the ubiquitous column.

Following a decade of research, scientists at the school said they have successfully made and test-flown a robot that's modeled after a bee and about the size of a fly.[36] It's dubbed "RoboBee," and while its first model still requires a tether to a power source to fly, scientists are optimistic that later models will cart their energy supply while flying.[37] Hopes are that the little robot bugs will also be able to carry tiny video cameras and recording devices and feed the surveillance data back into controllers' and users' iPads.

One can only wonder where all this drone technology might lead.

In January 2014 remarks during a Senate Commerce Committee hearing on drone policy, California Sen. Dianne Feinstein provided a little heads-up of where America was heading. She told a crowded room that she was in her home, listening to activists protest outside, and went to the window for a peek. Inches from her face was a drone. Apparently, she said, her appearance startled the operator of the drone and the device abruptly turned and flew from her window. But her message to other senators at the hearing was blunt: Go slow with this new technology. The negative repercussions on personal privacies could prove significant.[38]

12

ORWELLIAN TECHNOLOGY IS NOW THE NORM

Those people who will not be governed by God will be ruled by tyrants.

—William Penn

n mid-2013, the Equal Opportunity Employment Commission launched a lawsuit against Pennsylvania-based Consol Energy Inc., after an employee at one of the company's West Virginia mines refused to use a biometric hand scanner to log his work hours and was subsequently pressured to take an early retirement.[1]

The employee's argument, however, was that using the scanner would be tantamount to accepting the mark of the biblical beast, a violation of his Christian beliefs in Revelation 13:16–17: the beast "forced all people, great and small, rich and poor, free and slave, to receive a mark on their right hands or on their foreheads, so that they could not buy or sell unless they had the mark"(NIV).

Despite the fact that the employee had worked at the company for more than thirty-five years, the company refused to budge on its biometric scanning rule, characterizing it a necessary means of tracking employee attendance and work habits—a major feed into the company's bottom line.

Head south a few hundred miles to Muscogee County, Georgia, and there students at one school district in August 2013 were given a new option for buying lunch: hand scanners that read the web of veins on their palms. Students making a buy were told to simply hold one of their hands over a reader with infrared technology and wait a second or two. The scanner then analyzed the vein patterns and searched the database to identify and match the person to his or her account. Forget picture identification cards and cash. The process of checking out and paying took fewer than four seconds—the lunch line barely needed to come to a halt.[2]

Head northwest to Michigan and the creepiness factor increases.

In October 2011, the community of Farmington Hills took federal grant money and invested it in new "Intellistreets" technology from the creative minds of a company called Illuminating Concepts that placed specially designed lampposts with features right from Homeland Security's top spy wish list—and, simultaneously, from the dreams of environmentalists. The lamps are a curious mix of energy conservation and counterterrorism technology. On one hand, they automatically adjust to natural light patterns, thereby saving on city electricity costs. On the other, they monitor traffic, track pedestrians, and videotape and record passersby and their conversations, frequently without the pedestrians' knowledge.[3]

The idea behind the streetlamps—which contain sophisticated radio and speaker systems and high-tech video technology—is to alert authorities of impending dangers via breaking and real-time televised or broadcast information. But the privacy advocates fear, of course, is that government might use the technology for more sinister purposes.[4] First, the justification for the spy lamps is to track terrorists. Then, it's to root out high-profile and violent criminal suspects. And soon, the lampposts are recording and collecting video and conversation snippets on everyone who passes by, all in an ever-encroaching government quest to secure the citizens from attack and harm—for the good of the nation.

The line between security for all and freedom for one has certainly grown dim in recent years. At what point do we say, "Enough is enough; we have lost enough personal privacies"?

At what point do we admit that government cannot guarantee our security and save us from all harm?

The use of some of this technology has really gotten out of hand.

Parents in Polk County, Florida, were shocked to learn in May 2013 that school administrators had been scanning their children's irises, absent consent or even awareness. The cited reason? Administrators said they needed to give the students and their families some more security on their school buses.[5]

So they hired a private security company to install the program, which involved taking a quick scan of students' irises as they entered the school bus, then sending an alert via text or e-mail to parents to let them know their children had safety arrived at their destination. Orwellian factor aside, parents were also outraged that they weren't all given a heads-up that the program was being considered or implemented. One parent recalled to a local newspaper the complete shock she felt after learning her eight-year-old child was told to stare into a blue light until it changed color as he boarded his bus. An estimated 750 other students were subjected to the same order.[6]

School administrators said they meant to provide the parents an opt-out notice, but the staffer who was in charge of mailing those letters missed work due to a medical emergency, so the scanning went forth absent any resistance.[7] That's a pretty big snafu. The company in charge of scanning the irises has since said it's destroyed the database of information, but still—the story is chilling. For parents, it's a bit scary to realize how quick and easy it is for a government body to take control of children's privacies. It's doubly outrageous when that government body is a supposedly trusted source, like a school.

But iris scanning is growing technology in schools around the nation.

A South Dakota company named Blinkspot has made a whole business out of marketing eye-scan technology to school buses. One product targeted at the elementary level has children who are boarding a school bus first peer into a scanner that's fashioned to look like a pair of binoculars. If they're on the right bus, the scanner sounds a beep. If they're on the wrong bus, the scanner honks. Blinkspot also syncs its scanners to a mobile app for parents to track their children's whereabouts while riding the bus. When the student boards, the parent receives an e-mail, complete with the child's photograph, a Google map of the child's entrance on or exit from the bus, and the time and date of bus boarding and departure.[8]

The nation's places of higher learning are starting to catch the fever for tracking technology too.

In July 2013, Winthrop University in South Carolina tested out a new scanning technology program on its incoming freshman class, requiring that all new students take part in an eye scan as part of their identification card application process. The school also tested iris scanners at its Macfeat Early Childhood Laboratory School, where students who major in education receive training, and mulled installing scanners at the likes of the Lois Rhame West Health, Physical Education and Wellness Center. The reason for the technology there? University officials said it was inconvenient for students who want to work out or swim to carry their identification cards with them.[9]

Add to the list of justifications for spy technology: Stop terrorists. Catch criminals. And now, keep inconveniences at bay.

America's next generation won't have any concept of what constitutes personal privacy at all.

In 2007, a school system in Nashville, Tennessee, made waves with a first-in-the-nation data program that was billed as remembering the faces of staffers and students, and sounding the alarm on strangers on campus. The school district, which at the time served seventy-five thousand students, installed cameras equipped with facial recognition technology.[10] The program required that first, all students and staff, and others with cause to enter school grounds on a near-daily basis, have their photographs taken and uploaded into a database for storage. Whenever one of the many cameras that scoured the school property picked up a face that it could not match in the database, an alert would sound to security officials, who would then launch a query into the reasons for that person's presence.[11]

In addition to sounding alarms for would-be criminals, the face-remembering technology was also credited with identifying and alerting school officials to the presence of fired employees and suspended or expelled students. But as civil rights activists decried: What's to keep the technology from being used to watch students all the time and alert teachers and administrators to those who cut class?

Schools around the nation may be pushing the technology buttons a little too hard. It's a shame when even those who have nothing to hide are treated to schools that seem little more than jails, overseen by teachers and administrators with access to secret spy cameras and recording devices.

The technology's not going away anytime soon, though. Police, private entities, federal agencies—they're all on board the biometric bandwagon.

Facebook in August 2013 announced an update to its user policy to bring almost all of its one billion stored profile photographs into the company's facial recognition database as a means of speeding up the process of "tagging" friends. Facebook executives assured users that they could opt out of the system, which was intended to basically match faces in pictures with public profile features.[12] But privacy advocates were still concerned, and Federal Trade Commission officials announced an investigation into the policy change to see if Facebook was in violation of a 2011 agreement that was forged between the government and the company.[13] Why?

The agreement came at the end of a government finding that Facebook had violated the privacy of its users and shared personal data without first obtaining their permission.[14]

In other words, Facebook—despite its assurances that it has never given any federal entity complete access to its company databases and has supplied private information to intelligence or government agencies only as required by law—does not have a clean track record of upholding individual privacies. While the company may have promised its facial recognition photo database would never be used for purposes other than those known by users, a smart gambler wouldn't bet all the chips on that claim.

After all, once privacy is compromised, it's tough to get it returned. If Facebook lost control of its photo database to hackers, or worse, entered a partnership to grant government access to the data, what good is the company's promise to protect user privacy in the end?

Meanwhile, for the government sector, especially police, facial recognition data is proving a treasure chest.

Some of its use is valid—and necessary. For instance, facial reading technology on the battlefield has proven a substantial aid to US forces in Afghanistan and Iraq, trying to identify insurgents and terrorist leaders. It's also a proven technology for fighting crime on the domestic front, helping police sift through bleary store videotape images and pulling up matches of better pictures in facial photograph databases.[15]

But this same tool is ripe for civil rights infractions and privacy invasions.

In Pinellas County, Florida, alone, the sheriff's office has built a database of searchable facial photographs that includes more than 120 million individuals. Law enforcement's stated reason for assembling the database was to root out driver's license fraudsters—but in the mix are plenty of photographs of innocent bystanders. And that's the problem with the technology: it relies on storage of individual data that's very often collected absent the provider's knowledge and without notification to the provider of its intended use. Most people providing photographs think they're just taking a driver's license snapshot. But in June 2013, fully thirty-seven states allowed for facial recognition technology to be used in the driver's license permitting process—and that number is sure to grow in the coming years.[16]

For those with no criminal backgrounds, that's an alarming trend. After all, why should an innocent person with no arrest record be used in photograph form in a police lineup? Yet that's what police now have the technology to perform—digital lineups—in their own patrol vehicles, using portable laptops and a nationwide database of millions of photographs.

The bigger issue, of course, is what happens to that innocent person's photograph. As detractors of facial recognition technology have argued, these photograph databases are rapidly becoming a de facto national identification card system for government, law enforcement—anybody with a just cause, it would seem—to tap. And all unbeknownst to most Americans.

Against this backdrop, the Department of Homeland Security has been quietly bolstering local police agencies' ability to access the technology.

In August 2013, Homeland Security officials said they were developing spy technology capable of scanning huge crowds of people and searching for a specific individual based on inputted facial features, then alerting police to the person's presence. The technology—the Biometric Optical Surveillance System—was first a program of the Pentagon, but was then transferred to Homeland Security for eventual deployment to state and local law enforcement personnel.[17] A month later, federal officials sent their BOSS technology into the field for live testing—at the Tri-Cities Toyota Center's hockey game in Kennewick, Washington. The test was to see if Homeland Security officials could deploy BOSS and successfully locate and identify a handful of preselected faces among the sea of six thousand or so the rink holds. Hockey fans were told not to worry—if their photographs were taken, nobody would have access to them but government officials.[18]

That hardly seems a comfort.

Are those with privacy concerns to don hoodies or bandannas every time they enter a public space? Another simple way of beating facial technology is to, believe it or not, smile—thus, the no-smile rule while getting photographed for passports and driver's licenses.[19]

But even a beauty queen can't smile past all the Big Brother technology that's out there. Not all are image-based.

Voice biometrics that measure the tone, pitch, and rhythm of speech have been making gains in the security industry as a means of countering theft and fraud.[20] Like other touted security systems that depend on biometrics, the bigger issue is what becomes of the data that's collected. Biometric data that's hacked—including individual speech identification patterns—is not so easily recalled or replaced. Unlike a PIN, a user can't create a new voice, or a new set of palm veins, or an iris.

Other big data advances in recent years: fingerprint technology that can actually capture prints from feet away, from an Alabama company called IDair.[21] That means workers entering a secure employment facility need only wave at a scanner to obtain entry. And another emerging field: backscatter vans carrying military-grade technology that's been used by Transportation Security Agency officials to riffle through individuals' bags and clothing to search for banned items. Now, that technology is spreading among local law enforcement—giving police departments equipped with American Science & Engineering's Z Backscatter Vans, or with the more mobile backscatter radiation X-ray machines, the ability to simply look through the scope at nearby cars and individuals and conduct a quick and quiet, secret surveillance operation.[22]

The Electronic Privacy Information Group sued the Department of Homeland Security to stop TSA's usage of the technology, which revealed subjects' bodies beneath their clothes, calling it an abject violation of civil rights.[23] Bringing that same technology to the neighborhood and streets of small-town America can't be good news for privacy protectionists.

But by far the most egregious technological advance to hit the nation for the purpose of ravaging personal privacies is a piece of video surveillance software from BLS Labs called AISight—a tame enough sounding program with downright eerie capabilities and an even eerier mission.

The system itself is intelligence software that's equipped with behavior recognition technology that actually teaches itself, in time, to recognize deviations in a given sphere of coverage. As BLS Labs puts it, the technology measures structures, shapes and sizes, the speed of objects and the paths they pursue, and a dozen other factors, and records them for constant comparison and evaluation. The software is used in conjunction with video cameras, creating a system that's ultimately capable of predicting behaviors—and alerting when those behaviors don't meet expectations.[24] Moreover, AISight can be affixed to thousands of surveillance cameras at once. In a short period of time, each of those cameras is able to determine what's normal for the area it scopes, and what's not.[25]

The possibilities for its use are endless. If an AISight-equipped camera at a busy downtown city intersection picks up that at a certain time each day thousands of pedestrians walk through the area covered by its lens without stopping, and then suddenly a man stops that flow by pausing and pointing a gun at a subject, the software will flag that movement as abnormal.

Authorities can be quickly alerted and dispatched to the scene.

But AISight goes even further than issuing alerts. It's really a law enforcement dream come true—it provides the ability to practically predict crime before it even happens. Since the computer attached to the cameras constantly analyzes behaviors and compares the current findings to actions it previously recorded for identical time periods on different days, the software can also hit on what the human eye might consider as mundane behaviors, but ones that could really be step one of a crime in progress or an alert to a crime that's being planned.

They could also be innocent behaviors—and that's part of the problem with the technology.

For instance, in the aforementioned situation, where the AISight technology is attached to a camera that records a well-walked section of a city street, what if a man in the midst of the crowd paused for a split second to drop something on the ground? That simple act could mean radically different things: The man could actually be a terrorist, planting a packaged bomb. Or, he could be a guy on his way to work who dropped a piece of trash. There are dozens of other scenarios that could explain the act as innocent—and dozens more that are laced with criminal elements.

The point is, though, that regardless of advances in artificial intelligence, AISight can't read minds or intentions. It can only determine deviances in behaviors based on past predictors and past data, leaving open a real potential for civil rights infractions. Police say the technology is working for them. San Diego and other California cities tout the system as a solid crime-fighting tool, while dozens of other law enforcement departments around the nation have applied for Homeland Security grants to get their own versions.[26] And AISight isn't the only option for the so-called predictive policing technology.

A program called CompStat that tracks crime figures in real time and alerts police to the next likely target, and that creates crime patterns that give a larger look at a community's hot spots, has been making a splash among law enforcement agencies from Los Angeles to New York City.[27] The computer programming is based on the same type of model used to predict where earthquake aftershocks will hit, and several cities say it's been a tremendous aid, lowering burglary rates and other property crime statistics by significant margins in recent years.

IBM, meanwhile, has jumped into the policing game with its owner algorithm-based analysis program that helps police in Memphis, Tennessee, and Charleston, South Carolina, narrow down their likely crime targets and stop the acts before they occur.[28] Legal minds have questioned predictive policing policies, pondering their potential to violate the Fourth Amendment and wondering how court testimony might proceed for suspects who are arrested after a computer red-flagged them for crimes, and the police, in turn, initiated the arrests. How do you cross-examine a computer?

But AISight takes even these computer modeling programs to a new level that includes videotaping and analyzing behaviors of people on the street who aren't even guilty of a crime or suspected of an illegal act. Moreover, like other surveillance technology, it's rapidly moving from the cause of antiterrorism and anticrime to become yet another data tracking and collection tool—albeit even more intrusive—for government that turns citizens into suspects.

AISight has been installed by San Francisco Municipal Transit Authority to monitor its twelve MTA stations. Louisiana authorities contracted with BLS to use it for port security. And El Paso officials have pursued the technology to keep a constant computer eye on water treatment plants located near the border with Mexico.[29]

Talk about the meeting of science fiction fantasy with reality. It won't be long before innocent American citizens are ensnared in a prison of our own making—a cell built by well-meaning individuals who hyped our fears and sold us all on the need for layer upon layer of security. Between technology and politics, America's beacon of freedom is being slowly snuffed out.

13

PRESIDENT ON THE LOOSE!

The Tenth Amendment is the foundation of the Constitution.

—Thomas Jefferson

ost schoolchildren are taught in civics and history classes that America's government is based on a system that separates powers among three distinct entities: the judiciary, the executive, and the legislative. Legislators make the laws, courts interpret them, and the president swears an oath to the Constitution to uphold them.

Nowhere does the Constitution give the president the authority to declare laws with—as former aide to President Clinton, Paul Begala, famously said to a *New York Times* reporter after a July 1998 White House trip to China—a stroke of the pen.

Yet, that's what executive orders accomplish.

It's bad enough that this nation has already seen the near-complete destruction of its Tenth Amendment, guaranteeing that rights not already granted to the federal government are reserved to the states or to the people. It's equally dire that the Ninth Amendment, stipulating that individuals retain the rights that aren't specifically delegated or enumerated in the Constitution, is a long-forgotten memory.

But this steady centralization of power into the hands of Washington, DC, politicos has grown even narrower.

Executive orders in effect usurp the powers and authorities of the legislative and judicial branches, and centralize control in the hands of the executive. Our once-genius system of checks and balances, with a diverse spread of powers among the states, the people, and lastly the federal government, is torn apart and in its place stands a government that's more akin to what the Founding Fathers fled—a monarchy.

Still, even George Washington issued executive orders. Eight of them, in fact.[1] His first came on June 8, 1789, just three months after he was sworn in as the nation's first president. It wasn't actually called an executive order at the time; that term didn't come into common use until 1862, under President Abraham Lincoln. And it was rather generic in content, instructing all the leftover officers from the Confederate government to "impress me with a full, precise, and distinct *general idea* of the affairs of the United States" that they were tasked with overseeing. That's akin to an employer asking for employees to prepare and present reports on the state of their individual departments—quite proper and necessary. On top of that, the Constitution itself allows for the president to make such requests. Article 2, section 2, clause 1 states: "The president . . . may require the Opinion, in writing, of the principal Officer in each of the executive Departments, upon any Subject relating to the Duties of their respective Offices."

Washington's next executive order—defined as the nation's first presidential proclamation—came on the heels of a congressional committee request for the president to suggest the people of the United States engage in a national day of thanksgiving. On October 3, 1789, Washington signed a proclamation that declared Thursday, November 26, just that day.[2]

Contrast that to President Bill Clinton's multiple orders to label millions of acres of federal land as national monuments. Clinton may have been using existing law to justify his declarations—the Antiquities Act of 1906. But establishing a massive 1.7 million-acre national monument—the Grand Staircase-Escalante in Utah, declared on September 18, 1996, complete with all the accompanying federal land use restrictions—with a quick stroke of a pen is hardly a righteous presidential act.[3] That declaration sparked national outrage on several fronts: First, it came absent congressional approval. Second, it came during a highly charged presidential campaign season. Third, it completely disregarded the wishes of Utah state representatives, not to mention the then Republican governor. And fourth, it came as mining rights—and the accompanying million-dollar coal industry that was tied to the property—were coming under fire from the growing influential environmental lobby.

In other words, Clinton's sweeping decree was not exactly done in the spirit used by some earlier presidents to issue proclamations and orders. It was much more the act of an arrogant tyrant, set on fulfilling a personal agenda and simultaneously dismissive of the confines of constitutional law. Then interior secretary Bruce Babbitt's oft-repeated media quote summed up the attitude of that White House administration toward executive orders: to paraphrase, he bluntly said the executive had changed the rules of the Constitution and grabbed the powers of the legislative branch.[4] And that's the new law of the land.

President Obama has proven equally dismissive of constitutional confines on the executive branch, turning toward his pen rather than Congress to halt deportations of certain illegal immigrants.[5] In June 2012, Obama signed an order that open border activists were quick to defend as simply a directive, rather than an executive order, for the

Department of Homeland Security to show restraint in deportations of certain youth, particularly those with clear criminal backgrounds. But as clear eyes reveal, the directive had pretty much the same effect as an executive order. More than that, Obama's order came not long after the failed DREAM Act—the Development, Relief and Education for Minors Act, opposed by Senate Republicans as a step toward amnesty—and gave the impression of a president bypassing Congress to enact a personal agenda.[6]

A month later and Obama was at it again, with welfare policy, taking a backdoor approach rather than the more visible and diplomatic route through Congress, to issue a memorandum through Health and Human Services that ultimately gave states an opportunity to reform the work requirements for recipients.[7] Critics assailed the memo as providing the means by which states could broaden Temporary Assistance for Needy Families and relax restrictions so more could obtain welfare services without having to abide by 1998 work rules.[8] But this time, Obama's order would cause a bit of a stir among watchdog groups. The Government Accountability Office slapped back at his lone-star decree, saying he didn't have the authority as president to call for such reforms.[9] Rather, law required he take his policy proposal before Congress for approval.

Orders, memorandums, dictates, and proclamations—nowadays, they're all pretty much the same beast. The lingo may change, but what doesn't is the fact that the office of the presidency affords the seat holder plenty of opportunity to enact wide-reaching policy, without having to deal with Congress. Not all presidents through history took full advantage to the same degree, however.

Some presidents have actually exercised caution and restraint during leadership. Moreover, some congresses used to actually do their jobs and represent the interests of the people rather than cave and cower to presidential overreach.

At their most basic, executive orders are simply written directives that presidents send to their cabinet and department officials. Prior to the Lincoln administration, the written orders weren't classified by the now-accepted term of *executive orders. Rather, they were called directives, proclamations, policy decrees—or even left untitled.*[10] The president would simply sign them, like a letter that contained a political directive. Such written orders took a decidedly more formal turn during the Lincoln years, however, and researchers and historians began to number and categorize the directives.

Nowadays, executive orders are signed by the president—sometimes with much fanfare and publicity—and then assigned a number by the Office of the Federal Register. They're then printed in the Federal Register and formally recorded in the section "Title 3: The President, Code of Federal Regulations."[11]

Regardless, they're still not found in the enumerated powers for the president in the Constitution. Neither are presidential proclamations and presidential memorandums, two other means the executive branch has at its disposal to enact policies without legislative approval.

As of 1957, the generally accepted definition of executive orders, as put forth by that year's House Government Operations Committee, is that they are written presidential directives that carry the force of law. They are usually aimed at directing the actions of government officials and agencies and are to have only indirect impact on private citizens. But in addition to executive orders, presidents have the power to decree proclamations—signed orders that are aimed at influencing the private citizen more than a government agency.[12] Proclamations, however, are not considered legally binding since the president does not have the constitutional authority to order around the private citizen.

Presidential memoranda, meanwhile, seem to take on facets of both orders and proclamations, seeming at times tame-sounding in topic—like President Obama's September 17, 2013, memo to the secretary of state to compile data about human trafficking activities of several nations that receive US aid—and at other times much more controversial.[13]

On June 25, 2013, President Obama directed the Environmental

Protection Agency in a memorandum to "issue proposed carbon pollution standards, regulations or guidelines" for power plants by June 1, 2014.[14] The memorandum furthered an EPA standard from the previous year that targeted newly constructed power plants. Obama's memo specifically ordered the EPA to develop standards and regulations for existing plants too.[15] That's rather a sneaky way of pushing for more environmental mandates on power plants without having to go through Congress and the open-government route.

Obama's justification for the issuance of the memo was the Clean Air Act—that he was only giving the EPA a directive that carried out existing and congressionally approved law.[16] But his memorandum was hardly devoid of impact. What it did, with a stroke of the pen, was cut Congress out of the debate and set in motion the wheels for more and unfettered EPA regulation.

And in fact, it didn't take long for those additional environmental regulations to take shape. In October 2013, Obama announced a new executive order requiring federal agencies and local jurisdictions to factor in climate change—including controlling certain emission levels—while taking on new projects, like bridge construction or roadwork.[17] Congress still controlled the purse strings on any projects the government wanted to pursue in line with environmental mandates.[18]

Still, Obama's run around Congress was not exactly in the same spirit that guided our earliest presidents, who managed to exercise caution when it came to bypassing the Constitution with executive orders and dictates.

Our first six presidents, from George Washington through John Quincy Adams, only signed a total of eighteen of them. Andrew Jackson broke into double-digit land, with twelve. Presidents William Henry Harrison, Zachary Taylor, and James Garfield issued, in order, zero, five, and six.[19] Then came Abraham Lincoln, and civil libertarians found their foe.

History paints Lincoln kindly, and he may now be regarded as one of America's most revered presidents. But during his term, he actually caused a massive constitutional crisis with his issuance of an executive order during the unfolding of the Civil War, in 1861, at a time when federal troops were facing constant attack from militias in Virginia and Maryland.

Lincoln, hoping to quell the attacks, signed an executive order that suspended the right of habeas corpus—the right for an arrested individual to appear before a judge and hear the charges—for anyone detained for inciting acts of violence along the train route between Philadelphia and Washington.[20]

One of the militia's major leaders, a Maryland lawmaker named John Merryman, was subsequently captured and thrown in jail at Fort McHenry.[21] Merryman's legal team argued his imprisonment was illegal because his right of habeas corpus was wrongfully violated, a line of logic they turned to the Constitution to argue.[22] Article 1, section 9 reads: "The privilege of the writ of habeas corpus shall not be suspended, unless when in cases of rebellion or invasion the public safety may require it." They also argued that only Congress had the right to suspend habeas corpus, not the president, given that the section of the Constitution that spoke of the law, article 1, is the portion of the text that speaks to the powers of the legislative branch, not the executive.[23]

Yet Merryman stayed in prison for another seven weeks, after which he was never charged with a crime.[24] And in the legal fury that ensued, Congress actually passed a law that ceded to Lincoln the very same power he had already grabbed, via the Habeas Corpus Act of 1863.

A couple of years later, Lincoln again sparked a massive uproar with his Emancipation Proclamation, declaring on January 1, 1863, that "all persons held as slaves" in the rebel states "are, and henceforward shall be free."[25] Of course, its success depended wholly on a Union win—and contrary to what popular culture teaches, the order did not end slavery. It only addressed slavery among the states that had actually seceded from the Union.

But it did drive home the point that a pen in the hands of a president is a very powerful thing.

Still, in terms of sheer numbers, Lincoln—with a total of forty-eight—did exercise considerable restraint when it came to signing executive orders. It wasn't really until the progressive era and its accompanying nanny-type government mantra that presidents really started grabbing at the power of the legislative branch and decreeing by pen new laws of the land.

Theodore Roosevelt has the dubious honor of breaking the 1,000 mark with 1,081 signed orders, nearly five times more than any other president in history. Then came Woodrow Wilson, Calvin Coolidge, and Franklin Delano Roosevelt, and it was almost as if former White House chief of staff and key Democrat political strategist Rahm Emanuel had traveled back in time and whispered his famous words: never let a crisis go to waste. Plagued by war, economic depression, and a mind-set that government can solve all problems, these three presidents collectively issued more than 6,500 executive orders.[26]

Ten weeks after the Japanese bombed Pearl Harbor, in February 1942, FDR signed Executive Order 9066, granting the power to US authorities to remove anybody they "deemed necessary" from declared military areas. So the military labeled the entire West Coast a military area and began ordering its evacuation.[27] The region was heavily populated by those of Japanese descent, but within weeks of the executive order, 127,000 Japanese Americans had been pushed into internment camps around the nation.[28] One plaintiff, Fred Korematsu, did test the right of the president to issue such a far-reaching command against an entire segment of American citizenry without obtaining congressional authority. But in *Korematsu v. the United States*, the Supreme Court ultimately determined that the order was in line with the president's commander-in-chief powers over the military.[29]

With a quick stroke of the pen, Roosevelt was able to upset an entire population, prompting them to sell their homes and possessions, abandon their careers and jobs, and live in sometimes subpar conditions—under the watchful eyes of armed guards—while the war ensued.[30] The irony is that by war's end, a total of ten Americans were convicted on charges related to spying for Japan, but none were of Japanese heritage.[31]

In June 1933, Roosevelt signed an executive order that appointed a leader of the Federal Emergency Administrator of Public Works, a special board for his Public Works projects—and granted that agency the authority to spend up to $400 million to build highways and $238 million for the Navy to construct vessels.[32]

Among his other executive orders: He signed a proclamation the day after his inauguration, on March 5, 1933, to declare a bank holiday and shut down all financial transactions and exports of gold, silver, and other commodities for four days.[33] He issued a series of orders in about a three-week period in April 1933 that banned the export of gold and that removed gold as the standard of US currency.[34] He created the National Labor Board in August 1933 to bolster collective bargaining powers for unions by executive order.[35] And he established via a November 1933 executive order the Civil Works Administration, a project of the congressionally approved Federal Emergency Relief Administration to provide jobs for the unemployed.[36] But it was a poorly planned project: the CWA shut shop just a few months later under the weight of its own payroll demands. Four million were hired under the program, but taxpayers were shelling out $200 million each month to keep the workers employed.[37]

That's just a quick glance at FDR's first year in office. By the end of his terms, he issued a total of 3,522 executive orders and proclamations—by far, the most of all presidents. Woodrow Wilson is second, with 1,803.[38] But the number doesn't tell the full story.

Both Jimmy Carter and Ronald Reagan, two presidents at ideological opposites on the political spectrum, nevertheless both signed similar numbers of executive orders, at 320 and 381, respectively.[39]

What matters more than the number is how far an executive

order extends into the domain of another branch of government—the judicial and the legislative—and how much chipping to the natural order of the Constitution occurs with its issuance.

After the government shutdown of October 2013, Democratic Party strategists suggested that the standoff that waged between congressional members and White House officials for sixteen days would lead to President Obama's issuance of more executive orders.[40] The reason? He obviously couldn't work with Congress—so he had little recourse but to slam his agenda into law with a quick stroke of the pen.

In January 2014, Obama set off a firestorm with remarks made during his first official cabinet meeting of the year about the need to press forward with his desired agenda, with or without Congress. His words, captured by press around the nation: I've got a pen and I've got a phone, and I'm ready to use them. And I'm not just going to sit around and wait for Congress to pass legislation.[41] He then mixed the threat of executive order with a rather silly vow to work with Congress—much as a playground bully works with victims, so long as they turn over their lunch money.

That's not really the spirit that is supposed to guide this nation's government.

The three branches were created as separate but equal powers, and executive orders automatically tip the scales toward the president. For that reason alone, they should be tossed from America's system of governance and banned from future presidencies. But when presidents snatch that power to decree by pen for purposes of personal agenda and personal politics—only because Congress won't pass a pet policy, for example—that's an arrogant mock at Congress, the entire legislative process, and the Constitution, and America's entire rule of law takes a major hit.

Recall George Washington's response when the British surrendered at Yorktown, Virginia, in October 1781. This is the spirit that's supposed to guide our nation. Congress was reneging on its promise to pay the troops, and as the war wound down, Washington struggled to find a way to compensate his men. One of his officers,

Col. Lewis Nicola, wrote him a letter, suggesting that the inability of Congress to provide the military with its earned salaries was only proof that the new government was doomed to fail.[42] Nicola said Washington should take a bold step and use his popularity to seize control of the government—to declare himself king.[43]

Washington's response was swift.

In a letter sent back that same day, he first expressed shock at Nicola's suggestion and then abhorrence. He made clear, in just a few brief sentences, that he was about the last person in the world such an idea would appeal to and called on Nicola to turn quickly from that thought—and never again broach the topic.[44]

That's a sharp contrast to many of the presidents who followed with far less humble attitudes. And sad to say, but more presidents in modern-day America would probably agree with Nicola than with Washington.

14

THE BAFFLING WHITE HOUSE EMBRACE OF RADICAL ISLAMISM

It is our true policy to steer clear of permanent alliance with any portion of the foreign world.

—**George Washington, Farewell Address**

There's regular American logic. There's Inside the Beltway, career politician logic. And then there's American overseas policy logic. And when the three clash, as they did in 2013 over US policy in Egypt, chaos results.

Hosni Mubarak was appointed to the presidency in Egypt after Anwar Sadat was assassinated in 1981. He served in the role for three decades—the longest-serving Egyptian president ever—and enjoyed a mostly cordial relationship with the United States, helping the allied forces drive Iraqi troops from Kuwait in the 1991 Gulf War and joining with the Arab League's push for an Arab-Israel peace plan.[1] He also ruled his nation with an iron fist—but to the United States, that was actually an unspoken positive that kept in check more radical Islamic forces in the region.[2]

Corruption plagued his presidency, however, and he resigned amid a widespread and weeks-long protest that took over the streets of Cairo in 2011.[3] It was during these eighteen days of violence that tore at the nation, pitting pro-Mubarak supporters against a mostly youthful crowd that demanded a more democratic rule, that the United States distanced itself from the leader.[4]

In early February 2011, President Obama called for Mubarak to quickly leave office and put an end to the clashes. Cairo officials reacted to the swift and blunt order from their former White House friends with fury, accusing the United States of ratcheting up the violence and wrecking any chances for a peaceful Mubarak departure, complete with a smooth transition of power.[5]

Then came Mohamed Morsi, who won a narrow election in June 2012 to become Egypt's fifth president, and its first of pure Islamist belief.

Backed by the Muslim Brotherhood, a group that Mubarak had outright banned, Morsi took over the presidency with promises to govern for all of Egypt rather than for solely Islamist interests.[6] He also vowed to create a constitution that included input from Coptic Christians and women.[7] America welcomed him. President Obama made a personal telephone call to congratulate the Islamist leader on his win in late June 2012, pledging US support for his push to move Egypt toward democracy and touting a mutual respect for the new leader.[8] Then secretary of state Hillary Rodham Clinton traveled to Egypt in mid-July to personally welcome the new leader to his post and express America's support for his full transition to office.[9]

She largely ignored the elephant in the room, as did other American leaders: The military that controlled Egypt in the months between Mubarak and Morsi was still a thorn in the new president's side. Generals that had been loyal to Mubarak weren't so happy with Morsi or with his Muslim Brotherhood influences.

Meanwhile, Morsi basically took his US endorsement and ran. Shortly after taking office, he issued a decree that granted him dictator-type powers.[10] Egypt howled. Facing pressure from around the nation—pressure that included massive and violent protests that left several dead—Morsi ultimately softened the language in his decree.

But curiously missing from the swarms of domestic and international criticisms that hit at Morsi's move to become a modern-day pharaoh were any public rebukes from the United States leadership. Why was that?

His power grab came just days after he brought to fruition a cease-fire deal between Israel and Hamas that had been a pet goal of the Obama administration.[11]

Still, how awkward. Here's the United States—the bastion of freedom around the world—strangely silent as the newly seated Egyptian president practically took over the government. The United States only sent out the blandest of statements, hoping for a peaceful end to Morsi's decree and expressing desire for a government that truly reflected the will of Egypt's people.[12] No dramatic statements about the shock of Morsi's power grab. No outraged call for Morsi to abandon his pharaoh-like plans.

And this is where the three types of logic—regular American; Washington, DC, politician; and diplomatic policy wonk—begin to clash.

Regular America might start to wonder how a nation built on democratic-republican principles and rule of law could continue supporting a leader who basically declared himself an untouchable king. Capitol Hill politicians might start to take stock of the political winds and jump on the self-righteous bandwagon by condemning Morsi and calling for an end of US aid to Egypt, as then-ranking Senate Armed Services Committee Republican senator John McCain did—a truly fickle mirror of a call he made just a few months earlier for Mubarak.[13] And US overseas policy logic opted to continue the baffling path of support, despite the obvious signs of Morsi's walk toward authoritarianism, embrace of rigid Islamist principles, and upturned nose at previously touted principles of justice.

But the overseas policy logic got even weirder a few months later, when the Egyptian military—mostly loyal to the former leader, Mubarak—finally rose up and ousted Morsi from office, on July 3, 2013. By all definitions, this was a coup.

But America's leaders, from President Obama to his secretary of state, John Kerry, refused to label it such. Doing so would mean the United States would have to withdraw financial aid to the nation, according to laws guiding US taxpayer disbursements for unstable governments. Doing so would also prove a significant embarrassment for Obama and his administration, after they made such a show of calling for Mubarak to leave office.

Again, it was a clash of regular American logic, Capitol Hill logic and, in this instance, White House overseas policy.[14] While Sen. John McCain took to the media to insist that the overthrow of Morsi was a coup, John Kerry countered that it was simply a restoration of democracy—a rather odd turn of phrase that set the White House as a supporter of the military.[15]

Yet, for months, the White House had no problem backing Morsi and, by extension, his Muslim Brotherhood political partners—who stood largely against the military. And don't forget: this is the same military that supported Mubarak—whom America first supported before kicking to the curb.

It's dizzying.

Trying to sift through, make sense of, and keep pace with the Obama administration's overseas policy requires a scorecard: Are we friends with Morsi? Not now? Okay, we're enemies; got it.

But here's the golden light among all the Egypt unrest: at least regular America is now more aware of the Muslim Brotherhood than ever before.

And that's a good thing, because when career politicians, White House officials, and diplomats working for the administration try to tell us the Muslim Brotherhood is no threat—that it's not a radical Islamist faction with an anti-American bent—we know better.

But to listen to the Obama administration speak, the Muslim Brotherhood is a moderate political force with potential to assist with Middle Eastern and North African peace deals and democratic nation-building—that it's a necessary diplomatic partner.

In April 2012, with Egypt led by military rule, the White House invited representatives of the Muslim Brotherhood for a meeting with National Security Council officials at an undisclosed location in Washington, DC. What for? Obama spokesman Jay Carney harped on the need to reach out to what the administration described as new and emerging political players in Egypt.[16] A few months earlier, in December 2011, then senator John Kerry, chairman of the Senate Foreign Relations Committee, had traveled to Cairo for a meeting with top-ranking members of the Muslim Brotherhood, who assured him that their recent parliamentary wins—from the first elections held in the nation since Mubarak's departure from office—would not dampen the country's commitment to civil rights for all, despite gender or religion.[17]

But it wasn't long after this meeting, both before Morsi's rise to the presidency and during his year in office, that reports began to trickle in from around the world: radical Islamists are targeting Coptic Christians, the largest religious minority in the Middle East region, for persecution, burning their churches, killing their believers.[18] In May and June 2012, during the two rounds of voting that were held to elect a new president—an election Morsi won— witnesses told Arab media outlets that armed Muslim Brotherhood members had been blockading entire streets in Egypt to keep Coptic Christians from voting, threatening their families with violence for supporting a more secular candidate.[19]

Meanwhile, in March 2013, the Muslim Brotherhood in Egypt delivered a sharp rebuke of the United Nations draft declaration for women's rights that was billed as a call for the immediate end to all forms of violence against females.[20] Signing such a promise, the group said in a written statement, would upset Egypt's cultural traditions and lead to the "complete disintegration of society."[21]

Not all of their cited reasons for opposing the declaration were invalid. Some even mirrored what conservative, traditional, or Christian society in America might fear—that the declaration would open the doors for young girls to lawfully obtain birth control without their parents' knowledge, or that the United Nations' embrace of homosexuality as a right would usurp Egypt's religious prohibitions against the practice.[22]

But the group's general views of women are these, as summarized by Osama Yehia Abu Salama, an expert on Muslim Brotherhood beliefs, traditions, and philosophies: A woman should be confined and controlled by the man of the house. Even if the man beats the woman, the woman should be shown her responsibility in the beating. In the end, the man is only partly to blame for the beating— no matter what. He made those statements during a March 2013 seminar to train women to become marriage counselors.[23]

But here's the larger point that highlights the failed logic of Obama's overseas policy: The Obama administration doesn't have a problem with upsetting Christian traditions and beliefs by pushing gay rights in the military, in marriage, and in spite of traditional US church teachings. And the Obama administration doesn't have a problem imposing birth control mandates on private companies—via the 2010 Patient Protection and Affordable Care Act, i.e., Obamacare—even if those companies have religious objections to contraception. So why wouldn't this same administration denounce what it must perceive as a disdain for women's rights on the part of the Muslim Brotherhood—the very same type of disdain Hillary Rodham Clinton sought to end during her secretary of state travels under President Obama, when she harped on an international stage of the dire need to tear down gender walls?[24]

The only logical answer—the regular American logic answer—is that Obama must have a special place in his heart for the Muslim Brotherhood. In 2009, when the group was banned in Egypt and America still had a warm relationship with Mubarak, Obama nonetheless reached out to Muslim Brotherhood leaders with a special invitation to attend his now-famous Cairo speech and address to the Islamic community, June 2009.[25] He also invited a woman who presided over the Muslim Brotherhood–tied group, the Islamic Society of North America, or ISNA, to lead prayers at the National Cathedral, during his first inaugural event, January 19, 2009.[26]

It's just such messages of support from the Obama administration to the Muslim Brotherhood that are baffling—that defy regular, American logic. After all, it's not as if the aim of the group is top secret.

And they're not exactly pro-America.

The Muslim Brotherhood was founded in 1928 by Hassan al-Banna, who touted a combination of politics and charity to spread Islamist teachings around the world. Political struggles—Egyptians were fighting to rid their nation of British control—soon led the group to focus more on politics, and one of the Muslim Brotherhood's slogans became, "Islam is the solution."[27] Members hoped to spread Shariah law and create an Islamic state based on its rigid principles, and they quickly grew their ranks in the Arab world. By the mid-1940s, the Muslim Brotherhood touted a half million members—enough to start an offshoot wing devoted to paramilitary missions, including bombings and assassinations of mostly British officials.[28] By the late 1940s, Egypt's government had had enough of the violence and ordered the group to disband.[29]

Shortly after that order, Egypt's prime minister, Mahmoud al-Nuqrashi, was assassinated, and some pointed fingers at the Muslim Brotherhood. Banna, who still held a leadership role with the group, criticized the assassination as a travesty—and then he was shot and killed by an unnamed gunman.[30] The group's influence continued to spread worldwide during the next couple of decades, between the 1950s and 1980s, albeit mostly underground.[31] During this time, one member in particular rose to prominence, Sayyid Qutb, who in the mid-1960s called for Muslim Brotherhood members to launch jihads against those who weren't followers of the faith to bring about radical reform and instill Shariah principles.[32] He was executed by Egypt's government in 1966, but he died a martyr to many, and his words actually inspired the creation of later radical terrorist groups, including al-Qa'ida.[33]

In 1981, the Muslim Brotherhood—unhappy with the peace agreement Egypt forged with Israel—joined forces with the Islamic Group to carry out the assassination of then president Anwar Sadat.[34] A few years later, Muslim Brotherhood members tied the knot with socialists and liberals to form the Islamic Alliance and win sixty-five seats in the parliament—a significant gain that drove the group's radical influence deeper into the nation.[35] And in 1995, when Mustafa Mashhur headed the Muslim Brotherhood, the group worked hard to bring back the Islamic Caliphate—a hard-line, radical rule—as well as ratchet up the jihad against Israel and force the spread of Islam around the world.[36]

Notably, Mashhur said in his book, *Jihad Is the Way, that* the *only difference between* al-Qa'ida and the Muslim Brotherhood was strategy.[37] But both groups, he said, maintained the same goals.

In 2003, membership in the Muslim Brotherhood took a noticeable upswing due in part to the US invasion of Iraq.[38] A couple of years later, it made great inroads in the political walls of Egypt, securing 20 percent of all the seats that had been up for contest in the parliamentary elections.[39]

Mubarak subsequently persecuted the group, jailing and torturing hundreds of members throughout the years after that 2005 election. But membership continued to grow in secret underground cells as the group's call for eradication of Israel resonated among radical Muslims. Even in mid-2012, Egypt's then Muslim Brotherhood leader Mohammed Badie spoke openly of the need for all Muslims to wage jihad against Israel and reclaim holy sites by force.[40]

The point of the history lesson is brief: how is it possible to believe the Muslim Brotherhood is in any way moderate?

Downplaying the radical elements of the group—its mission of jihad, its hatred of Israel and the West, its overall aim of imposing radical Islamist rule throughout the world—is not only a political hazard for the United States. It's also a serious security threat. How can we even wage a war against terrorism, never mind win one, if we don't properly identify the enemy?

In September 2013, Egypt's high courts ordered the dissolution—yet again—of the Muslim Brotherhood and the seizure of its assets. A left-leaning political party in the nation, Tagammu, meanwhile, accused the group of terrorism and of using religion to bring about a personal political agenda.[41] But if history repeats, the Muslim Brotherhood will just continue its work in an underground setting. That same month, Obama spoke at the fiftieth annual convention of the Islamic Society of North America and gave a glowing nod to the group's legacy—which at that particular September 2013 gathering included an eight-course seminar from Imam Zaid Shakir about the inferiority of the Constitution to Shariah law.[42] Why? Because the Constitution professes equality among the religions—it does not grant Muslims special rights over those of other faiths.

Does that sound like a friend of the United States and a champion of our democratic-republican cause? Even Egypt's interim government, on Christmas Day 2013, declared the Muslim Brotherhood a terrorist organization—sparking a new round of violent protests in the streets.[43] But from the White House? In the hours after that announcement, the Obama administration still stood strong in the Muslim Brotherhood's camp.

On top of that, the organization that Obama lauded for its legacy—ISNA—was placed on the Federal Bureau of Investigation's radar as far back as 1987 as a front group tasked with advancing an Islamic revolution in America.[44]

Maybe there are four, not three, types of logic at play here: regular America, career politician, US overseas—and the logic of destruction from those who seek to shatter the very foundations of our American government.

Moreover, ISNA has been making great gains in America.

It was created in the early 1980s by the Muslim Brotherhood, as a way of centralizing the Islamic message and movement in the West.[45] One of its founding members, Sami al Arian, was later convicted by federal authorities of a conspiracy to aid the terror organization Palestinian Islamic Jihad.[46] Another who worked with the group for years, Adurahman Alamoudi, was caught by authorities for funding al-Qa'ida and sent to federal prison.[47]

Still, the early 1980s were good to ISNA, and by 1984 the group had established one hundred Islamic entities around the United States—schools, mosques, nonprofit groups, clinics, shelters, and other community outreach projects.[48] Nowadays, the United States is home to hundreds of chapters of such groups as the Muslim American Society, the Council on American-Islamic Relations, the Muslim Communities Associations, the Association of Muslim Scientists and Engineers, and the Association of Muslim Social Scientists.[49]

That is not to say all these groups are fronts for terrorists.

But it is to say that not all are completely up-front about their deep-seated intent to upset America's constitutional form of government and implement one more in line with Shariah law or Islamic principles. And many in positions of political leadership in this country either don't believe that—or worse, don't care.

If we're truly fighting a war on terrorism, shouldn't we toss aside political considerations and baffling diplomatic outreaches and meet the enemy with clear eyes, common sense, and genuine concern for the safety of the American people? A little more caution could be the order of the day for our national leaders. A little more caution, a little less political correctness—a lot more regular logic.

15

POLITICAL CORRECTNESS IS KILLING US— REALLY

Wherefore, all affronts to Christianity, or endeavors to depreciate its efficacy, in those who have once professed it, are highly deserving of censure.

—Sir William Blackstone, in Blackstone's Commentaries on the Laws of England

I n mid-June 2007, Army psychiatrist Maj. Nidal Malik Hasan stood before a group of his mental health colleagues at Walter Reed Army Medical Center in Maryland, where he was finishing his six-year internship and residency, and delivered what was supposed to be a routine presentation on a medical topic.[1] Instead, he gave them a lecture on Muslim beliefs—and more specifically, how the United States was waging an unwarranted and warlike campaign against Islam.[2]

He also remarked how difficult the US military life was becoming for Muslims who wanted to serve, yet who faced a moral dilemma by fighting what he characterized as the rising number of unjustified missions against those of the Islamic faith.[3] And one more claim classmates found odd: he mentioned that Muslims serving in America's militaries might one day face the dilemma of shooting at their fellow troops in order to uphold their faith.[4]

Apparently, his rhetoric became so inflammatory that his fellow graduate students in the audience shouted their objections, and a senior military member halted the presentation.[5]

A month later, Hasan was transferred to Fort Hood to serve as a psychiatrist and to prepare for deployment to Afghanistan.[6] He wasn't ultimately deployed, but he did voice some concerns via e-mails to superior officers about a handful of soldiers he was evaluating. In one case, he said he was disturbed about a report that US troops had contaminated Iraqi drinking water with fuel.[7] In another, he decried the US killing of an Iraqi woman who had wandered into an off-limits area.[8] He wanted his supervisors to advise him how to handle the cases—but apparently, he didn't wait long for any answer.

It was just days later, on November 5, 2009, that Hasan strode into the medical deployment facility at Fort Hood, touting a high-powered weapon and screaming, "Allahu Akbar"—God is great—and started firing off rounds, ultimately killing thirteen and injuring thirty-two.[9]

He later bragged of his murders—while pleading not guilty—and characterized them in court appearances as defensive acts to help his Muslim brothers, in response to America's unjustified and illegal war in Afghanistan.[10] He also described them as his way of protecting Taliban leaders in Iraq and Afghanistan.

On top of that, America further learned during the murder trial that Hasan had been engaging in e-mail correspondence with radical Islamic cleric Anwar al-Awlaki in Yemen since December 2008.[11] For that, one FBI counterterrorism agent later admitted that it would have been "prudent" to interview Hasan.[12]

Still, that same FBI agent didn't cop to political correctness and denied that Hasan's religious affiliation had anything to do with the intelligence failures that seemed to let the Muslim radical fall through the military cracks. Even when a former FBI director, William Webster, conducted an independent review of the e-mails and determined that agents should have looked a little deeper into Hasan and that the politically sensitive nature was part of the reason for their hesitation, nobody was disciplined.[13] Authorities did implement some of the eighteen recommended policy changes—but hitting political correctness head-on was not among the suggested reforms.[14]

Still, the worst face-slap was yet to come. When it came time to file charges against Hasan, the military characterized his bloody massacre as an act of workplace violence, not Islamic terrorism. He was found guilty in August 2013 on a range of premeditated murder and premeditated attempted murder charges, and sentenced to death. The Pentagon said labeling him a terrorist would taint the trial and compromise the government's ability to win its prosecution.[15]

But to most of America, calling it workplace violence was a betrayal.

The softer charge was a direct hit to victims' families and loved ones, effectively cutting them off from obtaining certain military benefits and honors and making any awards they won from ensuing civil claims that much smaller.[16] But more than that, it was a direct assault on logic and on America's justice system.

The evidence that Hasan killed for his radical Islamic principles out of martyr-driven-madman passion was obvious. The fact that the US government didn't want to stamp that in the history books is both travesty and shame, and just another sad example of how leadership pays lip service to living up to constitutional oaths to protect and serve and instead focuses on pleasing the politically correct crowd.

After all, it's a controversial statement—that radical Islam is no different from other faiths, that it's truly a religion of peace, marred and tainted by no more than a handful of wayward activists.

And countering that mantra can be dangerous and deadly.

Remember in the late 1980s when Salman Rushdie saw his *The*

Satanic Verses published, and the Ayatollah Khomeini issued a call for his death—a fatwa—claiming the book was blasphemous to Muslims? Rushdie, fearing for his life, spent years in hiding.

In 2012, he emerged for an interview with a United Kingdom media outlet to suggest the world had only grown even more fearful of radical Islam in recent years. He said he doubted his *Satanic Verses* would even be published today, because a nervous book world would regard it as too critical of Islam.[17] Rushdie also suggested that publishers should "be braver" and fight the intimidation and censorship. But they're hardly alone in their caution.

Right around the same time frame that Rushdie emerged from isolation, a television broadcaster dropped plans to show a second screening of *Islam: The Untold Story,* after the documentary's presenter, Tom Holland, received numerous threats and angry messages on Twitter.[18] A spokeswoman for the Channel 4 station issued a statement saying that security officials had counseled the show's cancellation and were especially concerned that Holland had received messages advising him to make sure he had bodyguards with him on the streets.[19]

The problem with the documentary? Show researchers raised too many questions about several stories in the Koran and about the prophet Muhammad, and shed light on the fact that there wasn't much written history about the genesis of the religion.[20] Followers of the faith considered some of the content blasphemous, and even Iranian state-run television weighed in with an objection, labeling the film an outright insult.[21]

A couple of years earlier, it was the cartoon *South Park,* created by Trey Parker and Matt Stone, that faced fire from the Islam community.

The Comedy Central series is known for its political incorrectness and fearless—albeit, often tasteless—mocks and attacks on leading figures and causes of the day. But even that reputation was not enough to shield the show creators from threats when an episode satirizing the prophet Muhammad raised the hackles of an Islamic group, the New York–based Revolution Muslim.[22] The group posted on its website what it declared was a statement of fact, rather than threat, that the show creators would likely end up like Theo van Gogh for the cartoon episode.[23] Van Gogh was a Dutch movie maker who was killed by a Moroccan Muslim waging jihad in 2004 on the streets of Amsterdam over his film about Muslim abuse of women.[24] Network executives took it as a threat.

A second *South Park* episode that included more mentions of Muhammad was outright censored by Comedy Central—even though Parker and Stone had already censored it themselves, putting bars with the word "Censored" over cartoon images of the prophet and bleeping out mention of his name.[25]

It's worth noting that *South Park* creators have freely made fun of other religious leaders, including Jesus, Moses, and Buddha, in previous episodes, without fear for their lives.

Cross the ocean to France and the Islamic war on cartoon images of Muhammad continues.

In 2011, the office of the satirical magazine *Charlie Hebdo*, a popular French production, was firebombed after an Arab Spring edition featured a cartoon of the prophet on the cover, portraying a guest editor role.[26] The magazine's editor, speaking on a variety of radio shows about the bombing, said the office had received numerous threats and angry messages on Twitter and Facebook that had been passed on to police in the days before the attack.[27] Yet he couldn't believe the attack was carried out by French Muslims—preferring instead to call them ignorant radicals—even though Islam militants threatened a similar attack against a Danish publication a few years earlier.[28]

In 2006, a Danish newspaper sparked widespread Muslim protests and boycotts on Danish products after publishing a dozen satirical cartoon images of Muhammad that were perceived by followers of the faith to be blasphemous.[29] One of the images put a bomb in place of a turban on Muhammad's head, leading outraged Muslim believers to burn Danish flags in the streets throughout the Middle East.[30] The *Jyllands-Posten* newspaper offices in Copenhagen and in Arhus were threatened with bombings, and workers were subsequently evacuated.[31] The editor was forced to write and post a lengthy apology on the newspaper website, entitled "Honorable Citizens of the Muslim World."[32]

So what is it about the Muslim religion that inspires such violence? It's hard to picture a self-proclaimed Christian tossing a firebomb at an office that publishes or displays an unfavorable picture of Jesus Christ or other biblically based figure—and that's a theory that's actually been tested too.

In 1999, the taxpayer-funded New York Museum of Art in Brooklyn was about to showcase a painting by Chris Ofili of the Mother Mary covered in elephant dung.[33] Outrage ensued, and Mayor Rudy Giuliani dubbed the exhibit—which also contained sexually explicit photos over the Virgin Mary's body—anti-Catholic.[34] He ultimately stepped in and closed the display, using the taxpayer angle as partial justification.[35] As angry and outraged as those of Christian faith became over the painting—no bombs.

In September 2012, religious organizations blasted President Obama and his administration over what they deemed hypocrisy and the administration's lackadaisical shrug at a horrific anti-Christian museum display. Called the *Piss Christ*, the display—it can't even be called artwork—featured a photograph of the crucifix, complete with Jesus Christ, submerged in the so-called artist's urine. The display was funded in part by prize money from the taxpayer-fed National Endowment for the Arts.[36] And while those of sane sense called it disgusting and offensive, the Obama administration—which has waded into other cultural controversies to defend the Islamic faith—stayed largely silent. But again—no bombs from those of Christian faith.

Here's the hypocrisy: when Muslims express objection to a perceived religious slight in a violent manner, the White House under Obama takes great care to smooth the ruffled feathers.

Recall the brief 2012 film *Innocence of Muslims*, which the White House denounced and at first pointed to as the spark that ignited the killings of four Americans at the US consulate in Benghazi, Libya—terrorist attacks that came on the anniversary of September 11.[37] Not only did the White House ask, unsuccessfully, for Google to remove the low-budget, fourteen-minute video from YouTube, blaming it for inciting widespread riots and violence in Muslim communities around the world.[38] Leading film critics Obama and then secretary of state Hillary Clinton also spent $70,000 of taxpayer dollars to run ads on seven different television stations in Pakistan to condemn the film and make clear the White House disapproved of its content.[39]

Around this time, one of Pakistan's leading ministers stepped forward and offered publicly to pay $100,000 to anyone who killed the film producer.[40]

The filmmaker, American citizen Nakoula Basseley Nakoula, was ultimately imprisoned in California on charges stemming from parole violations—a conviction that came from what many called a government-inspired, trumped-up case.[41]

Failing to regard radical Islamism with clear eyes is a danger to America's security. As former New York City mayor Rudy Giuliani famously said during July 2013 testimony to the House Homeland Security Committee, you can't fight an enemy you refuse to name or acknowledge.[42] He also said:

> We must purge ourselves of the practice of political correctness when it interferes with our rational and intellectually honest analysis of identifying characteristics that help us to discover these killers in advance. For example, there would have been a greater chance of preventing Fort Hood and maybe the Boston bombings if the relevant bureaucracies had been less reluctant to identify the eventual killers as potential Islamic extremist terrorists. But bureaucracies respond to the message they are getting from the top. . . . In the present climate, the message being conveyed from the top is that it is inappropriate to label someone an "Islamic extremist" no matter how compelling the suspicions. But you can't fight an enemy you don't acknowledge.[43]

His comments were blunt, unequivocal, fearless—and entirely truthful, given the years of special treatment that Muslims have been afforded under the Obama administration. Remember the special reach-out by Obama to those of the Islamic faith to make them feel they played an important role in the race to space?

In 2010, Charles Bolden, a retired Maine Corps major general, former astronaut, and former NASA administrator, said Obama gave him a set of basic instructions when he took on leadership duties at the space agency—the first, to inspire youth to tackle math and science;[44] the second, to expand relations in the international community; and the third, to target Muslims with a special pat on the back to bolster their self-esteem about their contributions to the space program.[45]

The White House fielded fire for what critics say was a substantial policy shift that skewed the mission of NASA. Administration staffers went on the defensive, issuing a statement that the president simply meant that space missions were now collaborative, rather than competitive, and that future endeavors would include partnerships with all countries, from Russia to Japan to Muslim-dominated nations.[46]

It's not only the White House.

In April 2012, Gen. Martin Dempsey, chairman of the Joint Chiefs of Staff, ordered the US military to go through all its training courses on radical Islamism and make sure nothing was in the text that could be perceived as anti-Muslim.[47] Earlier, the Pentagon had conducted a similar purge in its course for officers on Islam.[48] The investigation of the course materials had started because of student complaints. Their big objection? Some of the materials taught that Islam was at war with the West.[49]

But really, what's wrong with teaching that some, if not much, of Islamic principle demands war with the West?

As scholars on Islamic principle teach, the Koran defines infidels as anyone who rejects Islam, and infidels are considered enemies of the faith.[50] It's only political correctness that compels the belief that Islam, as taught through the Koran, is a religion of peace—and those who suggest otherwise are Islamophobes. But here's a test: if Islam is really that peaceful, then why can't believers withstand criticism with grace and dignity?

Why are those who speak against the religion's prophet, or show a cartoon image of Muhammad, subject to threats, bombings, and other acts of violence? Other religions don't teach believers to act that way. And other religions don't sprout a political or military offshoot that's then blamed for the acts of violence committed by the believers—as Islam does, with its attempt to differentiate between political Islam and religious Islam.[51] Books have been written and research conducted on both sides of the equation: Is Islam a religion of peace? Many say yes—and undoubtedly, many in the faith are themselves of peaceful mind and heart. But here's a thought. Whether Islam is a religion of peace or of violent takeover, one thing is clear: it sure is an easy religion to use to promote and justify acts of violence.

It'd be hard to cite the teachings of Jesus Christ and blow up the World Trade Center. Not many Christians would be on board with that line of logic.

Yet when it comes time to implement simple security measures, America's politicians are only too willing to cede to demands from special-interest Muslim groups. Remember the long-running fiascos with Muslim women decrying the forced removal of their head scarves to obtain their driver's licenses? CAIR once again had a hand in changing state laws to allow Muslim women to keep their headdresses, or hijabs, for photographs.[52] As a matter of fact, CAIR mounted an entire national campaign that spanned years and went after every state to change the Department of Motor Vehicle laws and accommodate Muslim religious dictates for women.[53] Yet women of faiths other than Islam are generally ordered by DMV workers to remove their hats or head scarves for license pictures.

It's a clash of First Amendment guarantees with Americans' security and safety rights, true. But in a war on terror, when Americans of all walks are seeing their rights ceded by government on a daily basis, why are those of Islamic faith given a pass on something that's not even a right, but rather a privilege—a driver's license?

Asking America's politicians to name the enemy in the War on Terror is not a new idea. Neither is it that outrageous, except for those of completely foggy mind or for those who want to purposely cloud the truth for evil intent. In 2011, New York's Rep. Peter King was put through the liberal and mainstream media wringer for a series of congressional hearings that dared to look at the trend of radical Islamism on American soil, especially after witnesses confirmed that US authorities were dismissing or outright ignoring homegrown threats.[54] Several lawmakers even criticized the hearings as pointless, arguing that a better use of House Homeland Security Committee members' time would be to investigate the Ku Klux Klan and criminal organizations—a blatant disregard for radical Islam's threat.[55] CAIR, meanwhile, characterized the entire hearing process as anti-Muslim.[56]

So we can't even talk about the threat of radical Islam? This culture of fear of being labeled anti-Muslim, biased, or bigoted has left America in a weakened position of defense. If elected leaders, who are sworn to defend this nation against all threats, foreign and domestic, can't even discuss one of the threats they're sworn to fight against—well, where does that leave the rest of us?

In a word—vulnerable.

And in mid-2012, some in Congress—once again—acknowledged that fact.

A report from the House Committee on Homeland Security based on the four hearings that King held on Islam's growing threats concluded: Political correctness was compromising America's national security. The United States was failing to recognize and deal with the deep dangers from al Qaeda and other radical and militant Islamist groups. From the report:

> This is no phantom threat. It shares no equivalency with threats posed by other domestic terrorists who have no foreign ties or any demonstrated capability of organizing themselves for spectacular attacks inside the homeland. In late 2010, Attorney General Eric

Holder said there had been 126 homegrown plots, threats and attacks since 2009—the year homegrown radicalized jihadis attacked military heroes at Fort Hood and in Little Rock. Since we began our investigation into the radicalization threat from within the Muslim-American community, many more violent Islamist extremists have been intercepted attempting to kill their fellow Americans. . . . The radicalization of Muslim-Americans by the violent Islamist extremist ideology, promulgated by al Qaeda and its affiliates is a problem that the United States cannot continue to simply ignore or deflect. Unfortunately, it appears that within the United States, political correctness has prevented many from sufficiently acknowledging and tackling this dangerous problem.[57]

A year later, and America—along with the international community—is still treading these dangerous waters.

In late 2013, the fifty-seven-member Organization of Islamic Cooperation gave the thumbs-up to a new, global Advisory Media Committee aimed at rooting out instances of Islamophobia around the world.[58] The recommendation for the panel's creation came on the heels of the OIC's September 2013 workshop, "The First International Conference on Islamophobia: Law & Media," which concluded that Europe and North America, primarily, held skewed views of Muslims.[59] The new OIC panel was tasked with the mission of countering these views.

You know what that means, don't you?

Bluntly, the panel will serve as a new attack dog that will work to build consensus on an international scale to compel America and European nations to tone down criticisms of Islam. Just what the United States needs—another force to instill even more political correctness about radical Islamism.

The research and survey Pew Forum group released a 226-page report on Muslim attitudes and beliefs in mid-2013 that gave some interesting insights about those of Islamic faith. Notably, the survey didn't include feedback from Muslims in India, Iran, China, or Saudi Arabia—where al Qaeda founder Osama bin Laden spent his formative years and where fifteen of the terrorists who attacked America on September 11, 2001, hailed from.[60] The survey also failed to include opinions from Muslims who live in America or other Western nations.[61]

Regardless, some of the statistics are both revealing and concerning.

Most in the Middle East and parts of Africa want to make Shariah the law of the land, with fully 99 percent in Afghanistan believing adherence to strict Islamic principles is the only way to live.[62] Ninety-one percent in Iraq felt similarly, followed by 89 percent in the Palestinian territories, 86 percent in Niger and Malaysia, 84 percent in Pakistan, and 74 percent in Egypt—large majorities that might lead one to wonder about the fate of US-driven democracy-building efforts in some of those regions.[63]

At the same time, views of what Shariah means differed across the regions and among the respondents. Most Muslims said they don't see a conflict between Shariah law and modern society—even though a large population regarded alcohol, birth control, and divorce as immoral and maintained that wives should always obey their husbands.[64] Of course, other religions teach similarly. But the difference is how those of Muslim faith react to those who commit immoral or criminal acts.

For instance, America's Constitution doesn't allow for the killing of one's wife as a means of saving the family's honor and good name—and that's just one blunt contrast between Shariah and modern society. In South Asia, a large median percentage of Muslims believe Shariah law should allow for authorities to cut off the hands of thieves or to impose the death penalty on those who renounce their Islamic faith.[65] In the Middle East and North Africa, more than half of the median want executions for those who convert from Islam.[66]

And while Pew researchers put forth that the majority of Muslims who responded to the survey said they strongly objected to bombings and other acts of violence in the name of Islam, the numbers are nonetheless threatening. Respondents were asked specifically to characterize their views of suicide bombings and whether those attacks were ever justified. Pew summarized their findings: "Clear majorities in most countries say such acts are rarely or never justified as a means of defending Islam from its enemies. In most countries where the question was asked, roughly three-quarters or more Muslims reject suicide bombing and other forms of violence against civilians."[67]

Isn't that kind of missing the headline? That's called, in newspeak, burying the lead.

After all, if a quarter of Christians thought suicide bombings against civilians in the name of Jesus was a justifiable act, depending on the circumstances, that just might lead the evening news—and it wouldn't be to announce that three-quarters of followers of Jesus don't believe in suicide killings.

The Pew report authors put a similar spin on honor killings too.

Muslims were asked if honor killings are ever justified for premarital or extramarital sex. Pew researchers wrote that "in 14 of the 23 countries where the question was asked, at least half say honor killings are never justified when a woman stands accused."[68]

That's the politically correct way of saying that in vast swaths across the Muslim world, large percentages of those of Islamic faith believe that women who commit morally unacceptable sexual acts should be killed.

Potato-potahto, right? It's all in how you look at it.

Unfortunately, the pressure to dismiss the truths of radical Islam is only growing stronger. Political correctness and a concerted campaign of disinformation are slowly eroding our constitutional government. And truly, given the realities of our current education system and the political correctness and propaganda dogma that's often substituted for accurate history by agenda-driven leftists and intellectuals, it's not looking as though America's future generations will be schooled with the tools needed to turn back the tide.

16

TRAINING THE NEXT GENERATION THAT GOVERNMENT IS GOD

Train up a child in the way he should go, and when he is old he will not depart from it.

—Proverbs 22:6 *NKJV*

I n 2009, first lady Michelle Obama announced, to much press fanfare, her plans to dig up portions of the South Lawn at the White House and plant a vegetable garden, complete with fifty-five different varieties. Her hope, she said, was the garden would become a conversation starter that would lead the select schoolchildren who helped farm the produce to bring home a healthy-eating message to their families and, ultimately, their communities.[1]

Just a few months later—and no doubt buoyed by the media success of her much-publicized garden—the first lady went a step further and introduced her signature Let's Move campaign aimed at combating national obesity rates. The launch was a star-studded White House affair that brought out top-ranking administration politicos—from agriculture secretary Tom Vilsack to Health and Human Services secretary Kathleen Sebelius—as well as congressional members and mayors from around the nation.[2] The president of the American Academy of Pediatrics was on hand; members of the 2009 National Championship Pee-Wee football team showed up.[3] And President Obama himself lent his executive support, signing his name to a presidential memorandum that brought into existence the nation's first Task Force on Childhood Obesity, tasked with developing a national plan to implement the first lady's goals for childhood nutrition and physical fitness within ninety days.[4]

Mrs. Obama said of Let's Move: "The physical and emotional health of an entire generation and the economic health and security of our nation is at stake."[5]

Really? That sounds ominous.

But Congress answered her call to fitness arms with the passage of the Healthy, Hunger-Free Kids Act of 2010, freeing up billions of dollars in funding for schools to adopt healthier menus in their cafeterias and putting the US Department of Agriculture in charge of setting nutrition standards, including caloric limits on offered meals.[6] The president signed it into law in December 2010.[7] It wasn't long after the mandates took effect—and around the same time Mrs. Obama was championing her 2012 book, *American Grown: The Story of the White House Kitchen Garden and Gardens Across America*, that students across the nation started complaining.[8]

The lunches were too small. Students were starving. The food tasted disgusting.[9] And student-athletes, in particular, were suffering, saying the menus left them hungry and weak by the time the school day ended and practice or games began. Schools, for their part, started complaining of difficulties with menu compliance, reporting the 650 to 850 lunch calorie limits—depending on grade level—were too low for students and many didn't like the new cafeteria offerings.[10] Some students tossed the food, others started bringing lunches from home, and school districts said regulations were becoming too onerous and costly to implement. In July 2013, New York's Burnt Hills–Ballston Lake school district opted out of the federal program, reporting a loss of $100,000 from trying out the new menu.[11]

So what was Mrs. Obama's and the federal government's response to the growing criticisms about their food?

Push harder.

In September 2013, the first lady jumped to the bully pulpit to sway the private sector—both television executives and food industry officials—to stand down on marketing unhealthy food to children and to do it quickly.[12] A month later, she joined with *Sesame Street* and announced the nonprofit that produces the television show was giving certain food companies permission and licensing to use Muppet characters free of charge to promote fruits and vegetables for the next two years.[13] Mrs. Obama was positively giddy about the free marketing campaign, predicting children who saw an image of Elmo at the local grocery's apple bin or a life-size cardboard of Big Bird by the banana display would literally beg their parents to buy the healthy snacks, in favor of chips or candy.[14]

Time will tell if that prediction holds true. But regardless, isn't it time to put the kibosh on this federal overreach?

It's not that healthy eating is a silly notion for a first lady to adopt. It's certainly a worthy cause—our nation is a bit on the hefty side and could stand to lose a collective few pounds and adopt some healthier habits. On top of that, healthy eating seems a bit reminiscent of former first lady Nancy Reagan's antidrug, "Just Say No" campaign. Both advocate generally accepted principles without much controversy: kids should eat healthy, and they shouldn't do drugs.

But it's all in the messaging.

A mild rebuke is not the same as a federal mandate. A gentle message and educational campaign is not a taxpayer-funded regulation. A cheerleader attitude and motivational speech are hardly akin to driving national policy with a presidential memorandum or to compelling Congress to pass laws. And nothing within the first lady's Let's Move campaign hails from the side of mild, but rather falls heavy on the side of regulation. It's nanny-state governance aimed at the nation's most vulnerable and, oftentimes, most gullible—the kids.

Really, Mrs. Obama's entire campaign—from Let's Move to lunch menu to putting the pressure on the private market—serves as an apt and long-running commentary on something that's been stabbing at our modern culture and cutting into our once-commonly accepted norms: the notion of who knows best—parents or government. To Mrs. Obama and her healthy eating initiative supporters, government just knows better than parents how to raise and develop children.

That's a belief that better belongs in Cuba than America.

Yet this is what we've become. The whole Let's Move debacle is just one example of how our nation's children are learning, step-by-step and day by day, that government is the answer—the provider, the sustainer, the solution to all. Government, it would seem, is the smarter caretaker.

In February 2012, a mother in the small town of Raeford, North Carolina, reported to a media outlet that she sent her daughter off to preschool with a homemade lunch of turkey and cheese on bread, a banana, potato chips, and apple juice.[15] Pretty routine-sounding. But apparently, that didn't sit well with health officials at the school who wanted the girl to eat vegetables.[16] They forced the girl to take a school lunch tray of chicken nuggets, milk, fruit, and vegetables, while saying she could still eat her bagged lunch.[17] The girl, age four, was intimidated by then—not to mention overwhelmed by the adult-size portion of double lunches—and ate only her chicken nuggets. The mother, who later learned of the lunchtime incident, was outraged and upset that the school wouldn't let her daughter alone.[18] Moreover, this wasn't the first time the school pushed its own version of a healthy lunch on the girl, despite the mother's repeated requests to let her parent and decide her own daughter's menu. In a later meeting of the school principal, the mother, and the girl's grandmother, the question was raised by the family: What is this, China?[19]

If the justification for such government oversight and intrusion is that officials just want to help—to extend a helping hand—then it seems warranted to point out that from good intentions often spring mischief and outright evil. Think zero-tolerance policy in schools around the nation.

In late 2010, a star student-athlete in her last year of high school in North Carolina was charged with a Class 1 misdemeanor and faced the possibility of six months in prison for bringing a paring knife to school in her bagged lunch.[20] School officials said the knife was actually in her purse and they found it while performing random searches on other students to look for drugs.[21] Either way, she said she took her father's lunch to school by mistake and that he had included the knife to slice his apple.[22] But school administrators refused to cut her a break, claiming the knife was a weapon and she violated policy by bringing it on campus. In addition to her charge, she was suspended for the remainder of the school year.[23]

If only such stories were few and far between. But tales like that have been making headlines around the country for years.

Head south to Fort Myers, Florida, and go back in time to 2001, and it was just the same for another high school senior—an honor student and National Merit Scholar, age eighteen, who watched her future tumble after administrators noticed a dinner knife on the floorboards in her parked car.[24] She was charged with a felony, despite the fact that the knife was about as sharp as a butter spreader and never left her locked car.[25] The principal in that case—as in the North Carolina case—refused to handle the matter with leniency, citing a law is a law is a law and all must follow the law.[26]

Now, what about the 2013 shocking story of the little Maryland boy who nibbled his Pop-Tart pastry into what school administrators deemed the shape of a gun and was subsequently suspended?

In June of that year, the parents were denied an appeal to have the boy's suspension expunged from his school records.[27]

His case—certainly one that tasks sane minds—is hardly in a corner all alone.

In mid-2013, Suffolk, Virginia, school officials suspended two second grade boys, both age seven, for pointing pencils at each other and making gun sounds—as no doubt 90 percent of America has done during youth.[28] One boy told his father he was playing a Marine, taking out the "bad guy" his friend was playing, but school officials didn't see it so innocently.[29] A spokesperson for the school system said a pencil, when pointed in a certain manner and when accompanied by gun sounds, is truly a weapon. And the school has a policy—a zero-tolerance policy—to maintain, the spokesperson added.[30]

Also in mid-2013, a six-year-old Palmer, Massachusetts, boy was given a school detention for the crime of carting a G.I. Joe Lego plastic toy gun—about the size of a quarter—onto the bus.[31] The kindergartner was then threatened with a suspension from riding the bus and forced to write an apology letter to the driver.[32] The school, meanwhile, took it upon itself to send a letter home to each and every parent who had a child on the bus to advise of the incident and calm any fears, admitting in the process that nobody was ever in danger.[33] After the mother protested the overkill and told of the trauma her son went through over the weekend, in dread of detention, the school consented to drop the punishment.[34] But how can a school on one hand admit no danger exists but then on the other hand inflict a punishment on a student for committing, ostensibly, an act of danger?

Zero-tolerance policy rears its illogical head yet again.

In January 2013, a five-year-old Pennsylvania girl was given a ten-day suspension for playing with a Hello Kitty "bubble gun" that blows soap bubbles.[35] She reportedly told friends at her bus stop that they could use the toy and shoot each other and play together. The principal, upon learning of the comment, said it was a terroristic threat and slapped on the harsh punishment.[36]

A six-year-old Washington boy who dared to talk about guns at school—just talk—was sent home in February 2013 after a classmate tattled to a teacher that he had a weapon.[37] He didn't—not even a toy one. But the boy was still sent home, leaving the parents to theorize that their son was suspended for the simple crime of discussing the Nerf guns the family bought during a recent out-of-state trip.[38] When the parents contacted the school to clarify, they said the girl who had reported their son to the teacher had expressed concerns about her safety.[39] And the father said school officials told them such matters are covered in the code of conduct and handbook given out to all students. The parents were puzzled, correctly realizing that talking about guns was not an act that was actually prohibited by policy, and planned to appeal.[40] But before they could take action, administrators reversed the decision and said the boy's record would be expunged of the suspension.[41]

Chances are, the incident wasn't so quickly expunged from the boy's mind—and that leads to a central issue: just what exactly are schools teaching children nowadays? Respect for authority and rule of law can't be high on the list.

But just when it's hard to imagine school zero-tolerance policy getting more ridiculous, there's this, from August 2012: Nebraska parents said their deaf son's school objected to the way he signed his name—Hunter—with the gesture of a gun and demanded he learn to spell it letter by letter instead.[42]

The boy, three, had been gesturing his name in accordance with Signing Exact English methods—which meant he shaped his fingers in the shape of a gun—since he was six months old.[43] But school officials wanted him to spell it letter by letter instead, using American Sign Language style.[44] Why? Once again, school policy prohibits any type of object on campus grounds that is a weapon, can be used as a weapon, or even looks like a weapon—zero tolerance.[45]

The list of ridiculous offenses seems endless.

But what's more alarming is that while schools are busy taking out all mention of guns, violence, and weapons from the classroom, from toys to pastry images to forms of speech, teachers are simultaneously adding in lessons that skew history, push leftist political agenda, and put at risk—to those of traditional principled mind—the healthy development of youthful minds.

Why do elementary-age children need sex education classes?

Chicago Public Schools implemented sex and health education classes for kindergartners in mid-2013. The new mandate requires three hundred minutes of teaching, spread out in thirty-minute increments on a monthly basis.[46] So in addition to reading, writing, and arithmetic, the city's five-year-olds will also learn the ins and outs, as well as dos and don'ts, of human sexuality. Some parents were outraged, asking why little children needed to know about such adult topics.[47] But administrators were largely unmoved, saying they would take care to teach the classes in a way that the children could understand, using age-appropriate language and graphics.[48]

As if that's supposed to ease concerns. Part of the course was to talk about same-sex partnerships, a topic that some parents preferred to keep under their own wraps based on family beliefs, teachings, morals, and values.[49]

But those boundaries are being broken by schools on a regular basis nowadays.

Massachusetts schools were ordered by state education authorities to provide transgender students access to opposite-gender bathrooms and locker rooms.[50] That policy was handed down on the heels of a November 2011 state law that prohibited all forms of discrimination based on transgender status.[51] And what that means on a practical level is that schools in Massachusetts now have to honor the demands of boys who state they're girls and vice versa, no matter what biology, genetics, and other physical evidence show.

My, how Massachusetts has changed. Home to one of the Founding Fathers' fiercest defenders of the faith, John Adams—home to some of the fiercest freedom fighters of the Revolutionary War era, a crew of patriots who stood strong against the world's greatest power of the time—Massachusetts is now known more as a bastion of liberalism. Even fifty years ago, though, it's hard to imagine that school transgender policy flying.

So really—my, how our nation has changed.

New York City in late 2013, just in time for the Christmas season, mulled a change in policy that would allow schools to close for Muslim holidays—specifically, the Eid al-Fitr and Eid al-Adha observances that often coincided with school testing schedules.[52] At least one county in Maryland considered the same policy amendment for its schools, in recognition of the growing Muslim community.[53] This as Christmas around the nation continues to come under attack by the same education system that seeks to be sensitive to Muslim needs.

How many schools now list Christmas break on their student calendars, as opposed to the more generic—and devoid of Christian religion—winter break? Headlines sprout every year in the lead-up to December about school Christmas pageants that are under attack for religious overtones. The nation's now to the point that the 1965 creation *A Charlie Brown Christmas*, with its biblical message and mention of Jesus—the real meaning of the holiday, after all—has become a controversy.

Christianity, Founding Father roots, and traditional beliefs are slowly being drummed from our schools, and soon, our national discourse. After this generation of children grows and graduates, the path toward government and away from God will be broadened even more. The signs are all there. In September 2013, a mother in Tennessee was outraged when her daughter, ten, was told by a teacher who wanted to know all the students' "idols" that, no, she couldn't name Jesus—she would have to choose someone else.[54] So the girl named deceased pop star Michael Jackson, and that was accepted.[55]

School textbooks can't even be trusted to teach the truth of our nation's history, or of worldwide issues of interest, anymore.

Parents in Florida in mid-2013 expressed outrage to school officials over a course book, named simply *World History*, that devoted thirty-six pages to Islam versus three small paragraphs to

Christianity.[56] One state lawmaker called the textbook decidedly biased in favor of Islam, complete with a skewed sugarcoating of how the Muslim religion really rose in the world ranks.[57]

Around that same time frame, in August 2013, politicians and education officials in Texas were in heated debate about a lesson plan in the state schools that many accused of teaching that the Boston Tea Party was staged by terrorists—at least in the minds of the British.[58]

A month later, and it was South Carolina that hit the spotlight.

A history book in at least one high school in the state was faulted for its waffling interpretation of the Second Amendment in the US Constitution. The book, furnished to Simpsonville, South Carolina, students, seemed to diminish the concept of the individual's right to own and bear arms by combining discussion of the Second Amendment with the Third Amendment—as if gun ownership were a preclusion to keep government soldiers from taking over private citizens' homes.[59] The book also emphasized the right to bear arms but not keep them—while in the actual Second Amendment, the text specifies that those rights go hand in hand.

But one of the worst lessons thrust on our nation's children has to be this, from Illinois: fourth-graders there in August 2013 were being taught in a lengthy worksheet, in question-and-answer form, about the true nature of government. The worksheet was titled, "What Is Government?"[60] And the answer, simply: government is family.[61]

The worksheet posed compare-contrast questions between family and government, ultimately leading students to realize that government—like family—keeps people safe, healthy, and educated.[62] The school, when asked for explanation, said it was only trying to give the children an example and analogy they could relate to and understand.[63]

That may be true. But fifty years ago, that same teacher would have been teaching that same lesson plan with an analogy of how government differed from family.

17

AMERICA'S REAL WAR: ARE WE STILL ONE NATION, UNDER GOD?

And can the liberties of a nation be thought secure when we have removed their only firm basis, a conviction in the minds of the people that these liberties are of the Gift of God? That they are not to be violated but with His wrath? Indeed, I tremble for my country when I reflect that God is just; that His justice cannot sleep forever.

—*Thomas Jefferson,* **Notes on the State of Virginia**

In November 2013, the Supreme Court of the United States agreed to take up a case that originated in Greece, New York, over a local government body's pre-meeting prayer practices. Over the span of eleven years, the town council opened its sessions with prayers that were primarily led by those of Christian faith. Specifically, the council opened with a Christian-based message between 1999 and 2007 and between January 2009 and June 2010.[1]

Council members deviated a bit from the Christian aspect of the prayer after two residents—an atheist woman and a Jewish woman—complained in 2008 that the town was endorsing one religion over another.[2] The council then allowed separate opening messages to be led by a Jewish person, a Wiccan priestess, and the head of a nearby Baha'i congregation.[3] Council members also allowed for other meetings in 2009, 2010, 2011, and 2013 to go forth with non-Christian opening prayers.[4]

But the two women weren't satisfied with the town's accommodations and they turned to the courts for redress. They accused the town council of unlawfully promoting one religion over another by selecting Christians more often than followers of other faiths to lead the public sessions in prayer.[5] They also claimed they felt pressured to participate in the prayer by standing when instructed to do so—that they were in effect coerced to take part in the Christian messages.[6]

They lost in US District Court. The judge ruled that the town wasn't proselytizing.

But the pair refused to give up their claim and turned to the Second US Circuit Court of Appeals for a new ruling. They won their appeal after the court found the town was pushing one religion over another and giving a silent endorsement to Christianity.[7]

So Greece officials took the matter to the highest court in the nation—to the same court that thirty years ago already ruled that government bodies may indeed open in prayer. In November 2013, the attorney for the two women asked that justices rule that pre-meeting prayers could not contain any specific Christian bent—that future prayers omit an appeal to or mention of Jesus Christ.[8]

Really? Do we really want our government in charge of dictating the content of our prayers?

But this case was such an apt illustration of where our nation now stands. Instead of waiting respectively for the prayers to wrap up or leaving the room if silent respect was too tough to swallow, these two women went on a legal hunt to overturn a centuries-long, court-upheld tradition in America—that of bowing the head and asking God for blessing before legislative proceedings. And toward what purpose?

To upset the order of America.

As many in the media covering the Supreme Court case already pointed out, the justices themselves always open session with a court marshal's appeal to the Almighty: "God save the United States and this honorable court."[9] So the 2013 *Greece v. Galloway* case against prayer before legislative sessions was being heard by a government body that opens its own sessions in prayer. That's quite a twist.

As the Supreme Court made clear in 1983, in *Marsh v. Chambers*—where justices ruled that Nebraska didn't break law by letting a Presbyterian minister open legislative sessions for sixteen years—prayer before government business is part of the fabric of America's society.[10] It's in our national DNA.

Yet you wouldn't know that, with all the attacks on God in politics, culture, the military, and schools in recent years.

In October 2013, the Jackson City School District in Ohio bowed to pressure from the American Civil Liberties Union and the Freedom from Religion Foundation and agreed to pay $95,000 to settle a complaint about a painting of Jesus Christ.[11] The painting had been hung among other pictures of notable historical figures as part of the Jackson City School District's "Hall of Honor" display on one of its building's walls.[12] On top of that, it had hung there since 1947, when it was gifted to the district by a school student club.[13]

But in February 2013, two students and three parents complained, saying the painting was tantamount to a school endorsement of Christianity and should be removed. Enter the ACLU and the FFRF.[14]

The school superintendent at first vowed to fight the looming suit, decrying the idea of a group from Madison, Wisconsin—the FFRF—crossing state lines to fight a local school issue.[15] But he soon stepped back from the battle after learning the district's insurance company wouldn't pay the legal fees. The school took down the Jesus painting and put it away in a closet at the school.[16]

But even that wasn't good enough for the ACLU and FFRF.

Plaintiffs then argued that the painting shouldn't be anywhere on school grounds.[17] After all, they asked, what if someone opened the closet door and saw the Jesus painting and was offended?

To stop the suit, school officials agreed to pay $95,000—and to get the painting off school grounds.[18] The superintendent said the school wasn't financially equipped to handle the double-barrel ACLU-FFRF suit and legal bills were piling up.[19] One small win for the school: the insurance company agreed to pay the $95,000, so taxpayers weren't hit with the bill.[20]

Unbelievable. It's almost as if some people know the suit-happy culture we live in and look for ways to take advantage. And the fact that in this case Jesus was being presented on a school wall as a historical figure—rather than a biblical one—only drives that suspicion deeper.

In November 2013, officials with the Watauga County School District in North Carolina told the local American Legion Post 130 that its members couldn't hang posters that included the mantra "In God We Trust" because they feared it might be unconstitutional.[21] The posters, about sixteen by twenty inches, were framed and portrayed the American flag with the text of the national motto along with the words "The national motto of the United States, adopted by Congress, July 30, 1956."[22] And the American Legion was distributing them, free of charge, as part of a statewide initiative to post the national motto in prominent places.[23] By the time the American Legion got around to asking the Watauga County schools, its members had already placed posters in 185 different businesses in the community.[24]

But the school's legal counsel suggested the school district ban them.[25] Why?

It was a preemptive move, in case somebody saw the posters, misinterpreted their contexts, and sued.[26]

As one poster supporter pointed out, though, it'd be hard to sue when most people already cart the motto around in their pockets, wallets, or purses. And as another argued, how come it's okay to put up pictures of witches on brooms for Halloween celebrations, or graphic images of the federal "Preparing for the Zombie Apocalypse" program, but not of the national motto?[27]

It's not the first time the national motto has come under attack.

In 2011, a California math teacher with thirty years of experience in the classroom was ordered by a court to take down his banner display that showcased the religious heritage of the United States. One banner touted the four messages, all in capital letters: "IN GOD WE TRUST," "ONE NATION UNDER GOD," "GOD BLESS AMERICA," and "GOD SHED HIS GRACE ON THEE."[28] Another banner stated, with the emphasis on the last word, "All Men Are Created Equal, They Are Endowed By Their CREATOR."[29]

The teacher had hung the banners for twenty years in one school, but transferred to another—Westview High School near San Diego—where he was told the messages were in violation of the Constitution because they promoted one particular belief over another.[30] The teacher tried to argue that it was his First Amendment rights that were actually being violated by the order, given that other teachers in the school displayed religious items for other faiths—a Tibetan prayer flag, for instance—but to no avail.[31]

The court ruled the banners had to come down, adding that the teacher was free to educate students about the religious heritage of the nation—just not in the classroom, or at school.[32]

Does that mean that the Declaration of Independence—or at least the portion that contains the same phrase as one of the teacher's banners—can't be hung in the classroom because it might be seen as an offense to those of different views?

The Pledge of Allegiance is under attack too.

In mid-2013, the Supreme Judicial Court of Massachusetts heard a complaint from a handful of parents and the American Humanist Association that school students were being wrongfully pushed to say the Pledge of Allegiance—specifically the phrase "under God."[33] The school defended its policy, arguing that students weren't forced to say the pledge.[34] Their participation was wholly voluntary.

But the plaintiffs, from the Acton-Boxborough School District, said the pledge unfairly marginalizes and stereotypes atheists. They wanted the school recitation brought to a halt.[35]

Why do these cases always start with a complaint from a single person or a small handful of people who suddenly decide that decades-old American traditions—that are supported by millions around the nation—are overtly offensive and demand immediate change? The pledge takes about ten seconds to recite. Nobody's holding a gun to compel recitation. Yet somehow, some disgruntled individual finds standing quietly and respectfully for that brief period of time to allow for classmates and schools officials to give a patriotic nod to a stark symbol of American pride and history is intolerable.

If atheists truly don't believe in God, why would they find someone else's mention and recognition of God so threatening? After all, most people don't feel the need to sue to stop mention of the tooth fairy or the Easter bunny.

As with the US Supreme Court in the Greece, New York, town council prayer case, the Massachusetts court that heard the pledge complaint heralded in the session with an appeal to the Almighty. The Massachusetts court officer opened the hearing: "God save the Commonwealth of Massachusetts."[36]

This isn't the first fight in the Bay State over the pledge, however.

In 2011, parents in Brookline started a war against the pledge in schools, arguing that even though its recitation was voluntary and that it was actually spoken from the main office and broadcast over the intercom into each classroom, some students might feel pressure to participate anyway.[37]

Once again, the battle was brought by a small minority. A Brookline resident who described himself as extremely patriotic said he nonetheless saw the classroom pledge as a form of indoctrination of youthful minds and complained that some children might feel compelled to recite something they don't really want to, or believe.[38] A handful of similarly minded parents formed a group, the Brookline Political Action for Peace, and joined him to petition the school to remove the pledge from the classroom.[39]

School administrators, meanwhile, said they had never heard any students complain they were bullied into reciting the pledge and couldn't understand the outrage.[40]

At least parents weren't arguing that the phrase "under God" was the problem. But still, the case represents the further erosion of traditional and common principles in our society—the outright rejection of core American values that once seemed ingrained.

Why care?

Tearing down the commonly accepted societal beliefs, habits, customs, and values of the many and imposing instead the arbitrary will of the few is an open door to tyrannical government. It's a rejection of the natural order, the universally accepted, the understood and unquestioned right versus wrong—for the imposition of a chaotic and confusing system of governance that's ever changing, based on whim and desire. If America doesn't stand for God and country, what does she stand for?

That's the attitude, and danger, that undercuts these fights against America's most treasured conviction—that God, not government, rules us. It's that core principle that's represented and showcased during both pre-legislative prayer and recitation of the Pledge of Allegiance.

We're not just battling a Pledge of Allegiance case or town council prayer protest. We're battling for the very heart and soul of America. Meanwhile, the battlefield only grows larger and wider.

In 2003, a teacher's aide in one Pennsylvania county filed a suit in federal court, accusing her employer of wrongfully suspending her for wearing a necklace with a Christian cross pendant to her job at Penns Manor Area Elementary School.[41] Ten years later and that same ban was being echoed on the West Coast, at Sonoma State University. There, in mid-2013, a student was ordered to take off her cross necklace by a school official who worried its Christian message might offend others.[42]

And it's not always the Christian cross that offends. In 1999, a school board in Mississippi sparked a court suit after banning the wearing of all Stars of David on district properties. The reason? The traditional Jewish symbol was believed to have been usurped by gang members, who were wearing the emblem as a sign of their affiliations.[43] Administrators also considered banning Christian crosses for the same reason.[44] But it didn't take long for the school to reverse its decision. Just a couple of months after its ban was announced—and in the face of numerous threats of lawsuits—the school changed its mind and tossed the prohibition.[45]

Not all religious freedom cases end so quickly. Not all are waged in the schools, either.

The American Civil Liberties Union was at the heart of a Mohave Desert case that raged fully ten years in several separate courts, pitting patriots, veterans, and Christians against atheists, civil rights activists, and those who decried a public memorial that included a seven-foot-high cross.[46] The memorial, a tribute to military members killed during the course of duty, had stood since the 1930s on a parcel of publicly owned park land known as Sunrise Rock.[47]

The site came under fire from the ACLU in 2001, when attorneys argued that the memorial was unconstitutional because it included a Christian symbol on property overseen by the National Park Service and that gave the impression the federal government was endorsing a particular religion over another.[48]

Once again, the suit arose from the complaint of one—a retired National Park Service employee.[49] Congress tried to stave off a judicial controversy by declaring the site a national memorial in 2002 and by passing a ban on the use of federal funds to take down the cross.[50] But that didn't have the desired effect of halting the court cases. Congress then tried to enact a land swap, exchanging the property on which the cross rested for another parcel in the same area—again, to no avail.[51]

Two separate federal courts nonetheless agreed with the ACLU that the cross had to go because it violated the separation-of-church-

and-state concept.[52] The courts also found that the congressional attempt to sidestep the issue with the property transfer proposal was illegal too.[53]

But memorial supporters kept up the fight, and the case finally reached the ears of the US Supreme Court.[54] In 2010, the nation's highest court ruled that the First Amendment doesn't require the complete eradication of all shows of religious symbols from the public sector and that the Mojave Desert cross was akin to the thousands of crosses that marked grave sites of fallen Americans all around the world. The court also found that the lower courts were too quick to dismiss the idea of swapping out the land and transferring the memorial property into private ownership hands.[55] And that's how the case was ultimately decided—the Veterans of Foreign Wars assumed control of the memorial land. In November 2012, the cross was formally reerected and rededicated.[56]

Unfortunately, that battle may have been won but the war was far from ended.

In 2012, the Washington, DC, Americans United for the Separation of Church and State launched a similar protest against the presence of a Christian cross on a parcel of public land in Riverside.[57] The Mount Rubidoux cross, as it was dubbed, has stood at the site since 1955.[58]

In June 2013, the American Humanist Association served a suit to Lake Elsinore government officials, claiming a planned veterans' memorial with an image of a soldier on bended knee before a Christian cross that was planted on a grave site would cross constitutional lines if constructed on public property.[59]

The monument, six feet tall and made of black granite and etched in white, was a beautiful and tasteful sentiment that showed a soldier with Kevlar and firearm bending before a cross planted in a mound of earth over the block words: "Freedom is never free."[60] Emblazoned across the American flag, with a bald eagle flying to the right, was the message: "Honoring our brave men and women whom by their service give life to our most precious gift—freedom."[61]

City Council members said the memorial, which they wanted to set on public property before the Diamond Stadium minor-league baseball field, wasn't meant to display a religious message, but rather a military one based on history.[62] But the atheist group argued that the message was darker: they said the depiction of the cross was a stark warning to nonbelievers that they are not welcome.[63]

The Mount Rubidoux cross dispute was put to rest when city officials decided to copycat the land transfer idea in the Mojave Desert case. In April 2013, the city sold the property at auction and the buyer, a group of nonprofits that banded together under the umbrella organization Totally Mt. Rubidoux, has vowed to keep the memorial intact.

The Lake Elsinore fight led city officials to amend their memorial design. The newest version presented during court hearings in October 2013 includes several Christian crosses, along with numerous stars of David, near the image of the kneeling soldier.[64] But the atheist group still argued the memorial was religious, rather than historical.

And you thought there were no atheists in foxholes.

The Lake Elsinore case plays into a worrisome trend that's been hitting at our nation's military. In October 2013, the US Air Force Academy decided cadets no longer have to say the "so help me God" portion of their honor oath. What was once time-honored tradition is now optional rhetoric—all due to the insistence of the Military Religious Freedom Foundation, which complained the tail end of the oath violated separation-of-church-and-state rules.[65]

The academy superintendent, Lt. Gen. Michelle Johnson, said that the aim of the school was to instill and foster positive character traits among recruits, including dignity and respect for all. It was in that spirit that she demoted the oath to the category of optional.[66] But even that move wasn't enough for the president of the MRFF, Mikey Weinstein.[67] Weinstein—a 1977 honor graduate of the US Air Force Academy himself—nonetheless accused school heads of taking the easy way out and demanded that the entire phrase containing reference to God be dropped from the oath or he'd sue.[68]

So why wasn't he satisfied with the optional caveat? He said academy recruits would feel pressured into reciting the entire pledge and that even those who withstood the pressure and declined to say the religious portion would worry about repercussions from academy leaders.[69]

That's a rather startling admission. Is that to say America's future fighters are so wimpy they can't even stand strong in their principle for the two seconds it would take for that portion of the oath to be uttered? Imagine how they would react to an enemy capture.

But this is a small example of the chaos that groups like the MRFF want to create. Upset long-held traditions by whatever means necessary—complaints, lawsuits, the media—and in their place establish arbitrary rules based on the will of a few. Root out and abolish all mentions of God from the public sector, proclaiming a revisionist form of history that argues—wrongly—this nation was built by secularists who wanted to keep God away from government. And bully those who protest into silence. The slippery slope is that once God is removed, the door opens wider for government to enter.

If God's not leading, who is?

Worse is when these groups actually purport to be doing Americans a good deed. Weinstein, for instance, insisted his push for the complete abolishment of the religious aspect of the academy oath was a righteous argument because he was making a case of principle and sticking with it. Whether or not cadets could opt out of saying the objectionable portion of the oath was not the point, he said.[70] The bigger issue was the fact that the oath violates law—at least his interpretation of law.[71] And he just didn't want his former academy tainted by the black mark of breaking law.

Weinstein isn't alone in his attacks on the military.

In early 2013, the Pentagon ignited a firestorm with a statement that those in the military of Christian and other faiths could be court-martialed for sharing their religious views.[72] The statement was issued after secretary of defense Chuck Hagel held a closed-door meeting with several members of the military and civilian activists who brought forth a list of concerns about threats facing the troops—among them, sexual assaults and religious proselytizing.[73]

Interestingly, Weinstein was part of that meeting, to make clear to military heads his belief that Islamophobia, anti-Semitism, and the concerted attempts of religious believers to push their faith on others were damaging troop morale and readiness—and ultimately weakening national security.[74]

From that meeting came a promise of the Pentagon to create and distribute guidelines for how soldiers could share their faith.[75] But it also led to the immediate stark and dire warning to those already in military service: don't share too much or push too hard, because court-martial is a possible repercussion as are other forms of nonjudicial punishments.[76]

In October 2013, the military's Christian believers took another direct hit to their faith when several dozen Army soldiers attending a briefing at Camp Shelby in Mississippi were warned off any affiliation with the pro-family, traditional-values ministry American Family Association.[77] The soldiers were reportedly told that the AFA ought to be classified as a hate group, alongside the likes of the Ku Klux Klan, the Black Panthers, neo-Nazis, and the Nation of Islam.[78] Apparently, one chaplain in attendance raised an objection to the AFA's classification, asking for explanation.[79] The instructor, however, maintained that the group was akin to the Westboro Baptist Church—the hateful organization with members who stage loud protests at military funerals—because both referred to gays as sinners.[80]

Then again, so does the Bible. Does that mean the Word of God is tantamount to hate speech?

But the concluding message at the meeting: those who participate in hate groups face punishment and disciplinary proceedings.

The AFA's classification generated widespread outrage, and an Army spokesman came forward a couple of days later to issue a retraction. He said the military briefing had been conducted by a soldier who pulled information from the Internet and who had wrongfully included the AFA in his list of hate groups.[81] That's a significant error that comes at a time when expressions of Christianity in the military are under widespread attack. The Congressional Prayer Caucus, a bipartisan group of about one hundred members of Congress who cast aside politics to gather and pray for our nation, report that hostility against the military is on the upswing and that lawmakers need to step up efforts to guarantee those in the service will be protected from prosecution just for exercising their faith—like opposition to same-sex marriage or homosexual lifestyles.[82]

And other groups and individuals are fighting back too.

In July 2013, the Alliance Defending Freedom—formerly known as the Alliance Defense Fund, dedicated to providing legal assistance in religious freedom and traditional family values cases—filed a court motion on behalf of ten different Indiana churches that were being sued by the ACLU.[83] Their alleged civil crime?

The churches were displaying Christian crosses on publicly owned properties.[84]

The case started in June 2013 when Evansville city officials gave the go-ahead to a consortium of churches to put several six-foot-tall, artistically designed crosses on display on riverfront property as part of a two-week fund-raising drive.[85] Just a few days after the city granted the churches their permits, the Indiana chapter of the ACLU launched a lawsuit—based on the complaints of two residents—accusing the governing board of endorsing one religion over another.[86]

The ADF jumped into the mix, however, filing against the ACLU on behalf of the ten churches in the US District Court for the Southern District of Indiana.[87] The ADF's view: just as the ACLU argues that government cannot hold one religion's view higher than another, the ACLU cannot prevent the government from recognizing the right of a religious view over that of a nonreligious viewpoint.[88]

The government can't cater to atheists at the expense of those who believe in God.

That would seem a commonsense argument rooted in First Amendment rights. But in today's litigious atmosphere, where Christianity is under constant attack and uttering even the word "God" has brought about radical outcry, common sense is in short supply.

For instance: common sense might dictate that a teacher at a Christian school would have to hold Christian beliefs—that it would be a requirement of the job. But in the months leading into 2013, in one California town, that assumption drew heavy fire. The issue unfolded in 2009 when Little Oaks Elementary school was purchased by Godspeak Church and teachers affiliated with the former were required to fill out a questionnaire that asked about their religious faith as a condition of hire.[89] Two teachers refused, and the church-affiliated school refused to rehire them.[90]

The teachers threatened to sue—but the school quickly countersued, saying religious freedom trumps state equal employment laws.[91] Attorneys for the school contended in paperwork filed in federal court that school officials certainly have the right to ensure teachers are of similar faith—or, at least, of a faith that's not at odds with the church teachings and mission.[92]

It seems that for every step forward in this fight for religious freedom comes another step back. In November 2013, a Pennsylvania lawmaker sponsored a bill to require every public school district in the state to post prominently in each and every building the motto "In God We Trust." The bill actually made it out of committee with a 14-9 vote.[93] But then opposition kicked in hard.

The president of the Delaware Valley chapter of Americans United for Separation of Church and State argued in a published opinion piece that the motto is clearly a religious message—not to mention divisive one—that wasn't even part of Founding Father language; it was, rather, adopted by Congress in 1956.[94]

Meanwhile, the ACLU state chapter roared onto the scene and vowed to sue if the motto mandate passed into law.[95]

But step back from all the legal brouhaha for a moment. What's the worst that could happen if the motto were allowed to be displayed at every public school in Pennsylvania—that students might be reminded that our nation is founded on a higher power and rooted in a spiritual presence?

It's not as if that realization would bring war, devastation, doom and gloom, and killing. It's not as if that motto—or the fact that America was founded by believers—is exactly a closely guarded secret in the nation, either. The motto is on our money; the evidence of America's belief in and reverence for a higher power dots our national landscape.

On October 3, 1789, right after completing a draft of the First Amendment, members of Congress passed a resolution that President George Washington might proclaim November 26, 1789, a day of "public thanksgiving and prayer" to acknowledge the blessings of God.[96] So he did. An excerpt:

> Whereas it is the duty of all nations to acknowledge the providence of Almighty God, to obey His will, to be grateful for His benefits, and humbly to implore His protection and favor; and—whereas both Houses of Congress have, by their joint committee, requested me "to recommend to the people of the United States a day of public thanksgiving and prayer, to be observed by acknowledging with grateful hearts the many and signal favors of Almighty God . . ." Now, therefore, I do recommend and assign Thursday, the 26th day of November next, to be devoted by the people of these States to the service of that great and glorious Being who is the beneficent author of all the good that was, that is, or that will be; that we many then all unite in rendering unto Him our sincere and humble thanks for His kind care and protection of the people . . . And also that we may then unite in most humbly offering our prayers and supplications to the great Lord and Ruler of Nations, and beseech Him to pardon our national and other transgressions.[97]

God—the source of all "good that was, that is, or that will be."

Notably, Washington didn't act alone on this proclamation—he only issued it at the request of members of Congress who recognized that the coming together of this great nation was not due to human hands, but rather heavenly guidance. Now fast-forward to November 2013 and this is the headline that blasts forward, a direct slap to Washington's humble recognition of higher power: "Atheist 'mega-churches' take root across US, world."[98]

The story stays true to its headline. In Los Angeles, as in other communities around the nation, Sunday mornings dawn with the opening of assembly doors that let in hundreds of people with a common denominator: they want to rub shoulders with inspirational messengers and listen to some good music and call that church. But noticeably missing from their worship is any mention of God.[99]

We're at a crossroads in America. Will we choose the path that Washington chose or the road that worships self?

That's the final frontier in the fight to maintain America's freedoms as envisioned by founders and encapsulated in our Constitution and guiding government documents. If God is pushed out and America loses the notion of "God-given," then government assumes full control and the police-state style of governance stays. That's just the natural order.

18

THROW THE BUMS OUT: WHY VIRTUE, ACCOUNTABILITY ARE KEY

Resistance to tyranny becomes the Christian and social duty of each individual. . . . Continue steadfast and, with a proper sense of your dependence on God, nobly defend those rights which heaven gave, and no man ought to take from us.

—John Hancock, first signer of the Declaration of Independence

Having a godly government doesn't mean scandals won't happen. What it does mean, however, is that when scandals strike, the guilty parties will be held accountable. And accountability is key in keeping the reminder in place for politicians: "You work for us." Once politicians and leaders forget that, the system of governance gets turned on its head and the balance of power shifts from the people to the politicos. That's part of the reason our nation is in such a mess today.

Remember Hillary Clinton's Capitol Hill meltdown during the Senate hearings on Benghazi?

On September 11, 2012, four Americans—including US ambassador to Libya Christopher Stevens—were killed in a horrific terrorist attack on America's diplomatic mission in Benghazi. The Obama administration vowed to root out the responsible party—but that was after a long and drawn-out denial that the attack was coordinated, well planned, and committed by terrorists who purposely timed the murderous rampage to mark the September 11, 2001, terrorism strike on domestic soil.[1] The White House mantra kept shifting on Benghazi.

First it was a random attack. Then it was a staged attack brought on by Muslim militants who were unhappy about an American-made online video that was perceived as negative to those of the Islamic faith. Then it was an act of terror. The White House said one thing, CIA and intelligence operatives another.[2] What did the Obama administration really believe? And why didn't the State Department provide the layers of additional security at the facility that had been requested in the lead-up to the attack?[3]

Then secretary of state Clinton was called to testify, and after weeks of delays—due in part to a stomach flu that then reportedly caused her to trip and fall, leading to her claim of concussion—she took the Senate hot seat.[4] When asked if the White House purposely misled the American people by blaming the attack on the video, saying it incited Muslim violence, Clinton lost her cool. She referred to the four dead Americans, the various narratives that had come from the White House, then blared forth the blunt question that resonated in media around the nation: "What difference at this point does it make?"[5]

To the American people, however, the difference is truth—versus not truth. And a government that can't provide truth doesn't deserve to hold the reins.

But the White House under Obama has experienced a particularly tough time delivering on that standard.

In mid-January 2014, a bipartisan Senate report shook the walls of the White House with a grim assessment of the Benghazi attack that left four brave Americans dead: It could have been prevented.[6]

And from the actual Senate Select Committee on Intelligence Report – three pretty blunt findings:

FINDING #1: In the months before the attacks on September 11, 2012, the IC [Intelligence Community] provided ample strategic warning that the security situation in eastern Libya was deteriorating and that U.S. facilities and personnel were at risk in Benghazi.[7]

FINDING #2: The State Department should have increased its security posture more significantly in Benghazi based on the deteriorating security situation on the ground and IC threat reporting on the prior attacks against Westerners in Benghazi – including two incidents at the Temporary Mission Facility on April 6 and June 12, 2012.[8]

FINDING #3: There was no singular "tactical warning" in the intelligence reporting leading up to the events on September 11, 2012, predicting an attack on U.S. facilities in Benghazi on the 9/11 anniversary, although State and the CIA both sent general warning notices to facilities worldwide noting the potential security concerns associated with the anniversary. Such a specific warning should not have been expected, however, given the limited intelligence collection of the Benghazi area at the time.[9]

But toward that last point, the Senate report adds this:

Although it did not reach the U.S. Intelligence Community until after the attacks, it is important to note that a former Transitional National Council (TNC) security official in Benghazi had received information of a possible attack against the Mission facility in advance. The official said that approximately four hours before the attack, he attempted to notify the Libyan Intelligence Service (LIS) that an attack was expected, but he was unable to reach two contacts he had in the LIS as they were out of the country.[10]

So why didn't the White House order a bolstering of security in Benghazi, in the face of so much warning and threat?

Yes, Mrs. Clinton. Yes, President Obama. Truth does in fact make a huge difference to Americans.

In mid-November 2013, as the Obamacare enrollment process continued its nosedive and the White House scrambled to contain the public relations nightmare, a Fox News poll showed fully half of voters thought the president "knowingly lied" when he promised Americans they could keep their existing health care plans if they wanted.[11] Fifty-eight percent also thought his apology to Americans who were booted off their health care plans—about 5 million by mid-November—was insincere, offered primarily for political reasons.[12]

Obama's approval ratings tanked, a direct result of the Obamacare fiasco and the president's fairy tale–like messaging that went something like this: *Perhaps if I keep telling the American people they can keep their insurance plans, they won't notice the millions of letters from their insurance companies cancelling their plans.*[13]

In mid-November 2013, a Quinnipiac University poll put his job approval among registered voters at 39 percent, his lowest rating ever.[14] Meanwhile, only 39 percent of respondents in that poll supported his signature health care law—down from 45 percent a month earlier.[15] But here's the kicker: 52 percent of the voters who participated in this Quinnipiac poll said the president was not "honest and trustworthy," the first time a majority of Obama's constituents said they felt that way toward him.[16]

Popular fact-checking sites, too, were busting out the Obama administration's Obamacare deceptions, calling out the White House for trying to blame insurance companies for the cancelled policies and for trying to sell the notion that the president never actually guaranteed all Americans could keep their health care plans.

In the first week of November 2013, the *Washington Post*'s Fact-Checker site issued to Obama and his press secretary, Jay Carney, a "Pinocchios" rating of 3 (out of 4)—the second-highest category for blatant lies—for telling Americans that insurance companies, not Obamacare regulations, were at fault for cancelling policies.[17]

Just one day earlier, the Pulitzer Prize–winning PolitiFact site gave Obama its highest ranking for dishonesty, the "Pants on Fire" label, for his attempt to revise history on his vow that Americans could keep their health care plans.[18] Obama tried to slide into November 4, 2013, remarks to the group Organizing for Action that he'd said only those Americans who had insurance plans that didn't change after the passage of Obamacare would be able to keep them.[19] As the fact-checkers at PolitiFact reported, however, Obama never included a caveat when he spoke of Americans' ability to keep their health care plans.[20]

He just simply promised they could—dozens of times. And seven of those vows came after the rollout revealed that some Americans would in fact be losing their plans due to Obamacare regulations.[21]

Skewing truths in the face of adversity has been the Obama administration's preferred modus operandi for years, though. And just as a sign of how deep the pit containing the White House under Obama's leadership spread: even liberals standing strong on the president's side started clamoring for accountability as 2013 drew to a close.

In October 2013, MSNBC's Chris Matthews—aka "Tingles," for his public pronouncement of Obama's ability to make Matthews's leg shiver with Obama's rhetoric—flew into a broadcast rant on his *Hardball* show and said he wouldn't rest until he received answers on Benghazi. Namely, he wanted to know what the State Department did during the time of the attack and why the United States didn't authorize an immediate rescue operation to save the Americans who were ultimately killed.[22] Of course, after the Senate report on Benghazi was released, Matthews' big reaction was not to condemn Clinton, but rather to kick at conservatives for criticizing Susan Rice, who used her national security advisor title the days after the attack to tamp down talk of terrorism.[23]

But the fact that months earlier he publicly ranted against the Democratic administration at all was significant on a couple of different fronts: It was a sign of Obama's dwindling favor among mainstream and liberal media personalities. And it was a subtle reminder that the president, once again, wasn't keeping his promise.

In October 2012, Obama had claimed responsibility for the Benghazi investigation.[24] He also said then that his top priority at that time was bringing to justice the guilty parties—he called them "folks"—and that the American people could count on that commitment.[25] But as the months dragged by and 2012 turned to 2013, it was still as Matthews said: what the heck happened in Benghazi? The Senate report may have shed some light – but not much retributive justice. As 2014 progressed, talk of a Clinton run for the White House still blared loudly in the press.

It's more than a shame that in the wings, still waiting for answers after months and months of promised investigation, were families and loved ones of the victims. It's also a travesty of truth that it took months to learn that, in addition to the four killed Americans, several other US citizens were injured.

It wasn't until March 2013, in response to insistent press inquiries, that the State Department confirmed that three diplomatic security agents and a federal contractor were hurt in the terrorist attack.[26] Still, the State Department wouldn't immediately confirm the exact injured count, and at least one lawmaker, Rep. Jason Chaffetz, who said he wanted to talk to the survivors, faulted the White House for putting up roadblocks, explaining the administration wouldn't even release the victims' names.[27]

Chaffetz, a few months later, also decried the State Department's denial of a House Oversight and Government Reform Committee request to interview injured diplomatic security agent David Ubben to learn why he had to sit on the rooftop of the CIA annex in Benghazi with massive leg injuries for about twenty hours—the length of time it took before administration officials sent in medical assistance.[28]

Is that how Obama upholds his pledge to the American people to uncover the details of the attack and hold the guilty parties responsible?

It wasn't until mid-November 2013 that details even started emerging about the seriousness of the injuries of the contractor and diplomatic security agents. Apparently, two were hit so badly by mortar fire—and their blood loss was so significant—that they nearly lost their lives too. As it was, the survivors had to undergo drastic and numerous surgeries to save limbs.[29]

But that information wasn't on a White House press release. It only leaked because survivors and witnesses who worked as contractors at the Benghazi facility were finally due to appear before the House Intelligence Committee and give closed-door testimony about the fateful evening.[30]

Most Americans can understand that certain intelligence information—including, perhaps, some of what Benghazi survivors and witnesses might say or even the identities of those who were injured—needs to be kept quiet for security purposes. But the Obama administration certainly doesn't inspire confidence that an investigation and attempt to hold guilty "folks" responsible are ongoing, concerted endeavors.

Still, that's the administration's fault. The hall of shame in the Obama White House is both long and wide.

Beginning in 2010, the Obama's Internal Revenue Service started separating out any applications for nonprofit status that contained the words "Tea Party," "Patriot," and the like for extra review.[31] That meant a delay in processing their requests for tax exemption. It was later learned that the head of the IRS unit in charge of deciding tax exempt applications, Lois Lerner, had been apprised of the practice in June 2011, but let it continue—a decision that stymied some groups' plans to enter the 2012 presidential election fray.[32]

For instance, TheTeaParty.net applied in March 2010 for tax-exempt status—and was approved on October 2, 2013.[33] As acting deputy inspector general for audit Michael McKenney wrote in his May 2013 report for the Treasury Department's inspector general for tax administration, or TIGTA:

The IRS used inappropriate criteria that identified for review Tea Party and other organizations applying for tax exempt status based upon their names or policy positions instead of indications of potential political campaign intervention. Ineffective management: 1) allowed inappropriate criteria to be developed and stay in place for more than 18 months, 2) resulted in substantial delays in processing certain applications, and 3) allowed unnecessary information requests to be issued.[34]

Lerner finally retired from her post in September 2013—with pension intact.[35] But the scandal didn't go with her.

Lawmakers on Capitol Hill vowed to press for more answers and more accountability in the scandal, which came at a time when the IRS was assuming even more power—acting as the Obamacare watchdog in charge of fining those who don't comply with the health care mandate.[36] And the nonprofit government watchdog group Judicial Watch, meanwhile, reported that IRS commissioner Douglas Shulman and his political assistant, Jonathan Davis, had made hundreds of trips to the White House at the very time the agency was busy targeting and delaying Tea Party–type tax exemption applications—a curious coincidence that raises the question, what exactly did the president or his confidants know about the actions of the IRS?[37]

Attorney General Eric Holder ordered a special investigation into the IRS in May 2013 to check for criminal violations.[38] But it didn't take long for the public to lose faith in his ability to conduct a fair investigation. Before the end of that month, a Quinnipiac University poll found that 76 percent of registered voters participating in the survey wanted a special prosecutor to look into possible IRS misconduct, in place of Holder. And that wasn't a particularly partisan response. While 88 percent of respondents who claimed to be Republicans wanted a special prosecutor to head up the IRS investigation, 63 percent of Democrats and 78 percent of Independents did too.[39]

Could that be because Holder's Department of Justice was caught, right around that time frame, seizing telephone records from reporters and editors with the Associated Press, à la the KGB?

Holder obtained about two months' worth of outgoing telephone calls placed by reporters working for the wire service in New York; Washington, DC; and Hartford, Connecticut, as well as those made from the AP's press gallery in the House of Representatives. The data seizure hit about twenty different telephone lines and spanned two months, March through April 2013.[40]

Federal authorities wouldn't say what they were looking for, but the AP speculated that it perhaps had something to do with February 2013 testimony from CIA director John Brennan, when he remarked that FBI agents had asked him if he had provided sensitive information for a story written by an AP reporter about US intelligence operations in Yemen a year earlier.[41] In September 2013, a former FBI agent, Donald Sachtleben, admitted he was the source of the information leak in the AP story—an admission made after federal authorities scrutinized the media outlet's phone records.[42]

Is that a happy ending for the Associated Press, though—or for the First Amendment?

The Department of Justice also secretly seized the telephone records of Fox News correspondent James Rosen as part of the agency's leak investigation on a report about North Korea.[43] Suspiciously, during this same time frame, CBS News' Sharyl Attkisson—an investigative journalist who had reported on many issues that put the Obama administration in a negative light—expressed outrage at the discovery that her computer had been compromised. A cybersecurity company hired by CBS confirmed that a third party had obtained access from a remote location to her computer files on numerous occasions in late 2012.[44]

Republicans in May and June of 2013 were toying with the idea of bringing Holder up on perjury charges for saying he had nothing to do with the tapping of media telephone records—even though he had personally approved the seizure of Fox News' telephone records—and rooting out the source for Rosen's 2009 North Korea reports.[45]

When that effort faded, a new one took its place. In November 2013, House Republicans pushed for Holder's impeachment—but this time over a different issue, the federal gun-running scandal known as Operation Fast and Furious.[46]

Fast and Furious was the federal operation run by the Bureau of Alcohol, Tobacco, Firearms and Explosives (ATF) that let illegal weapons filter from the United States into the hands of gun smugglers in Mexico in hopes they would lead to the location and apprehension of drug kingpins and cartel operators. ATF lost track of hundreds— by some estimates, fourteen hundred—of the operation's weapons, however.[47] And it was then learned that many of these guns were used in the commission of untold numbers of crimes—including the December 2010 murder of Border Patrol agent Brian Terry.[48]

Once again, Obama promised on national television to root out and hold responsible the guilty parties.[49] That was in October 2011, shortly after memos came to media light that revealed Holder himself had been briefed of the Fast and Furious program in July 2010—an interesting finding given the attorney general's May 3, 2011, testimony to Judiciary Committee members that he'd only learned of the program within the previous few weeks.[50]

In late 2012, family members of the killed Brian Terry launched a lawsuit against seven different federal officials and a gun shop owner, accusing them of negligence and wrongful death.[51] But Holder?

House members in June 2012 voted to hold him in contempt for refusing to provide enough Fast and Furious documents for officials to conduct a thorough investigation.[52] But the Department of Justice declined to go forth with a prosecution.[53] He kept his job. And as far as Obama's promise of bringing to justice any guilty parties—well, that seemed to go the way of the Benghazi vow.

It's not as if Obama and his cronies are the only politicians to skew truth, outright lie, or come under fire for various scandals.

The Democratic Party's John Edwards seemed to have the liberal political world in his hands in the mid-2000s. Touted in mainstream press as an honest candidate, a fearless defender of the military, and a rising political superstar, his eventual ascension to the White House seemed to some to be set in stone.[54]

Then the Rielle Hunter affair emerged—and it became public knowledge that Edwards wasn't really the loving husband to his cancer-stricken wife, Elizabeth, that he purported. His political career ultimately crashed; Hunter bore their baby in 2008, about two years before Elizabeth died. In 2011, Edwards was indicted by a federal grand jury over charges that he'd used campaign cash to try to keep his affair with Hunter quiet during his campaign.[55]

Equally as dramatic on the other side of the political aisle was Republican South Carolina governor Mark Sanford's mysterious 2009 traipse through what he initially claimed was the Appalachian Trail, but later admitted was a trip to Argentina to be with his "soul mate"—a characterization and admission that soon after led to his divorce.[56] Upon his return, Sanford gave a bizarre press conference to explain his six-day disappearance and his plans to step down as chairman of the Republican Governors Association and to apologize profusely to a long list of those he hurt—including his wife and their four children.[57] He also faced thirty-seven different ethics charges and in March 2010 agreed to pay a $74,000 fine for allegations that he used campaign cash for personal travel.[58]

Still, Sanford was able to follow his political disgrace with a rather speedy comeback, winning a special election in May 2013 for a House seat in Congress.[59] Edwards, meanwhile, escaped any punishment for his six fraud charges. A jury found him not guilty on one of the charges, and he skated on the other five—after jurors couldn't reach a decision and the judge declared a mistrial.[60] They both fielded some career dings and financial hits, saw the crumbling of their family foundations, and dealt with some public humiliations. But one can't help wonder: would Joe Q. Public have been let off so easily?

Unfortunately, the political world is filled with examples of similarly subpar displays of morals and values. But a dishonest president, leading a dishonest administration—including an attorney general whose primary job description is to uphold the rule of law—just takes the cake when it comes to influencing the direction of the nation.

What accountability has been brought on the Obama administration for all its deceptions, broken promises, and outright lies?

A government allowed to avoid accountability is a government that puts itself above the law. That the Obama administration has managed to skirt and escape liability for broken vows and unethical actions for so long only serves as a sad commentary on the state of our nation as well as an indication of how high a mountain we have to climb to return to our founding greatness. One framer of the First Amendment, Fisher Ames, said it succinctly: "Our liberty depends on our education, our laws and our habits . . . It is founded on morals and religion, whose authority reigns in the heart, and on the influence all these produce on public opinion before that opinion governs rulers."[61]

That's it, in a nutshell. A government without God is doomed to fall because a government without God leads to a slow erosion of all that is good, all that is virtuous. Another way to look at it: a government is only as moral and right as its people.

If we can't compel our leaders to act responsibly and honestly and to serve with honor and regard for law, then that's simply because we as a nation have lost our majority will on these points. Has the balance of power truly shifted where those with inferior character traits and tainted aspirations have overcome those with higher-minded ideals and pursuits?

Hopefully, no. But looking at the political world, it does seem we've lost our moral compass. We're turning into a nation ruled by fear—fear of political incorrectness, fear of attack, fear of being sued, fear of standing tall on the very principles that made us great. And out of that fear is rapidly emerging an intrusive government, a burdensome regulatory climate, a state of continuous federal overreach, and a police state atmosphere.

If we don't soon take back control—if we don't right this rudder and steer our ship back to a godly course—the vision of America, the shining city on the hill, will go dark. The notion of "God-given" will be gone, and in its place will stand a centralized government firmly in power to dole out only those rights it sees fit—a government no longer of the people, but rather by the elite.

And then where will our children go?

NOTES

INTRODUCTION: AMERICA ISN'T IMMUNE TO TYRANNY

1. "Former Top NSA Official: 'We Are Now in a Police State,'" *Washington's Blog*, December 18, 2013, http://www.washingtonsblog.com/2013/12/former-top-nsa-official-now-police-state. html.
2. Chester James Antieau, "Natural Rights and the Founding Fathers—The Virginians," *Washington and Lee Law Review* 17, no. 1: March 1, 1960.
3. The U.S. Environmental Protection Agency, "Landscape Characterization and Change Detection Methods Development Research," EPA Science Inventory, contact Katherine Coutros, http://cfpub.epa.gov/si/si_public_record_report.cfm?dirEntryId=11068, accessed November 9, 2013.
4. Reuters, "U.S. to Let Spy Agencies Scour American's Finances," *Chicago Tribune Business*, March 13, 2013, http://articles.chicagotribune.com/2013-03-13/business/chi-us-to-let-spy-agencies-scour-americans-finances-20130313_1_intelligence-agencies-spy-agencies-financial-data.
5. Larry O'Dell, "Brandon J. Raub, Former Marine, Detained after Anti-Government Facebook Postings," *Huff Post*, Politics, August 20, 2012, http://www.huffingtonpost.com/2012/08/21/brandon-j-raub-marine-detained_n_1817484.html.
6. Elise Hu, "Texas Teen Jailed for Sarcastic Facebook Comment," *All Tech Considered* (NPR blog), July 1, 2013, http://www.npr.org/blogs/alltechconsidered/2013/07/01/197669495/texas-teen-jailed-for-sarcastic-facebook-comment.
7. Associated Press, "Virginia Alcoholic Beverage Control Says 2 Agents Violated Policy During Student's Wrongful Arrest," *Washington Post*, November 7, 2013.
8. Peter Corbett, "Scottsdale Silent on Facility for Police," azcentral.com, July 8, 2012, http://www.azcentral.com/news/articles/2012/07/05/20120705scottsdale-police-facility-city-silent.html.
9. Michael R. Bloomberg and Thomas M. Menino, "About the Coalition: Message from the Co-Chairs," Mayors Against Illegal Guns, http://www.mayorsagainstillegalguns.org/html/about/about.shtml, accessed November 9, 2013.
10. Kirsten Andersen, "Public School District Agrees to Pay $95K Settlement after ACLU Sues over Jesus Picture," LifeSiteNews.com, October 9, 2013, http://www.lifesitenews.com/news/public-school-district-agrees-to-pay-95000-settlement-after-aclu-sues-over.

NOTES

11. Jay Dillon, "Ohio School District Agrees to Keep Portrait of Jesus Off Wall, Pay $95K Fine," Fox News, October 7, 2013, http://www.okcfox.com/story/23629831/ohio-school-district-agrees-to-keep-portrait-of-jesus-off-wall-pay-95g-fine.
12. Andersen, "Public School District Agrees to Pay $95K Settlement."

1: THE FOUNDING FATHERS' INTENT VERSUS TWENTY-FIRST-CENTURY REALITIES

1. United States District Court, District of Nevada, *Anthony Mitchell et al vs. City of Henderson, Nevada, et al*, Case 2:13-cv-01154-APG-CWH, http://online.wsj.com/public/resources/documents/henderson.pdf, accessed November 9, 2013.
2. Cheryl K. Chumley, "Third Amendment Scandal: Nevada Cops Sued for Storming Home They Wanted for Lookout," *Washington Times*, July 8, 2013, http://www.washingtontimes.com/news/2013/jul/8/nevada-cops-sued-storming-home-they-wanted-lookout/.
3. "Anthony Mitchell Lawsuit: Cops Violated Third Amendment, Occupied Home, Complaint States," *Huffington Post*, July 7, 2013, http://www.huffingtonpost.com/2013/07/07/anthony-mitchell-lawsuit-third-amendment-_n_3557431.html.
4. Megan Gallegos, "Police Commandeer Homes, Get Sued," Courthouse News Service, July 3, 2013, http://www.courthousenews.com/2013/07/03/59061.htm.
5. Mike Maharrey, "A Misguided Third Amendment Case in Nevada," Tenth Amendment Center, July 7, 2013, http://tenthamendmentcenter.com/2013/07/07/a-misguided-third-amendment-case-in-nevada/.
6. Associated Press, "Only One Gun Recovered from Tsarnaev Brothers Shootout in Watertown," CBS Boston, April 24, 2013, http://boston.cbslocal.com/2013/04/24/only-one-gun-recovered-from-tsarnaev-brothers-shootout-in-watertown/.
7. Globe Staff, "102 Hours in Pursuit of Marathon Suspects," *Boston Globe*, April 28, 2013, http://www.bostonglobe.com/metro/2013/04/28/bombreconstruct/VbSZhzHm35yR88EVmVdbDM/story.html.
8. Phillip Martin, James Edwards, and Hilary Sargent, "How Did Dzhokhar Tsarnaev Elude Police for So Long in Watertown?" WGBH, October 17, 2013, http://wgbhnews.org/post/how-did-dzhokhar-tsarnaev-elude-police-so-long-watertown.
9. Globe Staff, "102 Hours in Pursuit of Marathon Suspects."
10. Martin, Edwards, and Sargent, "How Did Dzhokhar Tsarnaev Elude Police for So Long in Watertown?"
11. Phillip Martin, "18 Hours: How Did Dzhokhar Tsarnaev Elude Police During Marathon Bombing Manhunt?" *Huffington Post*, October 29, 2013.
12. "Innocent Watertown Family Ripped from Their Home at Gunpoint; Police Storm the Property," YouTube video, posted by "12160info," April 21, 2013, http://www.youtube.com/watch?v=Op3TMliqBmA.
13. Stephen Kurkjian, "A Harrowing Incident During the Watertown Lockdown," *Boston Globe*, Opinion, June 29, 2013, http://www.bostonglobe.com/opinion/2013/06/28/podium-lockdown/kc02HXhjdWJNoiRxRn6IYO/story.html.
14. Ibid.
15. Kurkjian, "A Harrowing Incident During the Watertown Lockdown."
16. Hollie O'Connor, "School Districts Preparing for Demise of CSCOPE Lesson Plans," *Waco Tribune-Herald*, June 17, 2013, http://m.wacotrib.com/news/education/school-districts-preparing-for-demise-of-cscope-lesson-plans/article_292fee2e-d652-5a22-a4f9-60ae2586d8d0.html?mode=jqm.
17. "The 4th Amendment," Revolutionary War and Beyond, http://www.revolutionary-war-and-beyond.com/4th-amendment.html, accessed December 6, 2013.
18. "Writs of Assistance," How Stuff Works, http://history.howstuffworks.com/revolutionary-war/writs-of-assistance.htm, accessed Nov. 9, 2013.
19. Indiana Supreme Court, Appeal from the Vanderburgh Superior Court, No. 82S05-1007-CR-343, *Richard L. Barnes v. State of Indiana*, http://lawyersusaonline.com/wp-files/pdfs-3/barnes-v-indiana.pdf, accessed July 27, 2013.

20. Arnold Ahlert, "The Indiana Supreme Court Guts the Fourth Amendment," FrontPageMag. com, May 18, 2011, http://www.frontpagemag.com/2011/arnold-ahlert/the-indiana-supreme-court-guts-the-fourth-amendment/.

21. Pat Murphy, "Can homeowner resist unlawful entry by police?" *Benchmarks* (Lawyers USA blog), http://lawyersusaonline.com/benchmarks/2011/05/20/can-homeowner-resist-unlawful-entry-by-police/, accessed December 6, 2013.

22. Ahlert, "The Indiana Supreme Court Guts the Fourth Amendment."

23. Stephen C. Webster, "Indiana Court Strips Citizens of Right to Resist Unlawful Police Entry," *Raw Story*, May 16, 2011, http://www.rawstory.com/rs/2011/05/16/indiana-court-strips-citizens-of-right-to-resist-unlawful-police-entry/.

24. Indiana Supreme Court, Appeal from the Vanderburgh Superior Court, No. 82S05-1007-CR-343.

2: BIG GREEN TAKES THE WHEEL

1. Peter Brookes, "Is the Climate the Biggest Threat?" Heritage Foundation website, March 21, 2013, http://www.heritage.org/research/commentary/2013/3/is-the-climate-the-biggest-threat.

2. Ben Adler, "Liberals Shouldn't Fear Chuck Hagel's Environmental Record," *New Republic*, December 24, 2012, http://www.newrepublic.com/blog/111397/liberals-shouldnt-fear-chuck-hagels-environmental-record.

3. Matthew Cooper, "Chuck Hagel's Real Problem May Be Climate Change," *National Journal*, January 31, 2013, http://www.nationaljournal.com/domesticpolicy/chuck-hagel-s-real-problem-may-be-climate-change-20121220.

4. Matthew Daly, "John Kerry: Climate Change Is a 'Life-Threatening Issue' (VIDEO)," *Huffington Post*, January 24, 2013, http://www.huffingtonpost.com/2013/01/24/john-kerry-climate-change_n_2545406.html.

5. Chris Mooney and Julia Whitty, "The Navy Goes Green: Mother Jones and the Climate Desk Highlight a Major Energy Transformation in Our Military," *ThinkProgress* (blog), February 26, 2013, http://thinkprogress.org/climate/2013/02/26/1639981/the-navy-goes-green-mother-jones-and-the-climate-desk-highlight-a-major-energy-transformation-in-our-military/.

6. Cheryl Pellerin, "Pentagon Looks to Smart Grids for Battlefield Energy," U.S. Department of Defense, American Forces Press Service, October 20, 2011, http://www.defense.gov/news/newsarticle.aspx?id=65740.

7. Brian Frank, "10 Technologies Helping the Military Go Green," KCET, January 27, 2012, http://www.kcet.org/shows/socal_connected/content/environment/10-technologies-helping-the-military-go-green.html.

8. Mooney and Whitty, "The Navy Goes Green."

9. Mike McKinley, "The Cruise of the Great White Fleet," Navy Department Library, http://www.history.navy.mil/library/online/gwf_cruise.htm, accessed November 9, 2013.

10. Zack Colman, "Climate Change Causing Pentagon Planning Shift, says DOD Strategist," *The Hill*, June 7, 2013, http://thehill.com/blogs/e2-wire/304151-climate-change-causing-pentagon-planning-shift-says-dod-strategist.

11. Solomon M. Hsiang, Marshall Burke, and Edward Miguel, "Quantifying the Influence of Climate on Human Conflict," *Science* 341 no. 6151: August 1, 2013, https://www.sciencemag.org/content/341/6151/1235367.abstract.

12. Rebecca Morelle, "Rise in Violence 'Linked to Climate Change,'" BBC News, Science & Environment, August 2, 2013, http://www.bbc.co.uk/news/science-environment-23538771.

13. Ibid.

14. Elizabeth Landau, "Climate Change May Increase Violence, Study Shows," *CNN U.S.*, August 2, 2013, http://www.cnn.com/2013/08/01/us/climate-change-violence/.

15. United States Environmental Protection Agency, "Environmental Justice," www.epa.gov/environmentaljustice, upd. November 19, 2013.

16. Nicolas Loris, "Court Upholds Greenhouse Gas Rule; Congress Needs to Step Up," *The Foundry* (Heritage Foundation blog), June 26, 2012, http://blog.heritage.org/2012/06/26/court-upholds-greenhouse-gas-rule-congress-needs-to-step-up/.
17. Ibid.
18. U.S. Environmental Protection Agency, "U.S. Court of Appeals – D.C. Circuit Uphold EPA's Actions to Reduce Greenhouse Gases Under the Clean Air Act," http://www.epa.gov/climatechange/endangerment/ghgcourtdecision.html, accessed November 30, 2013.
19. U.S. Environmental Protection Agency, "Endangerment and Cause or Contribute Findings for Greenhouse Gases under Section 202(a) of the Clean Air Act," http://www.epa.gov/climatechange/endangerment/, accessed November 30, 2013.
20. IPCC: Intergovernmental Panel on Climate Change, http://www.ipcc.ch/, accessed November 30, 2013.
21. "About the NIPCC," NIPCCReport.org, http://www.nipccreport.org/about/about.html, accessed November 30, 2013.
22. Ibid.
23. Loris, "Court Upholds Greenhouse Gas Rule."
24. Nicolas Loris, "The Assault on Coal and American Consumers," Heritage Foundation, July 23, 2012, http://www.heritage.org/research/reports/2012/07/the-assault-on-coal-and-american-consumers.
25. Associated Press, with Jon Fahey, contrib., "Coal-Fired Power Plants Closing: First Energy Shutting Down Six Sites in Ohio, Pennsylvania, Maryland," *Huff Post Green*, January 26, 2012, http://www.huffingtonpost.com/2012/01/26/coal-power-plants-closing-firstenergy_n_1234611.html.
26. Loris, "The Assault on Coal and American Consumers."
27. Steve Goreham, "A Science-Based Rebuttal to Global Warming Alarmism," *Washington Times*, Communities, September 20, 2013, http://communities.washingtontimes.com/neighborhood/climatism-watching-climate-science/2013/sep/10/science-based-rebuttal-global-warming-alarmism/.
28. Environmental Protection Agency, "Environmental Justice: Basic Information: Background," http://www.epa.gov/environmentaljustice/basics/ejbackground.html, upd. May 24, 2012.
29. Ibid.
30. Environmental Protection Agency, "Plan EJ 2014, executive summary," http://www.epa.gov/environmentaljustice/resources/policy/plan-ej-2014/plan-ej-exec-sum.pdf, September 2011.
31. Ron Selak Jr., "Septic System Strife: Treatment Problem May Close Church," *Tribune Chronicle* (Warren, OH), July 15, 2012, http://www.tribtoday.com/page/content.detail/id/574145/Septic-system-strife.html.
32. Ed Runyan, "Outrageous: EPA Rule May Force Church to Close," July 12, 2012, http://epaabuse.com/8035/news/epa-rule-may-force-church-to-close/.
33. Ryan Holeywell, "Judge: EPA Can't Treat Stormwater as Pollutant," *FedWatch* (a *Governing* magazine blog), http://www.governing.com/blogs/fedwatch/Judge-EPA-Cant-Treat-Stormwater-as-Pollutant.html, January 8, 2013.
34. Fox News, "Federal Judge Rules EPA Overstepped Authority Trying to Regulate Water as Pollutant in Virginia," Politics, January 4, 2013, http://www.foxnews.com/politics/2013/01/03/virginia-judge-rules-epa-overstepped-authority-trying-to-regulate-water-as/.
35. Errin Haines, "EPA Won't Appeal Ruling on Storm-Water Regulation," *Washington Post*, March 5, 2013, http://articles.washingtonpost.com/2013-03-05/local/37466492_1_storm-water-storm-water-regulation-attorney-general-ken-cuccinelli.
36. "Editorial: EPA's Chilling Effect: Alaska's Liberty Goes Up in Smoke Under New Air Regulations," *Washington Times*, January 4, 2013, http://www.washingtontimes.com/news/2013/jan/4/epa-s-chilling-effect/.
37. Tara Dodrill, "EPA Bans Most Wood-Burning Stoves," Energy Justice Network, October 2, 2013, http://www.energyjustice.net/content/epa-bans-most-wood-burning-stoves.
38. U.S. Environmental Protection Agency, "Learn Before You Burn," Burn Wise (a program of U.S. EPA), http://www.epa.gov/burnwise/, accessed November 30, 2013.
39. Joe Saunders, "Democrats, EPA Crack Down on Wood Burning at Home," *BizPac Review*, November 17, 2013, http://www.bizpacreview.com/2013/11/17/democrats-epa-crack-down-on-wood-burning-at-home-87325.

40. U.S. Environmental Protection Agency, "Ordinances and Regulations: Community Action – Laws and Ordinances," Burn Wise website, http://www.epa.gov/burnwise/ordinances.html, accessed November 30, 2013.

41. Ronald Reagan, during a news conference in August 12, 1986, posted at the Ronald Reagan Presidential Foundation and Library website, http://www.reaganfoundation.org/reagan-quotes-detail.aspx?tx=2079.

42. Craig Havighurst, "Why Gibson Guitar Was Raided by the Justice Department," *The Record* (NPR Music blog), August 31, 2011, http://www.npr.org/blogs/therecord/2011/08/31/140090116/why-gibson-guitar-was-raided-by-the-justice-department.

43. Caitlin Clarke and Adam Grant, "Gibson Guitar Logging Bust Demonstrates Lacey's Act Effectiveness," World Resources Institute, August 10, 2012, http://www.wri.org/blog/gibson-guitar-logging-bust-demonstrates-lacey-act%E2%80%99s-effectiveness.

44. Andrew C. Revkin, "A Closer Look at Gibson Guitar's Legal Troubles," Dot Earth (*New York Times* blog), http://dotearth.blogs.nytimes.com/2012/08/10/a-closer-look-at-gibson-guitars-legal-troubles/?_r=0, upd. August 13, 2012.

45. Kelsey Harris, "Gibson Guitars: Forgotten Scandal?" *The Foundry* (Heritage Foundation blog), June 3, 2013, http://blog.heritage.org/2013/06/03/forgotten-scandal-gibson-guitars-still-being-persecuted-for-doing-no-wrong/.

46. The Department of Justice, Office of Public Affairs, "Gibson Guitar Corp. Agrees to Resolve Investigation into Lacey Act Violations" (press release), August 6, 2012, http://www.justice.gov/opa/pr/2012/August/12-enrd-976.html.

47. Revkin, "A Closer Look at Gibson Guitar's Legal Troubles."

48. Neela Banerjee, "Gibson Becomes Cause Celebre for Conservatives," *Los Angeles Times*, September 27, 2011, http://articles.latimes.com/2011/sep/27/nation/la-na-gibson-guitar-20110928.

49. Mike Reynard, "Blackburn Joins Energy and Commerce Committee Leaders in Demanding Answers from Obama Administration on Gibson Guitar Raid" (press release), official website of U.S. Congressman Marsha Blackburn, September 9, 2011, http://blackburn.house.gov/news/documentsingle.aspx?DocumentID=259187.

50. Mike Reynard, Blackburn Questions Motives Behind Gibson Guitar Raid" (press release), official website of U.S. Congressman Marsha Blackburn, May 29, 2013, http://blackburn.house.gov/news/documentsingle.aspx?DocumentID=335768.

51. Erin Durkin, "Mayor Bloomberg Attacks Styrofoam in Latest Citywide Ban," *New York Daily News*, June 12, 2013, http://www.nydailynews.com/news/politics/mayor-bloomberg-attacks-styrofoam-latest-ban-article-1.1371041.

52. Michael M. Grynbaum, "To Go: Plastic Foam Containers, If the Mayor Gets His Way," *New York Times*, February 13, 2013, http://www.nytimes.com/2013/02/14/nyregion/next-bloomberg-target-plastic-foam-cups.html.

53. District Department of the Environment, "Skip the Bag, Save the River," website of the District of Columbia, http://green.dc.gov/bags, accessed August 3, 2013.

3: WHEN BUSINESS TURNS BIG BROTHER

1. Martha C. White, "When a Retailer Asks, 'Can I Have Your Zip Code?' Just Say No," *Time*, Business & Money, July 11, 2013, http://business.time.com/2013/07/11/when-retailer-asks-can-i-have-your-zip-code-just-say-no/.

2. Ibid.

3. Becket Adams, "Here's the Ugly Story of What Happened to One Woman Who Didn't Want to Give a Store Her Zip Code (and Why You Probably Shouldn't)," *The Blaze*, June 24, 2013, http://www.theblaze.com/stories/2013/06/24/heres-the-ugly-story-of-what-happened-to-one-woman-who-didnt-want-to-give-a-store-her-zip-code-and-why-you-probably-shouldnt/.

4. "We Snoop to Conquer: Security Cameras are Watching Honest Shoppers, Too," *Economist*, February 9, 2013, http://www.economist.com/news/business/21571452-security-cameras-are-watching-honest-shoppers-too-we-snoop-conquer.

5. Melissa Kondak, "Retail Stores are Tracking Your Cell Phone," *New Day* (CNN blog), July 17, 2013, http://newday.blogs.cnn.com/2013/07/17/retail-stores-are-tracking-your-cell-phone/.
6. "We Snoop to Conquer."
7. Ms. Smith, "Creepy Surveillance: Mannequins Secretly Record Shoppers and Profile Behaviors," Network World, blog entry, November 26, 2012, http://www.networkworld.com/community/blog/creepy-surveillance-mannequins-secretly-record-customers-and-profile-behaviors.
8. Andrew Roberts, "Bionic Mannequins Spy on Shoppers to Boost Luxury Sales," Bloomberg, November 21, 2012, http://www.bloomberg.com/news/2012-11-19/bionic-mannequins-spy-on-shoppers-to-boost-luxury-sales.html.
9. *Daily Mail* reporter, "High-End Stores Using Facial Recognition Technology to Identify Celebrity Customers," *Mail Online*, July 22, 2013, http://www.dailymail.co.uk/news/article-2373125/High-end-stores-using-facial-recognition-technology-identify-celebrity-customers.html.
10. Brenda Salinas, "High-End Stores Use Facial Recognition Tools to Spot VIPs," *All Tech Considered* (NPR blog), July 21, 2013, http://www.npr.org/blogs/alltechconsidered/2013/07/21/203273764/high-end-stores-use-facial-recognition-tools-to-spot-vips.
11. Ibid.
12. *Daily Mail* reporter, "High-End Stores Using Facial Recognition Technology to Identify Celebrity Customers."
13. "Never Leave Home Without It: Ditch Your Credit Card and Pay for Purchases with Your Face," *New York Post*, July 24, 2013, http://nypost.com/2013/07/24/never-leave-home-without-it-ditch-your-credit-card-and-pay-for-purchases-with-your-face/.
14. Ibid.
15. Elizabeth A. Harris, Nicole Perlroth, Nathanial Popper, and Hilary Stout, "A Sneaky Path Into Target Customers' Wallets," *The New York Times*, Jan. 17, 2014.
16. Federal Trade Commission, "Protecting Consumer Privacy in an Era of Rapid Change: Recommendations for Businesses and Policymakers," March 26, 2012.
17. Lois Beckett, "Everything We Know about What Data Brokers Know about You," ProPublica, March 7, 2013.
18. Ibid.
19. Adam Tanner, "Data Brokers Are Now Selling Your Car's Location for $10 Online," *Forbes*, July 10, 2013, http://www.forbes.com/sites/adamtanner/2013/07/10/data-broker-offers-new-service-showing-where-they-have-spotted-your-car/.
20. Bill Vlasic, contrib., "Editoral: 'Black Boxes' Are in 96% of All New Cars," January 6, 2013, *USA Today*, http://www.usatoday.com/story/opinion/2013/01/06/black-boxes-cars-edr/1566098/.
21. Jaclyn Trop, "A Black Box for Car Crashes," *International New York Times*, Business Day, July 21, 2013, http://www.nytimes.com/2013/07/22/business/black-boxes-in-cars-a-question-of-privacy.html?_r=0.
22. Evan Halper, "A Black Box in Your Car? Some See a Source of Tax Revenue," *Los Angeles Times*, October 26, 2013, http://articles.latimes.com/2013/oct/26/nation/la-na-roads-black-boxes-20131027.
23. Doug Hornig and Alex Daley, "Is Big Data the Next Billion-Dollar Technology Industry?" *Technology Investor*, Casey Research, August 12, 2013, http://www.caseyresearch.com/cdd/big-data-next-billion-dollar-technology-industry.
24. Ibid.
25. Tom Kalil, "Big Data Is a Big Deal," White House blog, March 29, 2012, http://www.whitehouse.gov/blog/2012/03/29/big-data-big-deal.
26. Office of Science and Technology Policy | Executive Office of the President, *Fact Sheet: Big Data Across the Federal Government*, March 29, 2012, http://www.whitehouse.gov/sites/default/files/microsites/ostp/big_data_fact_sheet_final.pdf.
27. Federal Communications Commission, *Enforcement Bureau issues $25,000 NAL to Google Inc* (Commission Document), released April 13, 2012, http://www.fcc.gov/document/enforcement-bureau-issues-25000-nal-google-inc.

28. Paul Wagenseil "Google Spy Case Shows Why You Need to Encrypt Your Wi-Fi," SecurityNewsDaily, NBC News, April 30, 2012.
29. Federal Communications Commission, *Enforcement Bureau issues $25,000 NAL to Google.*
30. Wagenseil "Google Spy Case Shows Why You Need to Encrypt Your Wi-Fi."
31. Electronic Privacy Information Center, "National Security Letters," http://epic.org/privacy/nsl/, accessed December 3, 2013.
32. Dan Eggen, "FBI Found to Misuse Security Letters," *Washington Post*, March 14, 2008, http://articles.washingtonpost.com/2008-03-14/news/36785987_1_national-security-letters-e-mail-and-financial-records-fbi-agents.
33. Charles Doyle, "National Security Letters in Foreign Intelligence Investigations: A Glimpse of the Legal Background and Recent Amendments," Congressional Research Service, December 27, 2010, http://www.fas.org/sgp/crs/intel/RS22406.pdf.
34. Government Printing Office, *Public Law 107-56—Oct, 26, 2001: Uniting and Strengthening America by Providing Appropriate Tools Required to Intercept and Obstruct Terrorism (USA PATRIOT Act) Act of 2001*, http://www.gpo.gov/fdsys/pkg/PLAW-107publ56/pdf/PLAW-107publ56.pdf, accessed December 3, 2013.
35. Doyle, "National Security Letters in Foreign Intelligence Investigations."
36. FoxNews.com, "FBI 'Secretly Spying' on Google Users, Company Reveals," March 6, 2013, http://www.foxnews.com/tech/2013/03/06/fbi-ecretly-spying-on-google-users-company-reveals/.
37. Ibid.
38. Scott Cleland, "Google-Spy," *Somewhat Reasonable* (Heartland Institute blog), July 8, 2013, http://blog.heartland.org/2013/07/google-spy/.
39. Sara Malm, "Stop Using Google and Facebook If You Fear U.S. Spying, says Germany," *Daily Mail*, July 3, 2013, http://www.dailymail.co.uk/news/article-2354651/STOP-using-Google-Facebook-fear-US-spying-says-Germany.html.
40. Victoria Woollaston, "Big Brother Strikes Again: Now Twitter Wants to Start Tracking You on the Web," *Mail Online*, Science & Tech, July 4, 2013, http://www.dailymail.co.uk/sciencetech/article-2355983/Big-Brother-strikes-Now-TWITTER-wants-start-tracking-web.html.
41. Federal Judicial Center, "Olmstead v United States: The Constitutional Challenges of Prohibition Enforcement: Historical Documents: Dissenting opinion of Justice Louis D. Brandeis in *Olmstead v. United States*, accessed August 9, 2013, http://www.fjc.gov/history/home.nsf/page/tu_olmstead_doc_15.html.

4: THE PATRIOT ACT AND WHY YOU SHOULD CARE

1. This Day in History, "Oct. 26, 2001: George W. Bush Signs the Patriot Act," History, http://www.history.com/this-day-in-history/george-w-bush-signs-the-patriot-act, accessed August 19, 2013.
2. Paul Blumenthal, "Congress Had No Time to Read the USA Patriot Act," Sunlight Foundation Blog, March 2, 2009, http://sunlightfoundation.com/blog/2009/03/02/congress-had-no-time-to-read-the-usa-patriot-act/.
3. UShistory.org, "Congress: The People's Branch? 6e. How a Bill Becomes a Law," http://www.ushistory.org/gov/6e.asp, accessed August 19, 2013.
4. Laura Bruce, "Patriot Act Makes Banks Pry into New Accounts," Bankrate, September 2003, http://www.bankrate.com/brm/news/bank/20030930a1.asp.
5. The Federal Reserve Board, "Testimony of Herbert A. Biern . . . before the Committee on International Relations, U.S. House of Representatives, November 17, 2004," http://www.federalreserve.gov/boarddocs/testimony/2004/20041117/.
6. Ibid.
7. Ibid.
8. Federal Reserve Board, "Testimony of Herbert A. Biern."
9. Ibid.
10. Ibid.

11. Federal Financial Institutions Examination Council / Bank Secrecy Act/Anti–Money Laundering InfoBase, "Customer Due Diligence: Overview," *Bank Secrecy Act Anti-Money Laundering Examination Manual*, http://www.ffiec.gov/bsa_aml_infobase/pages_manual/OLM_013.htm, accessed August 24, 2013.

12. "Government Surveillance Will Affect Your Handling of Money," *In the Money*, CNN, aired August 31, 2003.

13. Olivia LaBarre, "Compliance Costs Still a Concern a Decade After the Patriot Act Passes," October 10, 2011, BankTech, http://www.banktech.com/regulation-compliance/compliance-costs-still-a-concern-a-decad/231900437.

14. Federal Reserve Board, "Testimony of Herbert A. Biern."

15. Board of Governors of the Federal Reserve System, "Enforcement Actions," Year: 2013, http://www.federalreserve.gov/newsevents/press/enforcement/2013enforcement.htm.

16. Timothy S. Hardy, "Intelligence Reform in the Mid-1970s," Central Intelligence Agency Library, approved for release in 1994, posted online July 2, 1996, https://www.cia.gov/library/center-for-the-study-of-intelligence/kent-csi/vol20no2/html/v20i2a01p_0001.htm.

17. American Civil Liberties Union, "How the Anti-Terrorism Bill Puts the CIA Back in the Business of Spying on Americans," October 23, 2001, https://www.aclu.org/national-security/how-anti-terrorism-bill-puts-cia-back-business-spying-americans.

18. Ibid.

19. Mary DeRosa, "Section 215: Access to Business Records Under FISA," *Patriot Debates*: A Sourceblog for the USA PATRIOT Debate, American Bar Association, 2005, http://apps.americanbar.org/natsecurity/patriotdebates/sections-214-and-215.

20. Edward C. Liu, "Amendments to the Foreign Intelligence Service Act (FISA) Extended Until June 1, 2015," Congressional Research Service, June 16, 2011, http://www.fas.org/sgp/crs/intel/R40138.pdf.

21. DeRosa, "Section 215."

22. Glenn Greenwald, "NSA Collecting Phone Records of Millions of Verizon Customers Daily," *Guardian* (UK), June 5, 2013, http://www.theguardian.com/world/2013/jun/06/nsa-phone-records-verizon-court-order.

23. Electronic Frontier Foundation, "Let the Sun Set on Patriot—Section 215. 'Access to Records and Other Items Under the Foreign Intelligence Surveillance Act,'" http://w2.eff.org/patriot/sunset/215.php, accessed August 24, 2013.

24. Charlie Savage, "Senators Say Patriot Act is Being Misinterpreted," *New York Times*, May 26, 2011, http://www.nytimes.com/2011/05/27/us/27patriot.html?_r=0.

25. Ron Wyden, "Wyden Statement on President Obama's Proposed Reforms to the FISC and Patriot Act," website of Ron Wyden, Senator for Oregon, August 9, 2013, http://www.wyden.senate.gov/news/press-releases/wyden-statement-on-president-obamas-proposed-reforms-to-the-fisc-and-patriot-act.

26. F. James Sensenbrenner, letter to Eric H. Holder Jr., June 6, 2013, http://www2.gwu.edu/~nsarchiv/NSAEBB/NSAEBB436/docs/EBB-063.pdf.

5: WHAT'S A PRISM? THE LONG HISTORY OF GOVERNMENT ABUSES

1. Glenn Greenwald and Ewen MacAskill, "NSA Prism Program Taps into User Data of Apple, Google and Others," *Guardian* (UK), June 6, 2013, http://www.theguardian.com/world/2013/jun/06/us-tech-giants-nsa-data.

2. Brennan Center for Justice at New York University School of Law, "Are They Allowed to Do That? A Breakdown of Selected Government Surveillance Programs," http://www.brennancenter.org/analysis/are-they-allowed-do-breakdown-selected-government-surveillance-programs, accessed August 27, 2013.

3. Ibid.

4. Ibid.

5. Ibid.

6. Greenwald and MacAskill, "NSA Prism Program Taps into User Data of Apple, Google and Others."

7. CBS/AP, "Google Asks FISA Court to Lift Gag Order on NSA Surveillance Program," CBS News, June 18, 2013, http://www.cbsnews.com/news/google-asks-fisa-court-to-lift-gag-order-on-nsa-surveillance-program/.

8. CNN Politics.

9. Ewen MacAskill, NSA Paid Millions to Cover PRISM Compliance Costs for Tech Companies," *Guardian*, August 22, 2013, http://www.theguardian.com/world/2013/aug/23/nsa-prism-costs-tech-companies-paid.

10. Brendan Sasso, "Report: NSA Paid Tech Companies to Comply With Surveillance," *Hillicon Valley* (*The Hill*'s technology blog), August 23, 2013, http://thehill.com/blogs/hillicon-valley/technology/318483-report-nsa-paid-tech-giants-to-comply-with-surveillance.

11. Ibid.

12. Associated Press, "PRISM Revelations: Germany Ends Surveillance Pact With U.S., Britain," *FirstPost*, World, August 2, 2013, http://www.firstpost.com/world/prism-revelations-germany-ends-surveillance-pact-with-us-britain-1006251.html.

13. Paul Ames, "Are America's Secretive Ways Destroying Its Relationship With Europe?" *Global Post*, July 31, 2013, http://www.globalpost.com/dispatch/news/regions/europe/130730/europe-data-wars-surveillance-nsa-snowden#1.

14. Ibid.

15. Zack Whittaker, "German Minister: Stop Using U.S. Web Services to Avoid NSA Spying," ZDNet, July 3, 2013, http://www.zdnet.com/german-minister-stop-using-u-s-web-services-to-avoid-nsa-spying-7000017631/.

16. Harriet Alexander, "NSA Employees Spied on Their Lovers Using Eavesdropping Programme," *Telegraph*, August 24, 2013, http://www.telegraph.co.uk/news/worldnews/northamerica/usa/10263880/NSA-employees-spied-on-their-lovers-using-eavesdropping-programme.html.

17. Barton Gellman, "Obama's Restrictions on NSA Surveillance Rely on Narrow Definitions of 'Spying,'" *The Washington Post*, January 17, 2014.

18. Carrie Johnson, "5 Takeaways From the President's NSA Speech," NPR, January 17, 2014.

19. Intelligence.gov, "A Complex Organization United Under a Single Goal: National Security," http://www.intelligence.gov/mission/structure.html; accessed September 4, 2013.

20. "U.S. Intelligence and Security Agencies," FAS Intelligence Resource Program official website, http://www.fas.org/irp/official.html, accessed September 4, 2013.

21. AARC: The Assassination Archives and Research Center, "Church Committee Reports," http://www.aarclibrary.org/publib/contents/church/contents_church_reports.htm, accessed September 4, 2013.

22. Senate Historical Office, Senate Stories, "1964–Present: January 27, 1975: Church Committee Created," United States Senate website, Art & History, http://www.senate.gov/artandhistory/history/minute/Church_Committee_Created.htm, accessed September 4, 2013.

23. "Select Committee on Presidential Campaign Activities," Mary Ferrell Foundation website, http://www.maryferrell.org/mffweb/archive/docset/getList.do?docSetId=1922, accessed December 9, 2013.

24. AARC Public Library, "Rockefeller Commission Reports," http://www.aarclibrary.org/publib/contents/church/contents_church_reports_rockcomm.htm; accessed September 4, 2013.

25. Scott Shane, "Spy Agencies Under Heaviest Scrutiny Since Abuse Scandal of the 70s," New York Times, July 25, 2013, http://www.nytimes.com/2013/07/26/us/politics/challenges-to-us-intelligence-agencies-recall-senate-inquiry-of-70s.html.

26. Maia Szalavitz, "The Legacy of the CIA's Secret LSD Experiments on America," *Time*, Health & Family, March 23, 2012, http://healthland.time.com/2012/03/23/the-legacy-of-the-cias-secret-lsd-experiments-on-america/.

27. Troy Hooper, "Operation Midnight Climax: How the CIA Dosed S.F. Citizens with LSD," *SF Weekly*, March 14, 2012, http://www.sfweekly.com/2012-03-14/news/cia-lsd-wayne-ritchie-george-h-white-mk-ultra/.

28. Josh Clark, "Did the CIA Test LSD on Unsuspecting Americans?" HowStuffWorks, http://history.howstuffworks.com/history-vs-myth/cia-lsd.htm, accessed September 4, 2013.

29. "Operation Midnight Climax: Weird and Twisted Tale from San Francisco Telegraph Hill," *SanFranciscoSentinel.com*, March 23, 2008, http://www.sanfranciscosentinel.com/?p=11209.

30. Hooper, "Operation Midnight Climax: How the CIA Dosed S.F. Citizens with LSD."

31. Jacob G. Hornberger, "The CIA's Murder of Frank Olson Goes to Court," Future of Freedom Foundation (Hornberger's blog), November 28, 2012, http://fff.org/2012/11/28/the-cias-murder-of-frank-olson-goes-to-court/.

32. Carl Bernstein, "The CIA and the Media: How America's Most Powerful News Media Worked Hand in Glove with the Central Intelligence Agency and Why the Church Committee Covered It Up," *Rolling Stone*, October 20, 1977; reprinted on the official website of Carl Bernstein, http://www.carlbernstein.com/magazine_cia_and_media.php, accessed November 10, 2013.

33. Rebecca Wazny, comp., "Operation Mockingbird and the Cult of the Modern Media," Amazon, http://www.amazon.com/Operation-Mockingbird-Cult-Media/lm/RI03LW2W5M56T, accessed November 10, 2013.

34. "The Church Committee Report" (executive summary), 1975, http://academic.brooklyn.cuny.edu/history/johnson/churchreport.htm, accessed December 10, 2013.

35. Bernstein, "The CIA and the Media."

36. Homeland Security Digital Library, "Military Human Experiments with Chemical Warfare Agents," https://www.hsdl.org/?view&did=466161, accessed September 4, 2013.

37. Ibid.

38. Centers for Disease Control and Prevention, "U.S. Public Health Service Study at Tuskegee: The Tuskegee Timeline," http://www.cdc.gov/tuskegee/timeline.htm, upd. September 24, 2013.

39. Barbara Loe Fisher, ed., "The Vaccine Reaction: Measles Vaccine Experiments on Minority Children Turn Deadly," National Vaccine Information Center, June 1996, http://www.nvic.org/nvic-archives/newsletter/vaccinereactionjune1996.aspx.

40. Marlene Cimons, "CDC Says It Erred in Measles Study," *Los Angeles Times*, June 17, 1996, http://articles.latimes.com/1996-06-17/news/mn-15871_1_measles-vaccine.

6: THE WAR ON TERRORISM AND THE RISE OF MILITARIZED POLICE

1. George W. Bush, "Address to a Joint Session of Congress and the American People," September 20, 2001; transcript available on the White House website, http://georgewbush-whitehouse.archives.gov/news/releases/2001/09/20010920-8.html.

2. Lawrence D. Rosenberg et al., "The War on Terror in United States Courts: A Summary of Selected Key Cases," American Bar Association Section of Litigation 2012, Section Annual Conference, National Security Law and Policy Forum, April 18–20, 2012, http://www.americanbar.org/content/dam/aba/administrative/litigation/materials/sac_2012/50-1_nat_sec_war_on_terror.authcheckdam.pdf, 2–3.

3. Ibid., 3–4.

4. Amanda Ripley, "The Case of the Dirty Bomber," *Time*, June 16, 2002, http://content.time.com/time/nation/article/0,8599,262917,00.html.

5. Rosenberg et al., "The War on Terror in United States Courts," 4.

6. Peter Whoriskey, "Jury Convicts Jose Padilla of Terror Charges," *Washington Post*, August 17, 2007, http://www.washingtonpost.com/wp-dyn/content/article/2007/08/16/AR2007081601009.html.

7. CBSMiami/AP, "Jose Padilla to Be Re-Sentenced Dec. 3 in Terror Case," CBS Miami, September 5, 2012, http://miami.cbslocal.com/2012/09/05/hearing-on-new-sentencing-date-for-terrorist-jose-padilla/.

8. Richard F. Grimmett, "CRS Report for Congress: Authorization for Use for Military Force in Response to the 9/11 Attacks: Legislative History," Federation of American Scientists, upd. January 16, 2007, http://www.fas.org/sgp/crs/natsec/RS22357.pdf, 1, 4, 6.

9. "Authorization for Use of Military Force 2001," *Lawfare* (blog), accessed September 8, 2013, http://www.lawfareblog.com/wiki/the-lawfare-wiki-document-library/post-911-era-materials/post-911-era-materials-legislative-materials/authorization-for-use-of-military-force/.

10. Ibid.

11. Carol D. Leonnig, "Report Rebuts Bush on Spying," *Washington Post*, September 7, 2006, http://www.washingtonpost.com/wp-dyn/content/article/2006/01/06/AR2006010601772.html.

12. The Offices of Inspectors General for the departments of Defense and Justice, and of the NSA, CIA and Office of the Director of National Intelligence, *Unclassifed Report on the President's Surveillance Program*," July 10, 2009, https://www.fas.org/irp/eprint/psp.pdf.

13. Dan Eggan, "Bush Authorized Domestic Spying," *Washington Post*, December 16, 2005, http://www.washingtonpost.com/wp-dyn/content/article/2005/12/16/AR2005121600021.html.

14. Leonnig, "Report Rebuts Bush on Spying."

15. Congress.gov, S. Res. 50 , 109ᵗʰ Congress (2005–2006), Introduced in Senate Jan. 20, 2006.

16. Matt Sledge, "Obama Call to Repeal 'Perpetual War' Law Contradicts Pentagon," *Huff Post*, Politics, May 23, 2013, http://www.huffingtonpost.com/2013/05/23/obama-aumf-repeal_n_3328667.html.

17. Patricia Zengerle and Matt Spetalnick, "Obama Wants to End 'War on Terror,' but Congress Balks," Reuters, May 24, 2013, http://www.reuters.com/article/2013/05/24/us-usa-obama-speech-idUSBRE94M04Y20130524.

18. Ibid.

19. Charlie Savage, "Debating the Legal Basis for the War on Terror," *New York Times*, May 16, 2013, http://www.nytimes.com/2013/05/17/us/politics/pentagon-official-urges-congress-to-keep-statute-allowing-war-on-terror-intact.html?_r=0.

20. Arthur Rizer and Joseph Hartman, "How the War on Terror Has Militarized the Police," *The Atlantic*, November 2011, http://www.theatlantic.com/national/archive/2011/11/how-the-war-on-terror-has-militarized-the-police/248047/.

21. Scott Israel, "Special Weapons and Tactics (SWAT) Team," website of Sheriff Scott Israel, Sheriff's Office, Broward County, FL, http://www.sheriff.org/about_bso/dle/units/swat.cfm, accessed November 10, 2013.

22. Radley Balko, "Jose Guerena's Family Sues Pima County over SWAT Raid Killing," *Huff Post*, Crime, upd. October 17, 2011, http://www.huffingtonpost.com/2011/08/17/jose-guerena-pima-county-lawsuit_n_926454.html.

23. Kim Smith, "Attorneys in Guerena Civil Case Told to Be Mindful," *At the Courthouse* (*Arizona Daily Star* blog), February 5, 2013, http://azstarnet.com/news/blogs/courthouse/attorneys-in-guerena-civil-case-told-to-be-mindful/article_288bb40c-6fd8-11e2-98f8-001a4bcf887a.html.

24. Liz Klimas, "Horrific Allegation: Couple Says Cops Climbed through Window without Warrant and Shot Their Dogs," *The Blaze*, August 9, 2013, http://www.theblaze.com/stories/2013/08/09/horrific-allegation-couple-says-cops-climbed-through-window-without-warrant-and-shot-their-dogs/#.

25. Ibid.

26. The Rutherford Institute, "Rutherford Institute Attorneys File Civil Rights Lawsuit over Wrongful Arrest, Detention in Psych Ward of Marine Brandon Raub Because of Facebook Posts," *On the Front Lines*, May 22, 2013, https://www.rutherford.org/publications_resources/on_the_front_lines/rutherford_institute_attorneys_file_civil_rights_lawsuit_over_wrongful_arre.

27. Craig Horowitz, "The NYPD's War on Terror," *New York* magazine, accessed September 9, 2013, http://nymag.com/nymetro/news/features/n_8286/.

28. Alyson Sheppard, "Police Shoot Cars with GPS Tags to Reduce High-Speed Chases," *Popular Mechanics*, November 6, 2013, http://www.popularmechanics.com/technology/military/news/police-shoot-cars-with-gps-tags-to-reduce-high-speed-chases-16127245.

29. Elaine Pittman, "Real-Life Police Technology Catches Up with Science Fiction," *Government Technology*, April 29, 2010, http://www.govtech.com/public-safety/Real-Life-Police-Technology-Catches-up-With.html.

30. Chad Vander Veen, "Top Law Enforcement Officials to Convene over Latest in Police Technology," *Government Technology*, September 4. 2013, http://www.govtech.com/public-safety/Top-Law-Enforcement-Officials-to-Convene-Over-Latest-in-Police-Technology.html.

31. Martin Kaste, "Can Software That Predicts Crime Pass Constitutional Muster?" NPR, July 26, 2013, http://www.npr.org/2013/07/26/205835674/can-software-that-predicts-crime-pass-constitutional-muster.

32. Heather Kelly, "Police Embracing Tech That Predicts Crimes," CNN Tech, July 9, 2013, http://www.cnn.com/2012/07/09/tech/innovation/police-tech.

33. Kaste, "Can Software That Predicts Crime Pass Constitutional Muster?"
34. Vander Veen, "Top Law Enforcement Officials to Convene over Latest in Police Technology."
35. Somini Sengupta, "Rise of Drones in U.S. Drives Efforts to Limit Police Use," *New York Times,* February 15, 2013, http://www.nytimes.com/2013/02/16/technology/rise-of-drones-in-us-spurs-efforts-to-limit-uses.html.
36. Ibid.
37. Natasha Lennard, "ACLU Challenges Bay Area Police Drone Plans," *Salon,* October 18, 2012, http://www.salon.com/2012/10/18/aclu_challenge_bay_area_police_drone_plans/.
38. Susan Greene, "Mesa County, Colo., A National Leader in Domestic Drone Use," *Huff Post Denver,* June 6, 2013, http://www.huffingtonpost.com/2013/06/06/mesa-county-colo-a-nation_n_3399876.html.
39. Scott Gordon, "North Texas Drivers Stopped at Roadblock Asked for Saliva, Blood," NBCDFW.com, November 20, 2013, http://www.nbcdfw.com/news/local/North-Texas-Drivers-Stopped-at-Roadblock-Asked-for-Saliva-Blood-232438621.html.
40. Bill Miller, "Fort Worth Police Chief Apologizes For Officers' Participation in Highway Safety Survey," Star-Telegram, November 21, 2013, http://www.star-telegram.com/2013/11/20/5356114/fort-worth-police-chief-apologizes.html.
41. Ibid.
42. NHTSA, *2007 National Roadside Survey of Alcohol and Drug Use by Drivers,* http://www.cicad.oas.org/apps/Document.aspx?Id=998, accessed December 4, 2013.

7: THE DOJ AND CIVIL FORFEITURES

1. American Civil Liberties Union, *"Morrow v. City of Teneha et al.* – Plaintiff Biographies," August 14, 2012, https://www.aclu.org/criminal-law-reform/morrow-plaintiff-biographies.
2. Jannell Ross, "Texas Police Shakedown Lawsuit Settled," *Huffington Post,* August 9, 2012.
3. American Civil Liberties Union, *"Morrow v. City of Teneha et al."*
4. Ross, "Texas Police Shakedown Lawsuit Settled."
5. Ibid.
6. American Civil Liberties Union, *"Morrow v. City of Teneha et al."*
7. United States Department of Justice, "Asset Forfeiture Program: Overview of the Asset Forfeiture Program," upd. January 2013, http://www.justice.gov/jmd/afp/.
8. The U.S. Marshals Service, "Asset Forfeiture: Asset Forfeiture Program," http://www.usmarshals.gov/assets/assets.html, accessed September 11, 2013.
9. Les Picker, "Forfeiture Laws, Policing Incentives, and Local Budgets," National Bureau of Economic Research, http://www.nber.org/digest/oct04/w10484.html, accessed September 11, 2013.
10. Brad Reid, "An Overview of Civil Asset Forfeiture and Recent Cases," *HuffPost,* Business, August 14, 2013, http://www.huffingtonpost.com/brad-reid/civil-asset-forfeiture-ch_b_3745209.html.
11. Steven L. Kessler, "The Civil Asset Forfeiture Reform Act of 2000," KesslerOnForfeiture.com, http://www.kessleronforfeiture.com/civil-asset-forfeiture-reform-act-of-2000/, accessed December 5, 2013.
12. Ibid.
13. Michael Saunders, ed., "Equitable Sharing Program: Number 16-922," Catalog of Federal Domestic Assistance, http://www.governmentgrantsmoney.com/program/16.922/, accessed September 11, 2013.
14. U.S. Marshals Service, "Asset Forfeiture Program," http://www.usmarshals.gov/assets/, accessed December 13, 2013.
15. U.S. Department of Justice, "FY 2012 Seized Property Inventory Valued Over One Million Dollars as of September 30, 2012," http://www.justice.gov/jmd/afp/02fundreport/2012affr/report7.htm, accessed September 11, 2013.
16. Ibid.

17. U.S. General Accountability Office, "Justice Assets Forfeiture Fund: Transparency of Balance and Controls over Equitable Sharing Should Be Improved," GAO-12-736, www.gao.gov/assets/600/592349.pdf, July 2012.

18. Brian J. Gottstein, "Cuccinelli Uses $245,000 Taken from Criminals to Buy Bulletproof Vests for Virginia Law Enforcement," website of Kenneth T. Cuccinelli, Attorney General of Virginia, http://www.ag.virginia.gov/Media%20and%20News%20Releases/News_Releases/Cuccinelli/120513_Bulletproof_Vests.html, December 5, 2013.

19. Reid, "An Overview of Civil Asset Forfeiture and Recent Cases."

20. Federal Bureau of Investigation, "White-Collar Crime: Asset Forfeiture," http://www.fbi.gov/about-us/investigate/white_collar/asset-forfeiture, accessed September 9, 2013.

21. Marian R. Williams, Jefferson E. Holcomb, and Kovandzie, "Asset Forfeiture Report: Part I, Policing for Profit," Institute for Justice, http://www.ij.org/part-i-policing-for-profit-2, March 2010.

22. Curt Anderson, "Fla. Police Cash Force Shows Forfeiture's Growth," Associated Press, May 10, 2013, http://bigstory.ap.org/article/fla-police-cash-force-shows-forfeitures-growth.

23. Williams, Holcomb, and Kovandzie, "Asset Forfeiture Report: Part I."

24. Information in the chart that follows was taken from Scott Bullock's, "Policing for Profit: Asset Forfeiture Report: Part II: Grading the States," Institute for Justice, http://www.ij.org/part-ii-grading-the-states-2. Used with permission.

25. The details of this case were taken from Sarah Stillman, "Taken," *New Yorker*, August 12, 2013, http://www.newyorker.com/reporting/2013/08/12/130812fa_fact_stillman.

26. John Burnett, "Seized Drug Assets Pad Police Budgets: First of a Four Part Series," NPR, June 16, 2008, http://www.npr.org/templates/story/story.php?storyId=91490480.

27. Stillman, "Taken."

28. Editorial board, "Forfeiture without Due Process," *Washington Post*, January 2, 2012, http://articles.washingtonpost.com/2012-01-02/opinions/35438128_1_forfeiture-laws-virginia-state-police-trooper.

29. Cases, Smith & Zimmerman PPLC, http://www.smithzimmerman.com/Cases.shtml, accessed December 6, 2013.

8: WHERE ARE THE WATCHDOGS?

1. "Transcript and Audio: Second Presidential Debate," NPR, October 16, 2012, http://www.npr.org/2012/10/16/163050988/transcript-obama-romney-2nd-presidential-debate.

2. Barack Obama, "Remarks by the President on the Deaths of U.S. Embassy Staff in Libya," The White House, Office of the Press Secretary, September 12, 2012, http://www.whitehouse.gov/the-press-office/2012/09/12/remarks-president-deaths-us-embassy-staff-libya.

3. Josh Voorhees, "The Townhall Debate Was One Giant Rule Violation," *The Slatest (Slate* blog), October 17, 2012, http://www.slate.com/blogs/the_slatest/2012/10/17/town_hall_debate_rules_candy_crowley_barack_obama_mitt_romney_throw_rule.html.

4. "Transcript and Audio: Second Presidential Debate."

5. Katie Reilly, "Respect for Journalists' Contributions Has Fallen Significantly in Recent Years," Pew Research Center, July 25, 2013, http://www.pewresearch.org/fact-tank/2013/07/25/respect-for-journalists-contributions-has-fallen-significantly-in-recent-years/.

6. Lisa O'Carroll, "Seymour Hersh on Obama, NSA, and the 'Pathetic' American Media," *Guardian Media Blog*, September 27, 2013. http://www.theguardian.com/media/media-blog/2013/sep/27/seymour-hersh-obama-nsa-american-media.

7. Donald H. Rumsfeld, "The Media War on Terror," Project Syndicate, February 22, 2006, http://www.project-syndicate.org/commentary/the-media-war-on-terror.

8. Rich Noyes, "Eight Years of Bias: The Liberal Media Versus the War in Iraq," Newsbusters, August 21, 2010, http://newsbusters.org/blogs/rich-noyes/2010/08/21/eight-years-bias-liberal-media-vs-war-iraq.

9. Claire Cozens, "Arnett Fired by NBC after Iraqi TV Outburst," *Guardian*, March 31, 2003, http://www.theguardian.com/media/2003/mar/31/broadcasting.Iraqandthemedia1.

10. Noyes, "Eight Years of Bias."

11. "Remarks by the President on Osama bin Laden," The White House, Office of the Press Secretary, May 2, 2011, http://www.whitehouse.gov/the-press-office/2011/05/02/remarks-president-osama-bin-laden.

12. Stephanie Condon, "Obama Monitored Osama bin Laden Attack in Real Time," CBS, May 2, 2011, http://www.cbsnews.com/news/obama-monitored-osama-bin-laden-attack-in-real-time/.

13. "Obama Describes Raid That Killed bin Laden," Today, May 2, 2012, http://www.today.com/video/today/47259832#47259832.

14. Matt Wilstein, "Reggie Love: Obama Took Break from Watching bin Laden Raid to Play Cards," Mediaite, August 15, 2013, http://www.mediaite.com/tv/reggie-love-obama-took-break-from-watching-bin-laden-raid-to-play-cards/.

15. Mark Memmott, "Obama Played Cards the Day bin Laden Was Killed: Important?" The Two-Way (NPR blog), August 15, 2013, http://www.npr.org/blogs/thetwo-way/2013/08/15/212312070/obama-played-cards-the-day-bin-laden-was-killed-important.

16. Jeff Poor, "Hersh Slams U.S. Media, Says 'Not One Word' of White House bin Laden Narrative Is True," Daily Caller, September 27, 2013, http://dailycaller.com/2013/09/27/hersh-slams-us-media-claims-bin-laden-narrative-is-not-true/.

17. "Chris Matthews: 'I Felt This Thrill Going Up My Leg' As Obama Spoke," Huff Post Media, March 28, 2008; rev. May 25, 2011, http://www.huffingtonpost.com/2008/02/13/chris-matthews-i-felt-thi_n_86449.html.

18. Mike Opelka, "Testy Chris Matthews Responds to 'Thrill Up His Leg' Question: 'Horse's A-- Right-Winger,'" The Blaze, May 25, 2012, http://www.theblaze.com/stories/2012/05/25/testy-chris-matthews-responds-to-thrill-up-his-leg-question-horses-a-right-winger/.

19. Frances Martel, "NYT's Apology for Tea Party Racism Accusation Not Enough for Breitbart," Mediaite, August 3, 2010, http://www.mediaite.com/online/nyts-apology-for-tea-party-racism-accusation-not-enough-for-andrew-breitbart/.

20. Robert Pear, "Spitting and Slurs Directed at Lawmakers," Prescriptions (New York Times blog), March 20, 2010, http://prescriptions.blogs.nytimes.com/2010/03/20/spitting-and-slurs-directed-at-lawmakers/?_r=0.

21. Matthew Balan, "Suzanne Malveaux Latest to Use Vulgar 'Teabagger' Label on CNN," Newbusters, November 23, 2009, http://newsbusters.org/blogs/matthew-balan/2009/11/23/suzanne-malveaux-latest-use-vulgar-teabagger-label-cnn.

22. Matt Hadro, "CNN's Malveaux Tells Van Jones He'd Be 'Good Spokesperson' for Occupy Movement," Newbusters, November 16, 2011, http://newsbusters.org/blogs/matt-hadro/2011/11/16/cnns-malveaux-tells-van-jones-hed-be-good-spokesperson-occupy-movement.

23. Matt Hadro, "CNN Ignored Illegality of 'Squatting,' Asks How it Can Help Occupy Movement," Newbusters, December 6, 2011, http://newsbusters.org/blogs/matt-hadro/2011/12/06/cnn-ignores-illegality-squatting-asks-how-it-can-help-occupy-movement.

24. Frances Martel, "Bernie Goldberg and Bill O'Reilly Make Fun of Liberals Labeling Tea Partiers 'Terrorists,'" Mediaite, August 1, 2011, http://www.mediaite.com/tv/bernie-goldberg-and-bill-oreilly-make-fun-of-liberals-labeling-tea-partiers-terrorists/.

25. Frances Martel, "Bernie Goldberg on Media Bias in Favor of Occupy Wall Street: 'There is No Hope for Them,'" Mediaite, October 31, 2011, http://www.mediaite.com/tv/bernie-goldberg-on-media-bias-in-favor-of-occupy-wall-street-there-is-no-hope-for-them/.

26. A.W.R. Hawkins, "Ayatollah Khameini Embraces Occupy Wall Street Movement," Predator Masters Forums, August 31, 2012, http://www.predatormastersforums.com/forums/ubbthreads.php?ubb=showflat&Number=2281478.

27. Joe Newby, "List Shows Communists, Islamists, Nazis Support Nationwide OWS Protests," Examiner, November 1, 2011, http://www.examiner.com/article/list-shows-communists-islamists-nazis-support-nationwide-ows-protests.

28. Erik Wemple, "Why Did New York Times Call George Zimmerman 'White Hispanic?'" Washington Post, Opinions, March 28, 2012, http://www.washingtonpost.com/blogs/erik-wemple/post/why-did-new-york-times-call-george-zimmerman-white-hispanic/2012/03/28/gIQAW6fngS_blog.html.

29. Isa Hopkins, "Is George Zimmerman White or Hispanic? That Depends," Salon, July 16, 2013, http://www.salon.com/2013/07/16/is_george_zimmerman_white_or_hispanic/.

30. Jerriann Sullivan, "Sharpton, Jackson to Speak at NAACP Convention as 1 Million Sign Petition," Orlando Sentinel, July 16, 2013, http://articles.orlandosentinel.com/2013-07-16/news/os-sharpton-jackson-speak-naacp-convention-20130716_1_george-zimmerman-trayvon-martin-naacp-convention.

31. Ibid.

32. Ibid.

33. Associated Press, "George Zimmerman Trial: Al Sharpton, Jesse Jackson, Urge Peace," upd. July 13, 2013, http://www.baynews9.com/content/news/baynews9/news/article.html/content/news/articles/cfn/2013/7/13/george_zimmerman_tri_0.html.

34. Daniel Politi, "Tucker Carlson: Al Sharpton and Jesse Jackson Are 'Hustlers and Pimps,'" Slate, July 14, 2013, http://www.slate.com/blogs/the_slatest/2013/07/14/carlson_sharpton_and_jackson_are_hustlers_and_pimps.html.

35. Tommy Christopher, "NBC Affiliate Aired Edited Zimmerman 911 Call Days Before Today Show Did," Mediaite, April 25, 2012, http://www.mediaite.com/tv/nbc-affiliate-aired-edited-zimmerman-911-call-a-week-before-today-show/.

36. Erik Wemple,"NBC Issues Apology on Zimmerman Tape Screw-Up," Washington Post, April 3, 2012, http://www.washingtonpost.com/blogs/erik-wemple/post/nbc-issues-apology-on-zimmerman-tape-screw-up/2012/04/03/gIQA8m5jtS_blog.html.

37. Christopher, "NBC Affiliate Aired Edited Zimmerman 911 Call Days Before Today Show Did."

38. Josh Feldman, "NBC News President Steve Capus Says Editing Zimmerman Tape Was 'Mistake,' Defends Al Sharpton," Mediaite, April 8, 2012, http://www.mediaite.com/tv/nbc-news-president-steve-capus-says-editing-zimmerman-tape-was-mistake-defends-al-sharpton/.

39. D'Vera Cohn, et al., "Gun Homicide Rate Down 49% Since 1993; Public Unaware," Pew Research Social & Demographic Trends, May 7, 2013, http://www.pewsocialtrends.org/2013/05/07/gun-homicide-rate-down-49-since-1993-peak-public-unaware/.

40. Michael A. Lindenberger, "Ten Years after Columbine, It's Easier to Bear Arms," Time, April 20, 2009, http://content.time.com/time/nation/article/0,8599,1891416,00.html.

41. Justin Peters, "After Newtown, We Vowed to Take Gun Control Seriously. Why Has Nothing Changed?" Crime (Slate blog), June 14, 2013, http://www.slate.com/blogs/crime/2013/06/14/newtown_anniversary_after_the_school_shooting_we_vowed_to_take_gun_control.html.

42. "First Amendment Research Information: Freedom of the Press History," Illinois First Amendment Center, http://www.illinoisfirstamendmentcenter.com/freedom_press_history.php, accessed December 11, 2013.

9: THE BATTLE AGAINST ZONING ZEALOTS

1. Del Webb, "Sun City Shadow Hills," http://www.delwebb.com/communities/ca/indio/sun-city-shadow-hills/12242/index1-about-the-area.aspx#.Uj2osRDYHIU, accessed September 21, 2013.

2. Jay Root, "Growing Disillusioned with HOAs," Texas Monthly, May 21, 2013, http://www.texasmonthly.com/story/growing-disillusioned-hoas.

3. Ibid.

4. Clifford J. Treese, "Statistical Review, 2012: For U.S. Homeowners Associations, Condominium Communities and Housing Cooperatives: National and State Data," Foundation for Community Association Research, http://www.cairf.org/foundationstatsbrochure.pdf, accessed September 12, 2013.

5. Ibid.

6. Ibid.

7. Mike Morris, "Marine Vet Battles HOA over His Too-Tall Flagpole," Houston Chronicle, January 6, 2011, http://www.chron.com/news/houston-texas/article/Marine-vet-battles-HOA-over-his-too-tall-flagpole-1684898.php.

8. "Retired Marine Wins Battle over Flagpole," *Community Association Management Insider*, July 17, 2011, https://www.communityassociationinsider.com/article/retired-marine-wins-battle-over-flagpole.

9. Morris, "Marine Vet Battles HOA Over His Too-Tall Flagpole."

10. "Retired Marine Wins Battle over Flagpole."

11. Cindy George, "HOA, Resident Go to Court in Flag Dispute," *Houston Chronicle*, May 18, 2013, http://www.houstonchronicle.com/news/houston-texas/houston/article/HOA-resident-go-to-court-in-flagpole-disagreement-4527260.php.

12. Ibid.

13. Rucks Russell, "Vet Protests HOA Restriction With Upside Down Flag Display," KHOU 11 News, May 21, 2013, http://www.khou.com/news/local/Vet-flies-flag-upside-down-in-protest-of-HOA-restriction--208236451.html.

14. George, "HOA, Resident Go To Court in Flag Dispute."

15. Russell, "Vet Protests HOA Restriction with Upside Down Flag Display."

16. George, "HOA, Resident Go To Court in Flag Dispute."

17. Ibid.

18. Russell, "Vet Protests HOA Restriction with Upside Down Flag Display."

19. Byron Harris, "HOA, Celina Homeowner Battle over Fines for Roof Color," WFAA-TV, September 13, 2013, http://www.wfaa.com/news/local/collin/Roof-Rights-223692861.html.

20. Ibid.

21. Jim McConnell, "Renegade Gardener Digs In, Fights HOA," *Chesterfield Observer*, June 19, 2013, http://www.chesterfieldobserver.com/news/2013-06-19/Front_Page/Renegade_gardener_digs_in_fights_HOA.html.

22. Jim McConnell, "Brandermill Gardener Wins Battle With HOA," *Chesterfield Observer*, August 14, 2013, http://www.chesterfieldobserver.com/news/2013-08-14/News/Brandermill_gardener_wins_battle_with_HOA.html.

23. Ibid.

24. Jonathan Wood, "Setting the Record Straight on Pepin," Pacific Legal Foundation *Liberty Blog*, June 28, 2013, http://blog.pacificlegal.org/2013/dear-editorialists-heres-what-pepin-is-about/.

25. Jonathan Wood, "Mess-achusetts: State Agency Attempts to Circumvent Limits on its Power, Ignores Property Rights," *Liberty Blog*, May 20, 2013, http://blog.pacificlegal.org/2013/mess-achusetts-state-agency-attempts-to-circumvent-limits-on-its-power-ignores-property-rights/.

26. Wood, "Setting the Record Straight on Pepin."

27. Ibid.

28. Conor Berry, "Bill Pepin's Quest to Build a Retirement Home in Hampden Derailed by Alleged Turtle Spotting Near His Land," *Mass Live* (blog), July 30, 2012, http://www.masslive.com/news/index.ssf/2012/07/bill_pepin_quest_to_build_retirement_home_in_hampden_eastern_box_turtle.html.

29. Wood, "Setting the Record Straight on Pepin."

30. Dan Ring, "Massachusetts Supreme Judicial Court Airs Challenge by William Pepin to Regulations on Endangered Species," *Mass Live*, October 8, 2013, http://www.masslive.com/politics/index.ssf/2013/10/massachusetts_supreme_judicial_4.html.

31. Kenric Ward, "Fauquier County Threatens Farmer with $5K Fines for Selling Food," Watchdog.org Virginia Bureau, August 1, 2012, http://watchdog.org/46098/va-fauquier-county-threatens-farmer-with-5000-fines-for-selling-food-at-her-farm/.

32. Sasha Bogursky, "Georgia Girls' Lemonade Stand Reopened at Local Water Park After Police Shut Them Down," Fox News, July 28, 2011, http://www.foxnews.com/us/2011/07/28/georgia-girls-lemonade-stand-reopened-at-local-water-park-after-police-shut/.

33. Associated Press, "Georgia Police Close Girls' Lemonade Stand," July 15, 2011, http://www.foxnews.com/us/2011/07/15/georgia-police-close-girls-lemonade-stand/.

34. Kristin Crowley, "Appleton Police Shut Down Lemonade Stand," Fox 11, upd. July 20, 2011, http://www.fox11online.com/news/appleton-pd-shut-down-lemonade-stand.

35. Lesley Conn, "Savannah to Allow Girl Scouts to Sell Cookies at Low House," Savannah Now, March 2, 2011, http://savannahnow.com/news/2011-03-02/savannah-allow-girl-scouts-sell-cookies-low-house.

36. Daniel Himebaugh, "Just an Old-Fashioned Land Grab," PLF *Liberty Blog*, August 7, 2013, http://blog.pacificlegal.org/2013/just-an-old-fashioned-land-grab/.
37. Ibid.
38. Jason Yurgartis, "Public Housing Ban on Guns Challenged," *News-Leader* (FL), September 20, 2013.
39. Ibid.
40. Second Amendment Foundation, "SAF Sues over Public Housing Gun Ban in Warren County, Illinois," April 4, 2012, http://saf.org/viewpr-new.asp?id=399.
41. *Dallas Morning News*, "Clinton Considers Banning All Guns in Public Housing," *Seattle Times*, February 5, 1994, http://community.seattletimes.nwsource.com/archive/?date=19940205&slug=1893619.
42. PJ Media, "Home Church Pastor Jailed 60 Days for 67 Zoning Violations," July 12, 2012, http://pjmedia.com/lifestyle/2012/07/12/home-church-pastor-jailed-60-days-for-67-zoning-violations/.
43. Bob Unruh, "Banished! City Forbids Bible Studies in Homes," WND, March 13, 2010, http://www.wnd.com/index.php?fa=PAGE.view&pageId=127793.
44. *Christianity Today*, "In-Home Prayer Forbidden by Connecticut Town Government," Rense Radio Network, December 10, 2000, http://rense.com/general6/inhomeprayer.htm.

10: THE DATA GRAB AND THE GROWTH OF SECRET GOVERNMENT CENTERS

1. Peter Corbett, "Scottsdale silent on facility for police," *Arizona Central*, July 8, 2012, http://www.azcentral.com/arizonarepublic/local/articles/2012/07/05/20120705scottsdale-police-facility-city-silent.html.
2. Ibid.
3. Ibid.
4. John Brandon, "Inside the NSA's Secret Utah Data Center," Fox News, June 11, 2013, http://www.foxnews.com/tech/2013/06/11/inside-nsas-secret-utah-data-center/.
5. Thomas Burr, "Shh . . . NSA's Utah Data Center May Be Open Already," *Salt Lake Tribune*, Politics, upd. September 26, 2013, http://www.sltrib.com/sltrib/politics/56915018-90/nsa-data-agency-center.html.csp.
6. Liz Klimas, "7 Stats to Know about NSA's Massive Utah Data Center as It Nears Completion," *The Blaze*, July 1, 2013, http://www.theblaze.com/stories/2013/07/01/seven-stats-to-know-about-nsas-utah-data-center-as-it-nears-completion/.
7. Nate Carlisle, "NSA Utah Data Center: Frequently Asked Questions," *Salt Lake Tribune*, upd. September 30, 2013, http://www.sltrib.com/sltrib/politics/56718440-90/nsa-utah-data-center.html.csp.
8. Brandon, "Inside the NSA's Secret Utah Data Center."
9. Rory Carroll, "Welcome to Utah, the NSA's Desert Home for Eavesdropping on America," Raw Story, June 14, 2013, http://www.rawstory.com/rs/2013/06/14/welcome-to-utah-the-nsas-desert-home-for-eavesdropping-on-america/.
10. Burr, "Shh . . . NSA's Utah Data Center May Be Open Already."
11. Ibid.
12. National Security Agency/Central Security Service, "NSA/CSS Core Values with NSA's Deputy Director, John C. Inglis," http://www.nsa.gov/about/values/core_values.shtml, accessed October 1, 2013.
13. Burr, "Shh . . . NSA's Utah Data Center May Be Open Already."
14. Carlisle, "NSA Utah Data Center: Frequently Asked Questions."
15. Ibid.
16. Carrie Johnson, "5 Takeaways From the President's NSA Speech," NPR, January 17, 2014.
17. Carroll, "Welcome to Utah, the NSA's Desert Home for Eavesdropping on America."
18. "Former Top NSA Official: 'We Are Now In a Police State,'" Washington's Blog, December 18, 2013, accessed January 18, 2014, http://www.washingtonsblog.com/2013/12/former-top-nsa-official-now-police-state.html.

19. Douglas Ernst, "NSA Spy Data Center Hit with Multiple Meltdowns; Electrical Explosions Delay Opening," *Washington Times*, October 8, 2013, http://www.washingtontimes.com/news/2013/oct/8/nsa-spy-data-center-hit-multiple-meltdowns-explosi/.

20. Siobhan Gorman, "Meltdowns Hobble NSA Data Center," *Wall Street Journal*, October 7, 2013, http://online.wsj.com/news/articles/SB10001424052702304441404579119490744478398.

21. Department of Homeland Security, "State and Major Urban Area Fusion Centers: National Network of Fusion Centers," http://www.dhs.gov/national-network-fusion-centers-fact-sheet, accessed October 2, 2013.

22. U.S. Senate, Permanent Subcommittee on Investigations, Committee on Homeland Security and Governmental Affairs, *Federal Support for and Involvement in State and Local Fusion Centers: Majority and Minority Staff Report*, October 3, 2012, 1, http://www.hsgac.senate.gov/download/?id=49139e81-1dd7-4788-a3bb-d6e7d97dde04.

23. Ibid., 1–2.

24. Ibid.

25. Charles S. Clark, "Homeland Security's Fusion Centers Lambasted in Senate Report," *Government Executive*, October 2, 2012, http://www.govexec.com/defense/2012/10/homeland-securitys-fusion-centers-lambasted-senate-report/58535/.

26. Robert O'Harrow Jr., "DHS 'Fusion Centers' Portrayed as Pools of Ineptitude, Civil Liberties Instrusions," *Washington Post*, October 2, 2012, http://www.washingtonpost.com/investigations/dhs-fusion-centers-portrayed-as-pools-of-ineptitude-and-civil-liberties-intrusions/2012/10/02/10014440-0cb1-11e2-bd1a-b868e65d57eb_story.html.

27. Michael McAuliff, "Homeland Security 'Fusion Centers' Target Fishing, Marriage Counseling, at Huge Cost," *Huff Post*, Politics, October 2, 2012, http://www.huffingtonpost.com/2012/10/02/homeland-security-fusion-centers_n_1933998.html.

28. *Recommendations for Fusion Centers: Preserving Privacy and Civil Liberties While Protecting Against Crime and Terrorism* (Washington, DC: Constitution Project, 2012), 4–7, http://constitutionproject.org/pdf/fusioncenterreport.pdf, accessed October 3, 2013.

29. Charles S. Clark, "Defenders of Fusion Centers Hit Back at Senate Panel's Criticisms," *Government Executive*, October 9, 2012, http://www.govexec.com/oversight/2012/10/defenders-fusion-centers-hit-back-senate-panels-criticisms/58652/.

30. Eileen R. Larence, et al., *Information Sharing: Agencies Could Better Coordinate to Reduce Overlap in Field-Based Activities* U.S. Government Accountability Office, April 2013, http://www.gao.gov/assets/660/653527.pdf.

31. Mickey McCarter, "Duplicative Efforts Among Fusion Centers Redundant, GAO Says," Homeland Security Today, April 5, 2013, http://www.hstoday.us/industry-news/general/single-article/duplicative-efforts-among-fusion-centers-redundant-gao-says/10afada2facc1028bbc3a6be3609f703.html.

32. Larence, et al., "What GAO Found," in *Information Sharing*.

33. George W. Bush, "President Bush Signs Homeland Security Act: Remarks by the President at the Signing of H.R. 5005 the Homeland Security Act of 2002," The White House: President George W. Bush, November 25, 2002, http://georgewbush-whitehouse.archives.gov/news/releases/2002/11/20021125-6.html.

34. George Bush, "Proposal to Create the Department of Homeland Security," official website of the Department of Homeland Security, from Bush, *The Department of Homeland Security* (June 2002), http://www.dhs.gov/proposal-create-department-homeland-security.

35. Department of Homeland Security, "2013 Fusion Center Success Stories," http://www.dhs.gov/2013-fusion-center-success-stories, accessed September 28, 2013.

36. Nationwide SAR Initiative, "About the NSI," http://nsi.ncirc.gov/about_nsi.aspx, accessed September 28, 2013.

37. *Recommendations for Fusion Centers*, 12.

38. Ibid.

39. Ibid, 13.

40. Federal Bureau of Investigation, "Stats & Services: eGuardian," FBI website, www.fbi.gov/stats-services/eguardian, accessed October 3, 2013, 13.

41. *Recommendations for Fusion Centers*.

42. Ibid., 12–13.
43. The Department of Homeland Security, "State and Major Urban Area Fusion Centers: Expanding the Nationwide Suspicious Activity Reporting (SAR) Initiative (NSI)," ISE, accessed October 3, 2013. http://www.ise.gov/nationwide-sar-initiative.
44. The Department of Homeland Security, "If You See Something, Say Something Campaign: About the Campaign," http://www.dhs.gov/if-you-see-something-say-something%E2%84%A2-campaign, accessed October 3, 2013.
45. Brennan Center for Justice, web page for *Domestic Intelligence: Our Rights and Our Safety,* November 8, 2013, http://www.brennancenter.org/publication/domestic-intelligence-our-rights-and-our-safety, foreword by Michael Waldman, http://www.brennancenter.org/sites/default/files/publications/Domestic%20Intelligence%20FINAL.pdf#page=6.

11: UNMANNED DRONES COMING TO A COMMUNITY NEAR YOU

1. MSNBC, "Department of Justice White Paper: Lawfulness of a Lethal Operation Directed Against a U.S. Citizen Who is a Senior Operational Leader of Al-Qa-ida or an Associated Force," http://msnbcmedia.msn.com/i/msnbc/sections/news/020413_DOJ_White_Paper.pdf, accessed October 5, 2013.
2. Sam Stein, "DOJ Drones Paper: Obama's Second Term Cabinet, Agenda Faces New Scrutiny," *Huffington Post,* upd. February 5, 2013, http://www.huffingtonpost.com/2013/02/04/doj-drones-paper_n_2619582.html.
3. John O. Brennan "The Ethics and Efficacy of the President's Counterterrorism Strategy," full remarks as prepared for delivery, April 30, 2012, video and transcript available from the Wilson Center, http://www.wilsoncenter.org/event/the-efficacy-and-ethics-us-counterterrorism-strategy.
4. The United States Department of Justice, "Attorney General Eric Holder Speaks at Northwestern University School of Law," remarks as prepared for delivery, March 5, 2012, http://www.justice.gov/iso/opa/ag/speeches/2012/ag-speech-1203051.html.
5. American Civil Liberties Union, "ACLU Comment on Eric Holder Speech on Targeted Killing Program," March 5, 2012, https://www.aclu.org/national-security/aclu-comment-eric-holder-speech-targeted-killing-program.
6. Eric H. Holder Jr., letter to "The Honorable Rand Paul," March 4, 2013, http://www.paul.senate.gov/files/documents/BrennanHolderResponse.pdf.
7. Stephen D. Kelly, letter to the Honorable Rand Paul, July 19, 2013, http://www.paul.senate.gov/files/documents/071913FBIresponse.pdf, 1–2.
8. Ibid., 1.
9. Ibid., 2.
10. Mark Mazzetti, Charlie Savage, and Scott Shane, "How a U.S. Citizen Came to Be in America's Cross Hairs," *New York Times,* March 9, 2013, http://www.nytimes.com/2013/03/10/world/middleeast/anwar-al-awlaki-a-us-citizen-in-americas-cross-hairs.html.
11. Tom Junod, "Obama's Administration Killed a 16-Year-Old American and Didn't Say Anything About It. This Is Justice?" *Esquire: The Politics Blog* August 2012, http://www.esquire.com/blogs/politics/abdulrahman-al-awlaki-death-10470891.
12. Mazzetti, Savage, and Shane, "How a U.S. Citizen Came to Be in America's Cross Hairs."
13. Michael Martinez, "U.S. Drone Killing of American al-Awlaki Prompts Legal, Moral Debate," CNN, September 30, 2011, http://www.cnn.com/2011/09/30/politics/targeting-us-citizens/.
14. Michael Martinez, "U.S. Drone Killing of American al-Awlaki Prompts Legal, Moral Debate," CNN, September 30, 2011, http://www.cnn.com/2011/09/30/politics/targeting-us-citizens/.
15. Simon McCormack, "Drones Targeting Chris Dorner? LAPD Won't Confirm UK Report," *Huff Post* Crime, February 11, 2013, http://www.huffingtonpost.com/2013/02/11/christopher-dorner-drones_n_2663871.html.
16. *Daily Mail* reporter, "Meet the North Dakota Family of Anti-Government Separatists Busted by Cops Using a Predator Drone . . . After 'Stealing Six Cows,'" *Mail Online,* upd. Dec. 13, 2011, http://www.dailymail.co.uk/news/article-2073248/Local-cops-used-Predator-drone-arrest-North-Dakota-farm-family-stealing-6-cows.html.

17. Ryan Gallagher, "Did a Surveillance Drone Help in the Arrest of a North Dakota Farmer?" *Future Tense* (blog), June 12, 2012, http://www.slate.com/blogs/future_tense/2012/06/12/rodney_brossart_north_dakota_farmer_arrested_in_case_involving_predator_surveillance_drone_.html.

18. *Daily Mail* reporter, "Meet the North Dakota Family of Anti-Government Separatists Busted by Cops Using a Predator Drone."

19. Gallagher, "Did a Surveillance Drone Help in the Arrest of a North Dakota Farmer?"

20. Jason Koebler, "Court Upholds Domestic Drone Use in Arrest of American Citizen," *U.S. News & World Report*, August 2, 2012, http://www.usnews.com/news/articles/2012/08/02/court-upholds-domestic-drone-use-in-arrest-of-american-citizen.

21. Ethan Rosenberg, "Report: FBI Spent $3 Million on Drones," *U.S. News & World Report*, September 27, 2013, http://www.usnews.com/news/newsgram/articles/2013/09/27/report-fbi-spent-3-million-on-drones.

22. Associated Press, "Justice Department Has Spent Nearly $5 Million on Drones, Watchdog Report Reveals," September 26, 2013, Fox News Politics, http://www.foxnews.com/politics/2013/09/26/justice-department-has-spent-nearly-5-million-on-drones-watchdog-report-reveals/.

23. Kimberly Dvorak, "Homeland Security Increasingly Lending Drones to Local Police," *Washington Times*, December 10, 2012, http://www.washingtontimes.com/news/2012/dec/10/homeland-security-increasingly-loaning-drones-to-l/.

24. Hunter Stuart, "Drone List Released by FAA Shows Which Police Departments Want to Fly Unmanned Aerial Vehicles," *Huff Post Politics*, upd. February 9, 2013, http://www.huffingtonpost.com/2013/02/08/drone-list-domestic-police-law-enforcement-surveillance_n_2647530.html.

25. Electronic Frontier Foundation, "FAA List of Certificates of Authorizations (COAs)," from EFF's Freedom of Information Act request to FAA, https://www.eff.org/document/faa-list-certificates-authorizations-coas.

26. Associated Press, "K-State Sees Role for Drones in Agriculture: Unmanned Aircraft Could Help Farmers Pinpoint Problem Areas," July 6, 2013, *Topeka Capital-Journal*, http://cjonline.com/news/2013-07-06/k-state-sees-role-drones-agriculture.

27. Pete Kasperowicz, "GOP Looks to Block EPA from Using Drones to Enforce Clean Water Rules," *The Hill: Floor Action* blog, June 20, 2012, http://thehill.com/blogs/floor-action/house/233741-gop-looks-to-block-epa-drone-surveillance-of-farms.

28. Congressional Budget Office, "H.R. 5961: Farmer's Privacy Act of 2012," September 12, 2012, http://www.cbo.gov/publication/43583.

29. The Library of Congress, "Bill Summary & Status, 112th Congress (2011–2012), H.R. 5961: CRS Summary," http://thomas.loc.gov/cgi-bin/bdquery/z?d112:HR05961:@@@D&summ2=m&, accessed December 16, 2012.

30. U.S. Environmental Protection Agency, EPA Science Inventory, "Landscape Characterization and Change Detection Methods Development Research (2005–2007)," http://cfpub.epa.gov/si/si_public_record_report.cfm?dirEntryId=11068, accessed October 6, 2013.

31. Ibid.

32. Alex Davies, "The FAA Has Shut Down 2 Journalism School Drone Programs," *Business Insider*, August 23, 2013, http://www.businessinsider.com/faa-ends-journalism-school-drone-use-2013-8.

33. Ryan Koronowski, "FAA Approves Use of Drones By ConocoPhillips to Monitor Oil Drilling Activities in Alaska," *ClimateProgress*, August 26, 2013, http://thinkprogress.org/climate/2013/08/26/2524731/drones-conocophillips-alaska/.

34. William Tapscott, "America's Smallest Military Spy Drone Can Land on Your Window Sill," *Yahoo! Voices*, February 19, 2011, http://voices.yahoo.com/americas-smallest-military-spy-drone-land-your-7895750.html.

35. *Popular Science*, "Robot Hummingbird Spy Drone Flies for Eight Minutes, Spies on Bad Guys," Fox News, February 18, 2011, http://www.foxnews.com/tech/2011/02/18/robot-hummingbird-spy-drone-flies-minutes-spies-bad-guys/.

36. Caroline Perry, "Robotic Insects Make First Controlled Flight," *Harvard Gazette*, May 2, 2013, http://news.harvard.edu/gazette/story/2013/05/robotic-insects-make-first-controlled-flight/.

37. Steven Poole, "Drones the Size of Bees: Good or Evil?" *Guardian*, June 14, 2013, http://www. theguardian.com/commentisfree/2013/jun/14/drones-size-bees-good-evil.

38. Kathryn A. Wolfe, "Dianne Feinstein Spots Drone Inches From Face," Politico, January, 15, 2014.

12: ORWELLIAN TECHNOLOGY IS NOW THE NORM

1. Homeland Security Newswire, "Hand Scanners as Mark of the Beast," September 30, 2013, http://www.homelandsecuritynewswire.com/dr20130930-hand-scanners-as-mark-of-the-beast.

2. Sarah Rich, "Palm Scanners Quicken Meal Purchases in Georgia High Schools," Government Technology, August 13, 2013, http://www.govtech.com/education/Palm-Scanners-Quicken-Meal-Purchases-in-Georgia-High-Schools.html.

3. Matt Roush, "Intelligent Street Lamps to Debut Friday," CBS Detroit, October 23, 2011, http://detroit.cbslocal.com/2011/10/23/225836/.

4. Daniel Miller, "Big Brother is Watching: Fears over 'Homeland Security' Streetlights That Can Record Your Conversations and Track Your Movements," *Daily Mail*, October 27, 2011, http://www.dailymail.co.uk/news/article-2054177/Big-Brother-watching-New-street-lights-Homeland-Security-applications-including-speakers-video-surveillance-emergency-alerts.html.

5. Erica Ritz, "Outrage: Fla. Schools Conduct Iris Scans on Children Without Parental Consent," *The Blaze*, May 30, 2013, http://www.theblaze.com/stories/2013/05/30/outrage-fla-schools-conduct-iris-scans-on-children-without-parental-consent/.

6. Chris Matyszczyk, "Schools Iris-Scanned Students Without Telling Parents," CNET, June 17, 2013, http://news.cnet.com/8301-17852_3-57589718-71/school-iris-scanned-students-without-telling-parents/.

7. Ritz, "Outrage."

8. Laurie Segall and Erica Fink, "Iris Scans Are the New School IDs," *CNN Money*, July 11, 2013, http://money.cnn.com/2013/07/11/technology/security/iris-scanning-school/.

9. Judy Longshaw, contact, "Winthrop Tests Iris Scan Technology and Is Featured on CNNMoney," Winthrop University, July 10, 2013, http://www.winthrop.edu/news-events/article.aspx?id=30599.

10. Keach Hagey, "Schools to Get Face-Remembering Cameras," CBS, February 11, 2009, http://www.cbsnews.com/news/schools-to-get-face-remembering-cameras/.

11. Thomas Frank, "School Security Cameras Go Cutting Edge," USA Today, November 1, 2007, http://usatoday30.usatoday.com/news/nation/2007-11-01-school-cameras_N.htm.

12. Alexei Oreskovic, "Facebook Considers Adding Profile Photos to Facial Recognition," Reuters, August 29, 2013, http://www.reuters.com/article/2013/08/29/us-facebook-facial-idUSBRE97S0UZ20130829.

13. Aurindom Mukherjee and Gerry Shih, "FTC to Scrutinize New Facebook Facial Recognition Feature," Reuters, September 11, 2013, http://www.reuters.com/article/2013/09/12/net-us-facebook-privacy-idUSBRE98B01V20130912.

14. Ibid.

15. Craig Timberg and Ellen Nakashima,"State-photo ID Databases Become Troves for Police," *Washington Post*, June 16, 2013, http://articles.washingtonpost.com/2013-06-16/business/40012903_1_databases-facial-recognition-systems-searches.

16. Ibid.

17. "DHS Developing Facial-Scanning Technology for Police," Fox News, Politics, August 21, 2013, http://www.foxnews.com/politics/2013/08/21/dhs-developing-facial-scanning-technology-for-police/.

18. Darlene Storm, "Homeland Security Testing Facial Recognition at Hockey Game," *ComputerWorld* (blog), September 16, 2013, http://blogs.computerworld.com/privacy/22821/homeland-security-testing-facial-recognition-hockey-game.

19. Sameer Padania, "How to Defend Yourself against Facial Recognition Technology," PBS, June 18, 2012, http://www.pbs.org/mediashift/2012/06/how-to-defend-yourself-against-facial-recognition-technology170/.

20. Lisa Myers, "An Explanation of Voice Biometrics," SANS Institute InfoSec Reading Room, April 19, 2004, https://www.sans.org/reading-room/whitepapers/authentication/exploration-voice-biometrics-1436.

21. "Touchless Fingerprint Products: Short Range Operation," the website of IDair, http://www.idairco.com/products/, accessed October 15, 2013.

22. Diane Macedo, "X-Ray Vans, Security Measure or Invasion of Privacy?" Fox News, October 22, 2010, http://www.foxnews.com/scitech/2010/10/19/x-ray-vans-security-measure-invasion-privacy/.

23. Electronic Privacy Information Group, "EPIC v. DHS: Suspension of Body Scanner Program," http://epic.org/privacy/body_scanners/epic_v_dhs_suspension_of_body.html, accessed October 15, 2013.

24. BRS Labs, "What is AISight," http://www.brslabs.com/aisight, accessed October 17, 2013.

25. Dave Summers, "New Surveillance Technology Tracks Every Move," NBC San Diego, June 29, 2013, http://www.nbcsandiego.com/news/local/AISight-New-Surveillance-Technology-Tracking-Every-Move-213612561.html.

26. Ibid.

27. Greg Risling, "LAPD Embraces 'Predictive Policing,'" PoliceONe.com, July 1, 2012, http://www.policeone.com/police-technology/police-software/articles/5790757-LAPD-embraces-predictive-policing/.

28. Ibid.

29. Ryan Gallagher, "U.S. Cities Embrace Software to Automatically Detect 'Suspicious' Behavior," *Future Tense* (blog), June 11, 2012, http://www.slate.com/blogs/future_tense/2012/06/11/aisight_from_brs_labs_and_other_technologies_to_detect_suspicious_behavior_.html.

13: PRESIDENT ON THE LOOSE!

1. John Woolley and Gerhard Peters, "Executive Orders: Washington–Obama," American Presidency Project, upd. July 20, 2013, http://www.presidency.ucsb.edu/data/orders.php#axzz2iB7aVxa1.

2. Harold C. Relyea, *CRS Report for Congress, Presidential Directives: Background and Overview*, Congressional Research Service, upd. November 26, 2006, http://www.fas.org/sgp/crs/misc/98-611.pdf, 1.

3. Paul Veravanich, "The Propriety of President Bill Clinton's Establishment of the Grand Staircase Escalante National Monument," *Environs* 20, no. 1, accessed October 19, 2013, http://environs.law.ucdavis.edu/issues/20/1/articles/veravanich.pdf.

4. Cliff Kincaid, "Clinton's Final Dangerous Days," Aim Report, December 8, 2000, http://www.aim.org/publications/aim_report/2000/12b.html.

5. FactCheck, "Obama's Executive Orders," September 25, 2012, http://www.factcheck.org/2012/09/obamas-executive-orders/.

6. Seth Hoy, "Immigration Impact: President Obama Issued a 'Directive,' Not an 'Executive Order' or 'New Law,'" American Immigration Council, June 19, 2012, http://immigrationimpact.com/2012/06/19/president-obama-issued-a-memo-not-an-executive-order/.

7. FactCheck, "Obama's Executive Orders."

8. Michael Tanner, "Obama Encouraging Americans to Get On Welfare," *Politico*, July 18, 2012, http://www.politico.com/news/stories/0712/78680.html.

9. U.S. Government Accountability Office, "Temporary Assistance for Needy Families: Information Memorandum Constitutes Rule for the Purposes of the Congressional Review Act: B-323772," September 4, 2012, http://www.gao.gov/products/B-323772.

10. Relyea, *CRS Report for Congress: Presidential Directives*.

11. Federal Register, "Executive Orders: Learn about Executive Orders," National Archives, accessed October 19, 2013, http://www.archives.gov/federal-register/executive-orders/.

12. Vanessa K. Burrows, "Executive Orders: Issuance and Revocation," Congressional Research Service, March 25, 2010, http://www.fas.org/sgp/crs/misc/RS20846.pdf.

13. The White House, Office of the Press Secretary, "Presidential Memorandum: Presidential Determination on Trafficking in Persons," memorandum for the Secretary of State, September 17, 2013.

14. The White House, Office of the Press Secretary, "Presidential Memorandum: Power Sector Carbon Pollution Standards," memorandum for the Environmental Protection Agency, June 25, 2013, http://www.whitehouse.gov/the-press-office/2013/06/25/presidential-memorandum-power-sector-carbon-pollution-standards.

15. Shelley Welton, "Deadlines for Regulating New and Existing Power Plant Carbon Emissions Set by Obama Memo," Center for Climate Change Law, *Climate Law Blog* June 26, 2013, http://blogs.law.columbia.edu/climatechange/2013/06/26/deadlines-for-regulating-new-existing-power-plant-carbon-emissions-set-by-obama-memo/.

16. The White House, "Presidential Memorandum: Power Sector Carbon Pollution Standards."

17. PBS News Hour, "An Executive Order Puts Climate Change Up Front," November 3, 2013, http://www.pbs.org/newshour/bb/politics/july-dec13/talev_11-03.html.

18. Ibid.

19. Woolley and Peters, "Executive Orders: Washington–Obama."

20. Ibid.

21. Ibid.

22. History.com, "This Day in History: President Lincoln Suspends the Writ of Habeas Corpus During the Civil War," http://www.history.com/this-day-in-history/president-lincoln-suspends-the-writ-of-habeas-corpus-during-the-civil-war, accessed October 20, 2013.

23. Ibid.

24. David Greenberg, "Lincoln's Crackdown: Suspects Jailed. No Charges Filed. Sound Familiar?" *Slate*, November 30, 2001, http://www.slate.com/articles/news_and_politics/history_lesson/2001/11/lincolns_crackdown.html.

25. National Archives and Records Administration, "The Emancipation Proclamation," http://www.archives.gov/exhibits/featured_documents/emancipation_proclamation/, accessed October 20, 2013.

26. Woolley and Peters, "Executive Orders: Washington–Obama."

27. History.com, "This Day in History: Roosevelt Signs Executive Order 9066," http://www.history.com/this-day-in-history/fdr-signs-executive-order-9066, accessed October 20, 2013.

28. U.S. History, "America in the Second World War: Japanese-American Internment," Independence Hall Association in Philadelphia, http://www.ushistory.org/us/51e.asp, accessed October 20, 2013.

29. Tony Konkoly, "Law Power and Personality: *Korematsu v. United States*, 1944," PBS, Supreme Court History page, http://www.pbs.org/wnet/supremecourt/personality/landmark_korematsu.html, accessed October 20, 2013.

30. U.S. History, "America in the Second World War."

31. History.com, "This Day in History: Roosevelt Signs Executive Order 9066."

32. Gerhard Peters and John T. Woolley, "Franklin D. Roosevelt: 89 – Executive Order 6174 on Public Works Administration," The American Presidency Project, http://www.presidency.ucsb.edu/ws/?pid=14671, accessed October 20, 2013.

33. Virginia.edu, "Chronology: The Making of the New Deal," http://xroads.virginia.edu/~ma02/volpe/newdeal/timeline_text.html, accessed October 20, 2013.

34. Philip Scranton, "When Roosevelt Ditched the Gold Standard," Bloomberg, April 22, 2013, http://www.bloomberg.com/news/2013-04-22/when-roosevelt-ditched-the-gold-standard.html.

35. Virginia.edu, "Chronology: The Making of the New Deal."

36. Ibid.

37. Princeton.edu, "Civil Works Administration," http://www.princeton.edu/~achaney/tmve/wiki100k/docs/Civil_Works_Administration.html, accessed October 20, 2013.

38. Woolley and Peters, "Executive Orders: Washington–Obama."

39. Ibid.

40. Jeff Mason, "Obama Will Have to Rely More and More on Executive Orders," *Business Insider*, October 20, 2013, http://www.businessinsider.com/obama-will-have-to-rely-more-and-more-on-executive-orders-2013-10.

41. Jim Acosta, "Obama Looks to Bypass Congress," CNN, January 14, 2014.
42. The Claremont Institute, "Rediscovering George Washington: Lesson Plan—George Washington and the Rule of Law," PBS, http://www.pbs.org/georgewashington/classroom/rule_of_law2.html, accessed October 21, 2013.
43. Ibid.
44. Ibid.

14: THE BAFFLING WHITE HOUSE EMBRACE OF RADICAL ISLAMISM

1. Hosni Mubarak, "A Peace Plan Within Our Grasp," New York Times, August 31, 2010, http://www.nytimes.com/2010/09/01/opinion/01mubarak.html?_r=0.
2. Yolande Knell, "Egypt Crisis: President Hosni Mubarak Resigns as Leader," BBC, February 12, 2011, http://www.bbc.co.uk/news/world-middle-east-12433045.
3. Ibid.
4. Helene Cooper, Mark Landler, and Mark Mazzetti, "Sudden Split Recasts U.S. Foreign Policy," New York Times, February 2, 2011, http://www.nytimes.com/2011/02/03/world/middleeast/03diplomacy.html?pagewanted=all.
5. Ibid.
6. BBC, "Profile: Egypt's Mohammed Morsi," September 2, 2013, http://www.bbc.co.uk/news/world-middle-east-18371427.
7. Arthur Stern, "Who Is Mohamed Morsi and Why Does Egypt Hate Him So Much?" PolicyMic, July 4, 2013, http://www.policymic.com/articles/52873/who-is-mohamed-morsi-and-why-does-egypt-hate-him-so-much.
8. Dave Boyer and Ashish Kumar Sen, "Obama Congratulates Morsi on Winning Egyptian Presidency," Washington Times, June 24, 2012, http://www.washingtontimes.com/news/2012/jun/24/obama-calls-to-congratulate-morsi-an-islamist-on-w/.
9. David D. Kirkpatrick, "Clinton Visits Egypt, Carrying a Muted Pledge of Support," New York Times, July 14, 2012, http://www.nytimes.com/2012/07/15/world/middleeast/clinton-arrives-in-egypt-for-meeting-with-new-president.html.
10. Bassem Sabry, "Absolute Power: Morsi Decree Stuns Egyptians," Al-Monitor Egypt Pulse, November 22, 2012, http://www.al-monitor.com/pulse/originals/2012/al-monitor/morsi-decree-constitution-power.html.
11. Hamza Hendawi, "Morsi's Gaza Ceasefire Deal Role Secures Egypt's President as Major Player," Huff Post World, November 21, 2012, http://www.huffingtonpost.com/2012/11/21/morsi-gaza-ceasefire_n_2173589.html.
12. Abdel-Rahman Hussein, "Mohamed Morsi Indicates Judicial Decree Will be Limited," Guardian, November 26, 2012, http://www.theguardian.com/world/2012/nov/26/mohamed-morsi-decree-sovereign-matters.
13. WorldConflictReport, "McCain to U.S. Government: Stop Foreign Aids to Egypt, Morsi Dictatorship," YouTube video with accompanying story, http://www.youtube.com/watch?v=_y7nTBT_mKM, November 27, 2012.
14. Martin Chulov, "Egypt's Ousting of Mohamed Morsi Was a Coup, Says John McCain," Guardian, August 6, 2013, http://www.theguardian.com/world/2013/aug/06/john-mccain-egypt-mohamed-morsi-coup.
15. Michael R. Gordon and Kareem Fahim, "Kerry Says Egypt's Military Was 'Restoring Democracy' in Ousting Morsi," New York Times, August 1, 2013, http://www.nytimes.com/2013/08/02/world/middleeast/egypt-warns-morsi-supporters-to-end-protests.html.
16. Fox News, "Muslim Brotherhood Envoys Met with White House Officials in D.C.," April 5, 2012, Politics, http://www.foxnews.com/politics/2012/04/05/muslim-brotherhood-envoys-met-with-white-house-officials-in-dc/.
17. Associated Press, "Senator John Kerry Meets with Egypt's Muslim Brotherhood in Cairo," December 10, 2011, Fox News, http://www.foxnews.com/politics/2011/12/10/senator-john-kerry-meets-with-egypts-muslim-brotherhood-in-cairo/.
18. Michael Terheyden, "Persecution of Christian Copts in Egypt on Rise as Muslim Brotherhood Consolidates Power," Catholic Online, August 27, 2012, http://www.catholic.org/international/international_story.php?id=47348.

19. Raymond Ibrahim, "Muslim Persecution of Christians, 2012: [Egypt's] Muslim Brotherhood Prevented the Copts, at Gunpoint, from Voting," Gatestone Institute, July 26, 2012, http://www.gatestoneinstitute.org/3203/muslim-persecution-of-christians-june-2012.

20. Amira Nowaira, "The Muslim Brotherhood Has Shown Its Contempt for Women," *Guardian*, March 18, 2013, http://www.theguardian.com/commentisfree/2013/mar/18/muslim-brotherhood-rejects-egyptian-womens-rights.

21. Muslim Brotherhood, "Muslim Brotherhood Statement Denouncing UN Women Declaration for Violating Sharia Principles," Ikhwan Web: The Muslim Brotherhood's Official English website, March 14, 2013, http://www.ikhwanweb.com/article.php?id=30731.

22. Ibid.

23. David D. Kirkpatrick and Mayy El Sheikh, "Muslim Brotherhood Statement on Women Stirs Liberals' Fears," *New York Times*, March 14, 2013, http://www.nytimes.com/2013/03/15/world/middleeast/muslim-brotherhoods-words-on-women-stir-liberal-fears.html.

24. Jonathan S. Tobin, "Obama Subsidizes Egyptian War on Women," *Commentary* magazine, March 15, 2013, http://www.commentarymagazine.com/2013/03/15/obama-subsidizes-egyptian-war-on-women-muslim-brotherhood/.

25. Luke Harding, "WikiLeaks Cables Show Close U.S. Relationship with Egyptian President," *Guardian*, January 28, 2011, http://www.theguardian.com/world/2011/jan/28/wikileaks-cairo-cables-egypt-president.

26. Robert Spencer, "The Muslim Brotherhood President," *FrontPage Magazine*, October 10, 2013, http://www.frontpagemag.com/2013/robert-spencer/the-muslim-brotherhood-president/.

27. BBC, "Profile: Egypt's Muslim Brotherhood," http://www.bbc.co.uk/news/world-middle-east-12313405, August 20, 2013.

28. Ibid.

29. Bryony Jones and Susannah Cullinane, "What Is the Muslim Brotherhood?" CNN, July 3, 2013, http://www.cnn.com/2013/07/03/world/africa/egypt-muslim-brotherhood-explainer/.

30. BBC, "Profile: Egypt's Muslim Brotherhood."

31. Ibid.

32. Ibid.

33. Ibid.

34. Julie Spears, "Muslim Brothers: Muslim Brotherhood," FAS Intelligence Resource Program, January 8, 2002, https://www.fas.org/irp/world/para/mb.htm.

35. Discover the Networks, "Muslim Brotherhood," http://www.discoverthenetworks.org/printgroupProfile.asp?grpid=6386, accessed October 23, 2013.

36. Ibid.

37. Ibid.

38. Jones and Cullinane, "What Is the Muslim Brotherhood?"

39. Ibid.

40. Discover the Networks, "Muslim Brotherhood."

41. David D. Kirkpatrick, "Egyptian Court Shuts Down the Muslim Brotherhood and Seizes Its Assets," *New York Times*, September 23, 2013, http://www.nytimes.com/2013/09/24/world/middleeast/egyptian-court-bans-muslim-brotherhood.html.

42. Ryan Mauro, "Obama's Shout-Out to Muslim Brotherhood Entity," *FrontPage Magazine*, September 5, 2013, http://www.frontpagemag.com/2013/ryan-mauro/unashamed-president-obama-thanks-muslim-brotherhood-entity/.

43. Salma Abdelaziz and Steve Almasy, "Egypt's interim Cabinet officially labels Muslim Brotherhood a terrorist group," December 25, 2013, http://www.cnn.com/2013/12/25/world/africa/egypt-muslim-brotherhood-terrorism/index.html.

44. Mauro, "Obama's Shout-Out to Muslim Brotherhood."

45. Ryan Mauro, "How the Muslim Brotherhood Is Winning in America," The Clarion Project, October 20, 2013, http://www.clarionproject.org/analysis/how-muslim-brotherhood-winning-america.

46. Erick Stakelbeck, "Muslim Brotherhood Influence Reaches White House," CBN News, August 28, 2013, http://www.cbn.com/cbnnews/us/2013/August/Muslim-Brotherhood-Influence-Reaches-White-House/.

47. Ibid.

48. Mauro, "How the Muslim Brotherhood Is Winning in America."
49. Ibid.

15: POLITICAL CORRECTNESS IS KILLING US—REALLY

1. Dana Priest, "Fort Hood Suspect Warned of Threats Within the Ranks," *Washington Post*, November 10, 2009, http://articles.washingtonpost.com/2009-11-10/news/36855074_1_nidal-m-hasan-fort-hood-muslim-soldiers.
2. Jon Swaine, "Fort Hood Shooter Nidal Hasan 'Left Free' to Kill," *Telegraph*, August 4, 2013, http://www.telegraph.co.uk/news/worldnews/northamerica/usa/10220449/Fort-Hood-shooter-Nidal-Hasan-left-free-to-kill.html.
3. Priest, "Fort Hood Suspect Warned of Threats Within the Ranks."
4. Swaine, "Fort Hood Shooter Nidal Hasan 'Left Free' to Kill."
5. Ibid.
6. Priest, "Fort Hood Suspect Warned of Threats Within the Ranks."
7. Manny Fernandez, "Fort Hood Gunman Told His Superiors of Concerns," *New York Times*, August 20, 2013, http://www.nytimes.com/2013/08/21/us/fort-hood-gunman-nidal-malik-hasan.html?_r=0&gwh=115818C7E47FEF41582C8F64E275BBC9&gwt=pay.
8. Ibid.
9. Swaine, "Fort Hood Shooter Nidal Hasan 'Left Free' to Kill."
10. Chelsea J. Carter,"Nidal Hasan Convicted in Fort Hood Shootings; Jurors Can Decide Death," August 23, 2013, CNN Justice, http://www.cnn.com/2013/08/23/justice/nidal-hasan-court-martial-friday/.
11. Carol Cratty, "FBI Official: Hasan Should Have Been Asked about Emails with Radical Cleric," CNN, August 2, 2012, http://www.cnn.com/2012/08/01/politics/hasan-fbi/.
12. Ibid.
13. Fox News, "Fort Hood Report Faults FBI for Missteps in Hasan Review, Cites Political Correctness," Fox News Politics, July 20, 2012, http://www.foxnews.com/politics/2012/07/19/fort-hood-report-recommends-many-changes-for-fbi-no-disciplinary-action/.
14. Lolita C. Baldor and Eileen Sullivan, "Fort Hood Shooting: FBI Ignored Evidence Against Nidal Hasan for Political Correctness, Report Says," *HuffPost* Crime, July 19, 2012, http://www.huffingtonpost.com/2012/07/19/fort-hood-shooting-fbi-nidal-hasan-political-correctness_n_1685653.html.
15. Michael Daly, "Nidal Hasan's Murders Termed 'Workplace Violence' by U.S.," *Daily Beast*, August 6, 2013, http://www.thedailybeast.com/articles/2013/08/06/nidal-hasan-s-murders-termed-workplace-violence-by-u-s.html.
16. Rick Moran, "Major Nidal Hasan Guilty on All Counts in 'Workplace Violence' Incident," *PJ Tatler*, August 23, 2013, http://pjmedia.com/tatler/2013/08/23/major-nidal-hasan-guilty-on-all-counts-in-workplace-violence-incident/.
17. BBC, "Salman Rushdie: Satanic Verses 'Would Not Be Published Today,'" BBC News Entertainment & Arts, September 17, 2012, http://www.bbc.co.uk/news/entertainment-arts-19600879.
18. Ibid.
19. John Hall, "Channel 4 Cancels Controversial Screening of Islam: The Untold Story Documentary after Presenter Tom Holland Is Threatened," *Independent* (UK), September 11, 2012, http://www.independent.co.uk/arts-entertainment/tv/news/channel-4-cancels-controversial-screening-of-islam-the-untold-story-documentary-after-presenter-tom-holland-is-threatened-8125641.html.
20. Channel 4, "Islam: The Untold Story," http://www.channel4.com/programmes/islam-the-untold-story, accessed October 29, 2013.
21. Hall, "Channel 4 Cancels Controversial Screening of Islam."
22. Dave Itzkoff, "'South Park' Episode Altered after Muslim Group's Warning," *New York Times*, Television, April 22, 2010, http://www.nytimes.com/2010/04/23/arts/television/23park.html?gwh=708466EFDC609C535A225FBBB484263E&gwt=pay.
23. Ibid.

24. Theodore Dalrymple, "Why Theo Van Gogh Was Murdered," *City Journal*, November 15, 2004, http://www.city-journal.org/html/eon_11_15_04td.html.
25. Itzkoff, "'South Park' Episode Altered After Muslim Group's Warning."
26. Angelique Chrisafis, "French Magazine Offices Petrol-Bombed after It Prints Muhammed Cartoon," *Guardian*, November 2, 2011, http://www.theguardian.com/world/2011/nov/02/french-magazine-bomb-muhammad-cartoon.
27. Ibid.
28. Associated Press, "French Satirical Magazine Office Fire Bombed Ahead of 'Muhammed Edition,'" Fox News, November 2, 2011, http://www.foxnews.com/world/2011/11/02/french-satirical-magazine-office-fire-bombed-ahead-muhammad-edition/.
29. Stephen Castle, "Mohamed Cartoons Provoke Bomb Threats against Danish Newspaper," *Independent* (UK), February 1, 2006, http://www.independent.co.uk/news/world/europe/mohamed-cartoons-provoke-bomb-threats-against-danish-newspaper-465246.html.
30. Stephanie Sy, "Bomb-Shaped Turban Cartoons Upset Muslims," ABC News, February 2, 2006, http://abcnews.go.com/International/story?id=1570095.
31. Ibid.
32. Castle, "Mohamed Cartoons Provoke Bomb Threats Against Danish Newspaper."
33. PBS Newshour, "The Art of Controversy," transcript of show on October 8, 1999, http://www.pbs.org/newshour/bb/entertainment/july-dec99/art_10-8a.html.
34. Ibid.
35. Matthew Brooks and Seth Leibsohn, "Virgin Dung: Art as Religious Bigotry," *Jewish World Review*, September 30, 1999, http://www.jewishworldreview.com/0999/virgin.dung.html.
36. Todd Starnes, "WH Silent over Demands to Denounce 'Piss Christ' Artwork," Fox News, September 21, 2012, http://radio.foxnews.com/toddstarnes/top-stories/wh-silent-over-demands-to-denounce-piss-christ-artwork.html.
37. Ibid.
38. Fox News, "Rep. Rogers Slams State Department for Pakistan Ads Denouncing Anti-Islamic Film," September 23, 2012, http://www.foxnews.com/politics/2012/09/23/rep-rogers-us-running-anti-islamic-film-ads-in-pakistan-horrible-idea/.
39. Ibid.
40. Ibid.
41. Andrew Kirell, "Red Eye Panel Gets Heated over Whether Feds Jailed Anti-Muslim Filmmaker as 'Scapegoat' for Benghazi," Mediaite, November 9, 2012, http://www.mediaite.com/tv/red-eye-panel-gets-heated-over-whether-feds-jailed-anti-muslim-filmmaker-as-scapegoat-for-benghazi/.
42. Lloyd Billingsley, "Tsarnaev, Hasan and Deadly Political Correctness," *FrontPage Magazine*, July 12, 2013, http://www.frontpagemag.com/2013/lloyd-billingsley/tsarnaev-hasan-and-deadly-political-correctness/.
43. "Remarks of the Honorable Rudolph W. Giuliani before the House Homeland Security Committee," July 10, 2013, http://docs.house.gov/meetings/HM/HM00/20130710/101108/HHRG-113-HM00-Wstate-GiulianiR-20130710.pdf.
44. Toby Harnden, "Barack Obama: NASA Must Try to Make Muslims 'Feel Good,'" *Telegraph*, July 6, 2010, http://www.telegraph.co.uk/science/space/7875584/Barack-Obama-Nasa-must-try-to-make-Muslims-feel-good.html.
45. Ibid.
46. Jake Tapper, "White House, NASA Defend Comments About NASA Outreach to Muslim World Criticized by Conservatives," *Political Punch* (blog), July 6, 2010, http://abcnews.go.com/blogs/politics/2010/07/white-house-nasa-defend-comments-about-nasa-outreach-to-muslim-world-criticized-by-conservatives/.
47. Meira Svirsky, "Entire Military, Pentagon Reviews All Islamic Training Materials," The Clarion Project, April 29, 2012, http://www.clarionproject.org/news/entire-military-pentagon-reviews-all-islamic-training-materials.
48. Omar Sacirbey, "Pentagon Probes Training Course on Islam," *Washington Post*, April 27, 2012, http://articles.washingtonpost.com/2012-04-27/national/35451893_1_joint-forces-staff-college-inquiry-report-islamic.
49. Ibid.

50. Jamie Glazov, "The Complete Infidel's Guide to the Koran," *FrontPage Magazine*, October 7, 2009, http://www.frontpagemag.com/2009/jamie-glazov/the-complete-infidels-guide-to-the-koran-by-jamie-glazov/.

51. The Center for the Study of Political Islam, "Political Islam: The Five Principles," http://www.politicalislam.com/principles/pages/five-principles/, accessed November 1, 2013.

52. Facebook, "CAIR: D.C. DMV Modifies Photo Policy Over Muslim Concerns," April 14, 2010, https://www.facebook.com/note.php?note_id=383868559441.

53. CAIR: Council on American-Islamic Relations Research Center, "Religious Accommodation in Driver's License Photographs: A Review of Code, Policies and Practices in the 50 States," CAIR, October 31, 2005, http://moritzlaw.osu.edu/electionlaw/litigation/documents/LWVJ.pdf.

54. Fox News, "Witnesses at King Hearing Say America 'Failing' to Confront Radical Islam," March 10, 2011, http://www.foxnews.com/politics/2011/03/10/king-draws-firing-radicalization-hearings-majority-supports-discussion/.

55. Ibid.

56. Council on American-Islamic Relations, "Rep. Peter King's Anti-Muslim Congressional Hearings," June 2012, http://www.cair.com/islamophobia/legislating-fear-2013-report/14-islamophobia/11638-rep-peter-king-s-anti-muslim-congressional-hearings.html, upd. February 15, 2013.

57. Committee on Homeland Security, "'The American-Muslim Response to Hearings on Radicalization Within Their Community,' June 20, 2012: The Radicalization of Muslim-Americans: The Committee on Homeland Security's Investigation of the Continuing Threat: Executive Summary and Key Findings," http://homeland.house.gov/sites/homeland.house.gov/files/06-20-12-Report.pdf.

58. Deborah Weiss, "International Effort by the OIC to Criminalize Criticism of Islam," The Clarion Project, October 24, 2013, http://www.clarionproject.org/analysis/international-effort-oic-criminize-criticism-islam.

59. Ibid.

60. Max Fisher, "What the Muslim World Believes, on Everything from Alcohol to Honor Killings, in 8 Maps, 5 Charts," *WorldViews* (blog), May 2, 2013, http://www.washingtonpost.com/blogs/worldviews/wp/2013/05/02/what-the-muslim-world-believes-on-everything-from-alcohol-to-honor-killings-in-8-maps-and-4-charts/.

61. Ibid.

62. James Bell et al., *The World's Muslims: Religion, Politics and Society* (Washington, DC: Pew Research Center's Forum on Religion & Public Life, April 30, 2013), http://www.pewforum.org/files/2013/04/worlds-muslims-religion-politics-society-full-report.pdf.

63. Ibid.

64. Ibid.

65. Ibid.

66. Ibid.

67. Ibid.

68. Ibid.

16: TRAINING THE NEXT GENERATION THAT GOVERNMENT IS GOD

1. Marian Burrows, "Obamas to Plant Vegetable Garden at White House," *New York Times*, March 19, 2009, http://www.nytimes.com/2009/03/20/dining/20garden.html?_r=0.

2. The White House, Office of the First Lady, "First Lady Michelle Obama Launches Let's Move: America's Move to Raise a Healthier Generation of Kids," February 9, 2010, http://www.whitehouse.gov/the-press-office/first-lady-michelle-obama-launches-lets-move-americas-move-raise-a-healthier-genera.

3. Ibid.

4. Ibid.

5. Ibid.

6. WhiteHouse.gov, "Let's Move: Child Nutrition Reauthorization, Healthy Hunger-Free Kids Act of 2010," http://www.whitehouse.gov/sites/default/files/Child_Nutrition_Fact_Sheet_12_10_10.pdf, accessed November 3, 2013.

7. The White House, Office of the Press Secretary, "President Obama Signs Healthy, Hunger-Free Kids Act of 2010 into Law," December 13, 2010, http://www.whitehouse.gov/the-press-office/2010/12/13/president-obama-signs-healthy-hunger-free-kids-act-2010-law.

8. The Shop Monticello, *American Grown*," Item 206240, http://www.monticelloshop.org/206240.html?gclid=CMrqt4CwyboCFQyZ4Aod_gEAOQ, accessed November 3, 2013.

9. Eric Owens, "Kentucky Students to First Lady Michelle Obama: Your Food 'Tastes Like Vomit,'" *Daily Caller*, August 27, 2013, http://dailycaller.com/2013/08/27/kentucky-students-to-first-lady-michelle-obama-your-food-tastes-like-vomit/.

10. Amy Bingham via World News, "Snacks: The USDA's Solution to Student's Healthy Lunch Complaints," ABC News, September 26, 2012, http://abcnews.go.com/Politics/OTUS/snacks-usdas-solution-healthy-school-lunch-protests/story?id=17324285.

11. News10 ABC, "Burnt Hills–Ballston Lake schools leave national lunch program," July 10, 2013, http://www.news10.com/story/22804698/burnt-hills-ballston-lake-schools-leave-national-lunch-program.

12. Darlene Superville, "Michelle Obama Calls Food Marketing Summit to Ask Companies to Stop Advertising Unhealthy Foods to Kids," *Huff Post*, Parents, September 18, 2013, http://www.huffingtonpost.com/2013/09/18/michelle-obama-food-marketing_n_3948115.html.

13. Darlene Superville, "'Sesame Street' Characters Join Michelle Obama's Healthy Food Campaign," *Christian Science Monitor*, November 1, 2013, http://www.csmonitor.com/The-Culture/Family/2013/1101/Sesame-Street-characters-join-Michelle-Obama-s-healthy-food-campaign.

14. Ibid.

15. Sara Burrows, "Preschooler's Homemade Lunch Replaced With Cafeteria 'Nuggets,'" *Carolina Journal Online*, February 14, 2012, http://www.carolinajournal.com/exclusives/display_exclusive.html?id=8762.

16. Ibid.

17. Matt Willoughby, "State Inspectors Searching Children's Lunch Boxes: 'This Isn't China, Is it?'" Civitas Institute, February 14, 2012, http://www.nccivitas.org/2012/state-inspectors-searching-childrens-lunch-boxes-this-isnt-china-is-it/.

18. Jonathon M. Seidl, "N.C. 'Inspector' Sends Girl's Lunch Home after Determining It's Not Healthy Enough," *The Blaze*, February 14, 2012, http://www.theblaze.com/stories/2012/02/14/n-c-food-inspector-sends-girls-lunch-home-after-determining-its-not-healthy-enough/.

19. Willoughby, "State Inspectors Searching Children's Lunch Boxes."

20. Brian W. Walsh, "17-Year-Old Ashley's So-Called 'Crime?' A Paring Knife in Her Lunch Sack," The Heritage Foundation, February 4, 2011, http://www.heritage.org/research/commentary/2011/02/17-yearold-ashleys-socalled-crime-a-paring-knife-in-her-lunch-sack.

21. WRAL.com, "School Board: Media 'Inaccurate about Student's Suspension," December 31, 2010, http://www.wral.com/news/education/story/8860447/.

22. Walsh, "17-Year-Old Ashley's So-Called 'Crime?'"

23. FoxNews.com. "Small Knife in Lunchbox Gets N.C. Student Suspended, Charged with Weapon Possession," December 29, 2010, http://www.foxnews.com/us/2010/12/29/nc-high-school-senior-suspended-charged-possesion-small-knife-lunchbox/.

24. Associated Press, "Fort Myers Honor Student Arrested Under Zero-Tolerance Policy," Fox News, May 23, 2001, http://www.foxnews.com/story/2001/05/23/fort-myers-honor-student-arrested-under-zero-tolerance-policy/.

25. Walsh, "17-Year-Old Ashley's So-Called 'Crime?'"

26. Associated Press, "Fort Myers Honor Student Arrested under Zero-Tolerance Policy."

27. Joe Burris, "Attempt to Expunge Boy's Suspension over Pastry Denied," *Baltimore Sun*, June 10, 2013, http://articles.baltimoresun.com/2013-06-10/news/bs-md-ar-pastry-student-appeal-20130610_1_county-school-board-pastry-school-official.

28. Anne McNamara, "Boy Who Held Pencil Like Gun Suspended," Fox43TV,http://www.fox43tv.com/news/local/suffolk/boy-who-held-pencil-like-gun-suspended upd. June 17, 2013.

29. Ibid.
30. Rebecca Klein, "School Gun Suspension: 2nd-Grade Boys, Booted for Pointing Pencils, Return to Class," *Huff Post*, Parents, May 8, 2013, http://www.huffingtonpost.com/2013/05/08/school-gun-suspension-suffolk-virginia-pencils_n_3239414.html.
31. CNN, "Toy Gun Causes Disturbance on Palmer School Bus," May 28, 2013, WHDH 7 News, http://www1.whdh.com/news/articles/local/western-ma/10010747200553/toy-gun-causes-disturbance-on-palmer-school-bus/.
32. WGGB (Palmer, MA), "Toy Gun Causes Disturbance on Palmer School Bus," May 24, 2013, http://www.wggb.com/2013/05/24/toy-gun-causes-disturbance-on-palmer-elementary-school-bus/.
33. Ibid.
34. CNN, "Toy Gun Causes Disturbance on Palmer School Bus."
35. Meredith Edwards, "Pennsylvania Girl, 5, Suspended for Talk of 'Shooting' a Hello Kitty 'Bubble Gun,'" CNN, January 22, 2013, http://www.cnn.com/2013/01/21/us/pennsylvania-girl-suspended/.
36. Ibid.
37. Ty Beaver, "Pasco School District Overturns 6-Year-Old's Suspension for Discussing Toy Gun," *Tri-City Herald*, March 7, 2013, http://www.tri-cityherald.com/2013/03/07/2302285/pasco-school-district-overturns.html.
38. Sara Noble, "Pasco County Suspends 6-Year-Old for Saying 'Gun,'" *Independent Sentinel*, March 7, 2013, http://www.independentsentinel.com/pasco-county-suspends-6-year-old-for-saying-gun/.
39. Beaver, "Pasco School District Overturns 6-Year-Old's Suspension for Discussing Toy Gun."
40. Ibid.
41. Ibid.
42. Tommy Christopher, "Deaf Child 'Forced' to Change Gun-Like Signing Name Not Actually Forced to Change Name," Mediaite, June 4, 2013, http://www.mediaite.com/online/deaf-child-forced-to-change-gun-like-signing-name-not-actually-forced-to-change-name/.
43. Jim Gold, "Deaf Child's Sign Language Name Looks Too Much Like Gun, Parent Says School Told Him," NBC News, August 28, 2012, http://usnews.nbcnews.com/_news/2012/08/28/13531342-deaf-childs-sign-language-name-looks-too-much-like-gun-parent-says-school-told-him.
44. Ibid.
45. Ibid.
46. Steven Ertelt, "Chicago Public Schools Mandate Sex Ed Classes for Kindergarten Students," LifeNews.com, August 30, 2013, http://www.lifenews.com/2013/08/30/chicago-public-schools-mandate-sex-ed-classes-for-kindergarten-students/.
47. Ibid.
48. Susan Berry, "Chicago Public Schools Mandate Sex Ed For Kindergartners," Breitbart, August 30, 2013, http://www.breitbart.com/Big-Government/2013/08/30/Chicago-Public-Schools-Mandate-Sex-Ed-for-Kindergartners.
49. Ibid.
50. Mary C. Tillotson, "Massachusetts Schools Adopt New Transgender Policy," The Heartland Institute, March 22, 2013, http://news.heartland.org/newspaper-article/2013/03/22/massachusetts-schools-adopt-new-transgender-policy.
51. Ibid.
52. Chris Nichols, "New York Schools May Close For Muslim Holidays," *The Signal: Predictions from Yahoo! News*, October 18, 2013, http://news.yahoo.com/new-york-schools-may-close-for-muslim-holidays-185517679.html.
53. Donna St. George, "In Push for Muslim School Holiday, Some Montgomery Students Will Stay Home," *Washington Post*, October 13, 2013, http://www.washingtonpost.com/local/education/in-push-for-muslim-school-holiday-some-montgomery-students-will-stay-home/2013/10/13/b26b8f6e-2d22-11e3-8ade-a1f23cda135e_story.html.
54. Charles C. Haynes, "American Idol: God Does Belong in Public Schools, If a Student Wants Him There," *Washington Post*, September 23, 2013, http://www.faithstreet.com/onfaith/2013/09/23/american-idol-god-does-belong-in-public-schools-if-a-student-wants-him-there.

55. Ibid.
56. Billy Hallowell, "Uproar over High School Textbook's 36 Pages of Content About Islam Continues—But Will This New Plan Temper the Storm?" *The Blaze*, August 14, 2013, http://www.theblaze.com/stories/2013/08/14/new-fix-proposed-to-assuage-furor-over-textbook-that-includes-36-pages-on-islam-and-3-paragraphs-on-christianity/.
57. Ibid.
58. Will Weissert, "Debate Again Thrusts CSCOPE into Texas Spotlight," statesman.com, August 24, 2013, http://www.statesman.com/news/news/debate-again-thrusts-cscope-into-texas-spotlight/nZbxF/.
59. Jason Howerton, "You Won't Believe What We Found in Another 'Widely Adopted' High School Textbook," *The Blaze*, September 17, 2013, http://www.theblaze.com/stories/2013/09/17/publisher-of-ap-history-book-containing-questionable-second-amendment-summary-has-direct-ties-to-common-core-and-theres-more/.
60. Laurie Higgins, "Government = Family According to Elementary School in Skokie," Illinois Family Institute, September 4, 2013, http://illinoisfamily.org/education/governmentfamily-according-to-elementary-school-in-skokie/.
61. Ibid.
62. Ibid.
63. Fred Lucas, "'What Is Government?' Elementary Students Taught It's Your 'Family,'" *The Blaze*, August 30, 2013, http://www.theblaze.com/stories/2013/08/30/what-is-government-elementary-students-taught-its-your-family/.

17: AMERICA'S REAL WAR: ARE WE STILL ONE NATION, UNDER GOD?

1. Mark Sherman, "High Court Wrestles With Prayer in Government," Fox News, November 9, 2013, http://www.foxnews.com/politics/2013/11/06/supreme-court-wrestling-with-prayer-at-ny-town-meetings/.
2. Timothy M. Phelps, "Public Prayer Case Appears to Perplex Supreme Court," *Los Angeles Times*, November 6, 2013, http://articles.latimes.com/2013/nov/06/nation/la-na-court-prayer-20131107.
3. Sherman, "High Court Wrestles With Prayer in Government."
4. Ibid.
5. Robert Barnes, "Supreme Court Hears Case on N.Y. Town's Practice of Opening Meetings with a Prayer," *Washington Post*, November 6, http://www.washingtonpost.com/politics/2013/11/06/bd818344-46ff-11e3-a196-3544a03c2351_story.html.
6. Sherman, "High Court Wrestles With Prayer in Government."
7. Ibid.
8. Phelps, "Public Prayer Case Appears to Perplex Supreme Court."
9. Supreme Court of the United States, "The Court and Its Procedures," http://www.supremecourt.gov/about/procedures.aspx, accessed November 12, 2013.
10. Barnes, "Supreme Court Hears Case on N.Y. Town's Practice of Opening Meetings with a Prayer."
11. Jay Dillon, "Ohio School District Agrees to Keep Portrait of Jesus off Wall, Pay $95K Fine," Fox 25, October 7, 2013, http://www.okcfox.com/story/23629831/ohio-school-district-agrees-to-keep-portrait-of-jesus-off-wall-pay-95g-fine.
12. Ibid.
13. Kirsten Andersen, "Public School District Agrees to Pay $95K Settlement after ACLU Sues over Jesus Picture," LifeSiteNews.com, October 9, 2013, http://www.lifesitenews.com/news/public-school-district-agrees-to-pay-95000-settlement-after-aclu-sues-over.
14. Ibid.
15. Michael Gryboski, "Ohio School District Settles with ACLU, Agrees to Remove Jesus Portrait, Pay $95,000 Fine," *Christian Post*, October 7, 2013, http://www.christianpost.com/news/ohio-school-district-settles-with-aclu-agrees-to-remove-jesus-portrait-pay-95k-fine-106092/.
16. Andersen, "Public School District Agrees to Pay $95K Settlement After ACLU Sues Over Jesus Picture."

17. Ibid.
18. Gryboski, "Ohio School District Settles With ACLU."
19. Andersen, "Public School District Agrees to Pay $95K Settlement After ACLU Sues Over Jesus Picture."
20. Ibid.
21. Heather Clark, "School District Refuses to Hang 'In God We Trust' Posters Due to 'Separation of Church and State,'" Christian News Network, November 12, 2013, http://christiannews. net/2013/11/12/school-district-refuses-to-hang-in-god-we-trust-posters-due-to-separation-of-church-and-state/.
22. Todd Starnes, "North Carolina School District Rejects 'In God We Trust' Posters," Fox News, November 7, 2013, http://www.foxnews.com/opinion/2013/11/07/north-carolina-school-district-rejects-in-god-trust-posters/.
23. Ibid.
24. Ibid.
25. Clark, "School District Refuses to Hang 'In God We Trust' Posters Due to 'Separation of Church and State.'"
26. Starnes, "North Carolina School District Rejects 'In God We Trust' Posters."
27. Clark, "School District Refuses to Hang 'In God We Trust' Posters Due to 'Separation of Church and State.'"
28. Robyn Hagan Cain, "Bradley Johnson Banner Order Does Not Violate First Amendment," *U.S. Ninth Circuit* (blog), September 15, 2011, http://blogs.findlaw.com/ninth_circuit/2011/09/bradley-johnson-banner-order-does-not-violate-first-amendment.html.
29. Ibid.
30. "Bradley Johnson, California Math Teacher, Has No Constitutional Right to Use Banners Referring to God, Judge Rules," *Huff Post* Education, http://www.huffingtonpost. com/2011/09/14/bradley-johnson-californi_n_962553.html, upd. November 14, 2011.
31. Ibid.
32. Cain, "Bradley Johnson Banner Order Does Not Violate First Amendment."
33. A. J. Kritikos, "Kritikos: Expelling God from School," *Washington Times*, September 8, 2013, http://www.washingtontimes.com/news/2013/sep/8/kritikos-expelling-god-from-school/?page=all.
34. Associated Press, "Massachusetts Court Hears Pledge of Allegiance Challenge," Fox News, September 4, 2013, http://www.foxnews.com/us/2013/09/04/massachusetts-court-hears-pledge-allegiance-challenge/.
35. Kritikos, "Kritikos: Expelling God from School."
36. G. Jeffrey MacDonald, "Mass. Justices Review Pledge of Allegiance," *USA Today*, September 5, 2013, http://www.usatoday.com/story/news/nation/2013/09/04/massachusetts-pledge-of-allegiance/2768071/.
37. Tovia Smith, "Parents Fight over Pledging Allegiance in Schools," NPR, September 19, 2011, http://www.npr.org/2011/09/19/140600621/parents-fight-over-pledging-allegiance-in-schools.
38. Ibid.
39. Associated Press, "Brookline Political Action for Peace, Massachusetts Group, Seeks School Pledge of Allegiance Ban," November 8, 2011, *Huff Post* Education, http://www.huffingtonpost. com/2011/09/08/brookline-political-actio_n_953710.html.
40. Smith, "Parents Fight over Pledging Allegiance in Schools."
41. Torsten Ove, "Suspended Teacher's Aide Sues Employer over Wearing Cross on Necklace," *Pittsburgh Post-Gazette*, May 7, 2003, http://old.post-gazette.com/localnews/20030507cross0507p2.asp.
42. Todd Starnes, "University Tells Student to Remove Cross Necklace," Fox News, July 2, 2013, http://radio.foxnews.com/toddstarnes/top-stories/university-tells-student-to-remove-cross-necklace.html.
43. Jeremy Leaming, "School Board Sued over Policy That Bans Star of David," Freedom Forum, August 8, 1999, http://www.freedomforum.org/templates/document.asp?documentID=8755.
44. The Catholic League, "School Board Ban on Star of David Fails," *Catalyst*, October 1999, http://www.catholicleague.org/school-board-ban-on-star-of-david-fails/.

45. Ibid.
46. Anugrah Kumar, "Veterans Resurrect Mojave Desert Cross in Calif. after Decade-Long Dispute," *Christian Post*, November 12, 2012, http://www.christianpost.com/news/veterans-resurrect-mojave-desert-cross-in-calif-after-decade-long-dispute-84782/.
47. Ibid.
48. David Olson, "Mojave Desert: Cross Stands Again," *Press-Enterprise*, November 11, 2012, http://www.pe.com/local-news/san-bernardino-county/san-bernardino-county-headlines-index/20121111-mojave-desert-cross-stands-again.ece.
49. Ibid.
50. Jess Bravin, "Court Says Cross Can Remain," *Wall Street Journal*, April 29, 2010.
51. Ibid.
52. Kumar, "Veterans Resurrect Mojave Desert Cross in Calif."
53. Bravin, "Court Says Cross Can Remain."
54. Kumar, "Veterans Resurrect Mojave Desert Cross in Calif. After Decade-Long Dispute."
55. Olson, "Mojave Desert: Cross Stands Again."
56. Ibid.
57. Alicia Robinson, "Mount Rubidoux Cross: Auction Outcome Satisfies Americans United," *Press-Enterprise*, April 18, 2013, http://blog.pe.com/news/2013/04/18/mount-rubidoux-cross-auction-outcome-satisfies-americans-united/.
58. Ibid.
59. NBC Southern California, "Lake Elsinore Sued over Cross on Planned City Monument," June 4, 2013, http://www.nbclosangeles.com/news/local/Lake-Elsinore-Sued-Over-Cross-on-Planned-City-Monument-210126731.html.
60. Hemant Mehta, "Judge Stops Lake Elsinore City Council from Putting up a Religious Monument for Veterans," Patheos, July 17, 2013, http://www.patheos.com/blogs/friendlyatheist/2013/07/17/judge-stops-lake-elsinore-city-council-from-putting-up-a-religious-monument-for-veterans/; no longer accessible.
61. Ibid.
62. NBC Southern California, "Lake Elsinore Sued over Cross on Planned City Monument."
63. Ibid.
64. Michael J. Williams, "Lake Elsinore: Vets Memorial Decision in Judge's Hands," *Press-Enterprise*, October 2, 2013, http://www.pe.com/local-news/riverside-county/lake-elsinore/lake-elsinore-headlines-index/20131002-lake-elsinore-vets-memorial-decision-in-judges-hands.ece.
65. Stephen Losey, "Academy Makes 'God' Optional in Cadets' Oath," *Air Force Times*, October 25, 2013, http://www.airforcetimes.com/article/20131025/NEWS/310230013/.
66. Ibid.
67. Military Religious Freedom Foundation, "Michael L. 'Mikey' Weinstein," http://www.militaryreligiousfreedom.org/about/michael-l-mikey-weinstein/, accessed November 13, 2013.
68. Billy Hallowell, "Megyn Kelly's Tense Interview with Military Church-State Separatist: 'Chill, Mikey,'" *The Blaze*, October 24, 2013, http://www.theblaze.com/stories/2013/10/24/mikey-chill-megyn-kelly-battles-with-military-church-state-separatist-over-removal-of-god-from-air-force-oath/.
69. Losey, "Academy Makes 'God' Optional in Cadets' Oath."
70. Hallowell, "Megyn Kelly's Tense Interview With Military Church-State Separatist."
71. Ibid.
72. John Jalsevac, "Pentagon: Christians in Military Could Be Court-Martialed for Promoting Their Faith," LifeSiteNews.com, May 2, 2013, http://www.lifesitenews.com/news/pentagon-christians-in-military-could-be-court-martialed-for-promoting-thei.
73. Sally Quinn, "U.S. Military Should Put Religious Freedom at the Front," *Washington Post*, April 26, 2013, http://articles.washingtonpost.com/2013-04-26/national/38838247_1_sexual-assault-pentagon-budget-chaplain.
74. Ibid.
75. Jalsevac, "Pentagon: Christians in Military Could Be Court-Martialed for Promoting Their Faith."

76. Ibid.

77. Todd Starnes, "U.S. Army Defines Christian Ministry as 'Domestic Hate Group,'" Fox News, October 14, 2013, http://www.foxnews.com/opinion/2013/10/14/us-army-defines-christian-ministry-as-domestic-hate-group/.

78. CBN News, "Mea Culpa: Army Withdraws 'Hate Group' Label," October 17, 2013, http://www.cbn.com/cbnnews/us/2013/October/Mea-Culpa-Army-Withdraws-Hate-Group-Label-/.

79. Starnes, "U.S. Army Defines Christian Ministry as 'Domestic Hate Group.'"

80. Ibid.

81. CBN News, "Mea Culpa."

82. The Congressional Prayer Caucus, Current Issues, "Opposing Hostility Towards Faith in the Air Force," http://forbes.house.gov/prayercaucus/issues.aspx, accessed November 13, 2013.

83. Alan Sears, "ACLU Continues Its Assaults on Public Expressions of Faith Nationwide," Alliance Defending Freedom, July 30, 2013, http://blog.alliancedefendingfreedom.org/2013/07/30/aclu-continues-its-assaults-on-public-expressions-of-faith-nationwide/.

84. Michael Gryboski, "ADF Defends 10 Indiana Churches Sued by ACLU for Displaying Crosses," Christian Post, July 17, 2013, http://www.christianpost.com/news/adf-files-motion-supporting-ind-churches-sued-by-aclu-100303/.

85. Ibid.

86. Sears, "ACLU Continues Its Assaults on Public Expressions of Faith Nationwide."

87. Gryboski, "ADF Defends 10 Indiana Churches."

88. Ibid.

89. Gordon Tokumatsu and Frava Burgess, "Thousand Oaks Christian School Files Religious Liberty Lawsuit Against Former Teachers," NBC Southern California, January 28, 2013, http://www.nbclosangeles.com/news/local/Thousand-Oaks-Christian-School-Files-Religious-Liberty-Lawsuit-188773861.html.

90. Ibid.

91. "Little Oaks Elementary Lawsuit: School Sues Two Former Teachers Who Refused to Prove Their Faith," Huffington Post, January 29, 2013, http://www.huffingtonpost.com/2013/01/29/little-oaks-elementary-lawsuit_n_2575002.html.

92. Tokumatsu and Burgess, "Thousand Oaks Christian School Files Religious Liberty Lawsuit Against Former Teachers."

93. Janice Rael, "DVAU President Ed Joyce: 'PA House Bill Promotes a Divisive Religious Message,'" Delaware Valley Americans United, dvau.org/?p=3141, accessed November 13, 2013.

94. Ibid.

95. Tony Romeo, "Some Pa. Lawmakers Seeking 'In God We Trust' in Every Public School," CBS Philly, November 13, 2013, http://philadelphia.cbslocal.com/2013/11/13/some-pa-lawmakers-want-in-god-we-trust-posted-in-every-public-school/.

96. The Heritage Foundation, "Washington's Thanksgiving Proclamation: October 3, 1789," http://www.heritage.org/initiatives/first-principles/primary-sources/washingtons-thanksgiving-proclamation, accessed November 13, 2013.

97. Ibid.

98. Gillian Flaccus, "Atheist 'mega-churches' take root across US, world," Yahoo! News, November 11, 2013, http://news.yahoo.com/atheist-mega-churches-root-across-us-world-214619648.html.

99. Ibid.

18: THROW THE BUMS OUT: WHY VIRTUE, ACCOUNTABILITY ARE KEY

1. Charles Krauthammer, "White House Wordplay," National Review, May 16, 2013, http://www.nationalreview.com/article/348559/white-house-wordplay-charles-krauthammer.

2. Ibid.

3. Anne Gearan, "State Dept. Acknowledges Rejecting Requests for More Security in Benghazi," *Washington Post*, October 10, 2012, http://www.washingtonpost.com/world/national-security/state-dept-downgraded-security-in-libya-before-deadly-attack-ex-officer-claims/2012/10/10/d7195faa-12e6-11e2-a16b-2c110031514a_story.html.

4. Kristen A. Lee,"Rep. Allen West Accuses Hillary Clinton of Faking Concussion to Avoid Benghazi Testimony," *New York Daily News*, December 20, 2012, http://www.nydailynews.com/news/politics/fox-news-guests-call-hillary-concussion-fake-article-1.1224556.

5. WSJ Staff, "Text of Hillary Clinton's Senate Testimony on Benghazi," *Wall Street Journal*, January 23, 2013; "Hillary Clinton at Benghazi Hearing: 'What Difference, Does It Make?'" posted by Joe Bunting, http://www.youtube.com/watch?v=Ka0_nz53CcM, accessed November 14, 2013.

6. "Senate Benghazi Report Damns Both Obama and Clinton," *Investor's Business Daily*, January 15, 2014, accessed January 18, 2014, http://news.investors.com/ibd-editorials/011514686514-benghazi-report-exposes-obama-and-clintons-incompetence.htm.

7. U.S. Select Senate Committee on Intelligence, "Review of the Terrorist Attacks on U.S. Facilities in Benghazi, Libya, September 11–12, 2012," January 15, 2014, http://www.intelligence.senate.gov/benghazi2014/benghazi.pdf, p. 10.

8. Ibid, p. 12.

9. Ibid. pp. 24–25

10. Ibid, p. 25.

11. Fox News, "Fox News Poll: Half of Americans Think President Lied about Obamacare; Majority Want Benghazi Probe to Continue," http://www.foxnews.com/politics/interactive/2013/11/13/fox-news-polls-half-voters-think-president-lied-about-obamacare-majority-want/, accessed November 14, 2013.

12. Dana Blanton, "Fox News Poll: Half Think Obama 'Knowingly Lied' to Pass Health Care," Fox News, November 13, 2013, http://www.foxnews.com/politics/2013/11/13/fox-news-poll-half-think-obama-knowingly-lied-to-pass-health-care-law/.

13. Avik Roy, "The Obamacare Exchange Scorecard: Around 100,000 Enrollees and Five Million Cancellations," *The Apothecary* (*Forbes* blog), November 12, 2013, http://www.forbes.com/sites/theapothecary/2013/11/12/the-obamacare-exchange-scorecard-around-100000-enrollees-and-five-million-cancellations/.

14. Aaron Blake, "Obamacare Disapproval Hits New High, as Obama Hits New Low," *Post Politics*, November 12, 2013, http://www.washingtonpost.com/blogs/post-politics/wp/2013/11/12/second-poll-shows-obama-hitting-new-low/.

15. Chris Cillizza and Aaron Blake, "How President Obama Can Stop the Bleeding on Obamacare," *The Fix*, November 13, 2013. http://www.washingtonpost.com/blogs/the-fix/wp/2013/11/13/how-president-obama-can-stop-the-bleeding-on-obamacare/.

16. Quinnipiac University, "Obama Job Approval Drops to Lowest Point Ever," http://www.quinnipiac.edu/institutes-and-centers/polling-institute/national/release-detail?ReleaseID=1975, November 12, 2013.

17. Glenn Kessler, "The White House Effort to Blame Insurance Companies for Lost Plans," *Doc's Talk* (blog), November 7, 2013, http://docstalk.blogspot.com/2013/11/the-white-house-effort-to-blame.html.

18. PolitiFact, "Barack Obama Says That What He'd Said Was You Could Keep Your Plan 'If It Hasn't Changed Since the Law Passed,'" November 6, 2013, http://www.politifact.com/truth-o-meter/statements/2013/nov/06/barack-obama/barack-obama-says-what-hed-said-was-you-could-keep/.

19. "Obama: 'What We Said Was You Can Keep It If It Hasn't Changed Since the Law Passed," *Real Clear Politics*, November 4, 2013, http://www.realclearpolitics.com/video/2013/11/04/obama_what_we_said_was_you_can_keep_it_if_it_hasnt_changed_since_the_law_passed.html, posted by Ian Schwartz.

20. PolitiFact, "Barack Obama Says That What He'd Said Was You Could Keep Your Plan 'If It Hasn't Changed Since the Law Passed.'"

21. Ibid.

22. Ibid.

23. Janeen Capizola, "Chris Matthews: The Right Owes Susan Rice an Apology for Benghazi," BizPacReview, January 18, 2014.

24. Guy Benson, "Obama: 'My Biggest Priority' Is Bringing the Benghazi 'Folks' to Justice," October 26, 2012, Townhall.com, http://townhall.com/tipsheet/guybenson/2012/10/26/obama_my_biggest_priority_is_bringing_the_benghazi_folks_to_justice.

25. Ibid.

26. Catherine Herridge, "Details Emerge about Americans Badly Injured in Benghazi Attack," Fox News, November 13, 2013, http://www.foxnews.com/politics/2013/11/13/details-emerge-about-americans-badly-injured-in-benghazi-attack/.

27. Fox News, "Lawmakers Demand Access to Survivors Injured in Benghazi Attack," March 6, 2013, http://www.foxnews.com/politics/2013/03/06/lawmakers-demand-access-to-survivors-injured-in-benghazi-attack/.

28. *Investor's Business Daily*, "Will David Ubben Blow Roof Off 'Phony' Benghazi Scandal?" IBD Editorials, August 1, 2013, http://news.investors.com/ibd-editorials/080113-666079-congress-seeks-david-ubben-benghazi-testimony.htm.

29. Herridge, "Details Emerge about Americans Badly Injured in Benghazi Attack."

30. Ibid.

31. Linda Feldmann, "Why Retirement of Lois Lerner Doesn't End IRS Tea Party Scandal," *DC Decoder* (blog), September 23, 2013, http://www.csmonitor.com/USA/DC-Decoder/2013/0923/Why-retirement-of-Lois-Lerner-doesn-t-end-IRS-tea-party-scandal-video.

32. Tom Fitton, "Judicial Watch Sues IRS for Tea Party Scandal Records," *Judicial Watch*, October 18, 2013, http://www.judicialwatch.org/press-room/press-releases/judicial-watch-sues-irs-for-tea-party-scandal-records/.

33. Paul Bedard, "Three Years Later, TheTeaParty.net Finally Gets IRS Tax-Exempt OK," *Washington Examiner*, October 2, 2013, http://washingtonexaminer.com/three-years-later-theteaparty.net-finally-gets-irs-tax-exempt-ok/article/2536672.

34. *Treasury Inspector General for Tax Administration: Inappropriate Criteria Were Used to Identify Tax-Exempt Applications for Review*, May 14, 2013, http://www.treasury.gov/tigta/auditreports/2013reports/201310053fr.pdf.

35. Feldman, "Why Retirement of Lois Lerner Doesn't End IRS Tea Party Scandal."

36. Ibid.

37. Fitton, "Judicial Watch Sues IRS for Tea Party Scandal Records."

38. Rachel Weiner, "Holder Has Ordered IRS Investigation," *Post Politics*, May 14, 2013, http://www.washingtonpost.com/blogs/post-politics/wp/2013/05/14/holder-has-ordered-irs-investigation/.

39. Meghasham Mali, "Poll: 76 Percent Want Special Prosecutor to Investigate IRS Scandal," *Briefing Room* (blog), May 30, 2013, http://thehill.com/blogs/blog-briefing-room/news/302479-poll-76-percent-want-special-prosecutor-to-investigate-irs-scandal.

40. Mark Sherman, "Gov't Obtains Wide AP Phone Records in Probe," Associated Press, May 13, 2013, http://bigstory.ap.org/article/govt-obtains-wide-ap-phone-records-probe.

41. Ibid.

42. Mark Sherman "Ex-FBI Agent to Plead Guilty to Being AP Source," Associated Press, September 23, 2013, http://bigstory.ap.org/article/ex-fbi-pleads-guilty-being-ap-source-sentenced.

43. Fox News, "DOJ Seized Phone Records for Fox News Numbers, Reporter's Parents," May 23, 2013, http://www.foxnews.com/politics/2013/05/23/correspondents-association-concerned-government-too-aggressive-in-tracking/.

44. Katie Pavlich, "Confirmed: CBS News Investigative Reporter Sharyl Attkisson's Computer Compromised," Townhall.com, June 14, 2013, http://townhall.com/tipsheet/katiepavlich/2013/06/14/confirmed-cbs-news-investigative-reporter-sharyl-attkissons-computer-compromised-n1620273.

45. Reuters, "Eric Holder Signed Off on Decision to Subpoena Fox News Telephone Records," *Huff Post* Politics, http://www.huffingtonpost.com/2013/05/29/eric-holder-fox-news_n_3349945.html, upd. May 29, 2013.

46. Rebecca Kaplan, "Several House Republicans to Seek Impeachment of Eric Holder," CBS News, November 7, 2013, http://www.cbsnews.com/news/several-house-republicans-to-seek-impeachment-of-eric-holder/.

47. Todd Schwarzschild and Drew Griffin "ATF Loses Track of 1,400 Guns in Criticized Probe," CNN Politics, July 12, 2011, http://www.cnn.com/2011/POLITICS/07/12/atf.guns/.

48. Katie Pavlich, "More Fast and Furious Weapons Show Up at Violent Crime Scenes in Mexico," Townhall.com, August 15, 2013, http://townhall.com/tipsheet/katiepavlich/2013/08/15/more-fast-and-furious-weapons-show-up-at-violent-crime-scenes-in-mexico-n1665076.

49. Becket Adams, "Obama Vows to Hold Those Responsible For Fast and Furious Accountable," *The Blaze*, October 18, 2011, http://www.theblaze.com/stories/2011/10/18/obama-vows-to-hold-those-responsible-for-fast-and-furious-accountable/.

50. Sharyl Attkisson, "ATF Fast and Furious: New Documents Show Attorney General Eric Holder Was Briefed in July 2010," CBS, October 3, 2011, http://www.cbsnews.com/news/atf-fast-and-furious-new-documents-show-attorney-general-eric-holder-was-briefed-in-july-2010/.

51. Sharyl Attkisson, "Brian Terry Family Sues ATF Officials in Fast and Furious," CBS, December 17, 2012, http://www.cbsnews.com/news/brian-terry-family-sues-atf-officials-in-fast-and-furious/.

52. Leigh Ann Caldwell, "House Charges Holder with Contempt of Congress," CBS, June 28, 2012, http://www.cbsnews.com/news/house-charges-holder-with-contempt-of-congress-28-06-2012/.

53. Kaplan, "Several House Republicans to Seek Impeachment of Eric Holder."

54. Justin McCarthy, "NBC's Lauer Applauds Honesty of 'Superstar' John Edwards," NewsBusters, February 6, 2007, http://newsbusters.org/node/10651.

55. Marc Dorian and Lauren Effron, "John Edwards and the Mistress: A Breakdown of One of America's Most Sensational Scandals," ABC News, November 12, 2013, http://abcnews.go.com/Politics/john-edwards-mistress-breakdown-americas-sensational-scandals/story?id=20854336.

56. Emily Friedman, "Judge Grants Jenny Sanford a Divorce from Cheating Gov. Mark Sanford," ABC News, February 26, 2010, http://abcnews.go.com/2020/TheLaw/jenny-sanford-granted-divorce-gov-mark-sanford/story?id=9955400.

57. CNN, "South Carolina Gov. Sanford Admits Extramarital Affair," CNN Politics, http://www.cnn.com/2009/POLITICS/06/24/south.carolina.governor/, upd. June 24, 2009.

58. Robbie Brown, "Gov. Sanford Accepts Fine in Ethics Case," *New York Times*, March 18, 2013, http://www.nytimes.com/2010/03/19/us/19sanford.html?_r=0.

59. Catalina Camia, "Mark Sanford Wins Special Election for Congress," *USA Today*, May 7, 2013, http://www.usatoday.com/story/news/politics/2013/05/07/mark-sanford-colbert-busch-congress-election-south-carolina/2140591/.

60. TMZ, "John Edwards Not Guilty!!!" May 31, 2012, http://www.tmz.com/2012/05/31/john-edwards-not-guilty.

61. Fisher Ames, *An Oration on the Sublime Virtues of General George Washington*, (Boston: Young & Minns, 1800), 23, quoted in WallBuilders, "Importance of Morality and Religion in Government," January 2000, http://www.wallbuilders.com/libissuesarticles.asp?id=63, accessed November 14, 2013.

INDEX

Revolution Muslim, 163–64
Right to Financial Privacy Act, 32
rights, our true source of, xv, xxi, 6, 79, 99, 101
Right of Way Preservation Ordinance (FL), 101–2
riot control, testing of substances at US Army Laboratories for use in, 55
Robobee (Harvard's bee-sized robot), 126–27
robot bugs, 126–27
Rockefeller, John D., 61
Rockefeller Commission, 42, 53
Romney, Mitt, 83, 84
Roosevelt, Franklin Delano, 146–47
Roosevelt, Theodore, 12–13, 146
Rosen, James, xvi, 207
Rumsfeld, Donald, 85
Rushdie, Salman, 162–63

S

Sachtleben, Donald, 207
Sadat, Anwar, 150, 157
Salama, Osama Yehia Abu, 155
Salon, 90
same-sex marriage, 195
San Antonio, TX, 114
San Francisco Housing Authority, 102
Sanford, Mark, 209
SAR (Suspicious Activity Report), 40, 115, 116
Satcher, David, 56
scanners, 128–29, 131, 135
school lunches, government regulation of, 174–76

schools
  and holidays, 181
  and left-leaning curriculum, 180, 181–82
  and ridiculous student "offenses" and punishments, 177–79
Scott, Bobby, 37
Scottsdale, AZ, xix–xx, 105–6
search and seizure, 2–5, 7, 9, 79
Seattle, WA, 66–67
Sebelius, Kathleen, 174
Second Amendment, xx, 92, 182
secret government centers, growth of, 105–16
Secret Service, 28, 43
section 215 (PATRIOT Act), 43–45
section 702 (FISA), 48, 51
Senate Commerce Committee, 127
Senate and House Intelligence Committees, 53
Senate Intelligence Committee, xvii, 61
Senate Select Committee on Intelligence Report on Benghazi, 201
Senate Watergate Committee, 52–53
Sensenbrenner, Jim, 45–46
September 11, 2001 terrorist attacks (*aka* 9/11), 6, 36, 51, 56, 61, 63, 86, 119, 166, 171, 200, 201
Sesame Street, 175
Shakir, Zaid, 158
Shariah law, 156, 158, 159, 171
Sharpton, Al, 90–91
Shulman, Douglas, 206
SIGAD US-984XN, xvi. *See also* PRISM
Singer, Fred, 16
Skype, 47
Slate, 92
Snowden, Edward, xv–xvi, 33, 48, 49–50, 108

PRESENTS

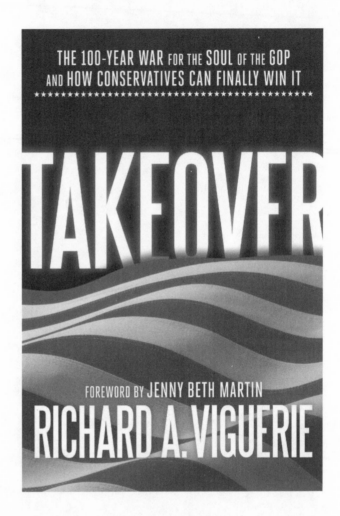

More than one hundred years ago Teddy Roosevelt abandoned the Republican Party to advance his progressive agenda. Over fifty years ago conservatives began a battle for control of the party. Now is the time for conservatives to finish the job and take back the Republican Party. In *TAKEOVER*, prominent Republican strategist and political direct-marketing pioneer Richard Viguerie offers practical advice and outlines the steps necessary for conservatives to win the civil war in the GOP and govern America by 2017.

WND Books • A *WND* COMPANY • WASHINGTON DC • WNDBOOKS.COM

PRESENTS

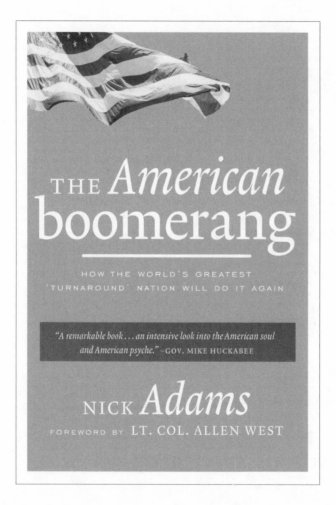

THE *American* boomerang

HOW THE WORLD'S GREATEST 'TURNAROUND' NATION WILL DO IT AGAIN

"*A remarkable book . . . an intensive look into the American soul and American psyche.*" -GOV. MIKE HUCKABEE

NICK *Adams*

FOREWORD BY LT. COL. ALLEN WEST

Birthed on the principal of freedom from tyranny and sustained by dependence on the divine power to grant freedom, justice, and liberty for all men and women, America rose to become the most extraordinary country on earth. She has overcome insurmountable odds and bounced back from repeated setbacks only to set the standard and remain a beacon for the world. America is the greatest turnaround nation ever. America must boomerang back.

WND Books • A **WND** COMPANY • WASHINGTON DC • WNDBOOKS.COM